# WORLD LITERATURE AND THE
# GEOGRAPHIES OF RESISTANCE

This book proposes a new definition of world literature: an archive of democratic mechanisms external to state power. Accordingly, *World Literature and the Geographies of Resistance* takes shape as an exploration of nonstate space – territories of self-government that contest the vertical command structures of the state. Joel Nickels argues that literature devoted to these processes of spatial occupation can help us imagine democratic alternatives to state space and to the regime of legalized dispossession that goes under the name of globalization. Conceptualized in these terms, world literature can be viewed not as the corollary of 1990s-era cosmopolitanism, but as a document of strategies for the militant reorganization of social space. This ambitious book addresses the work of Patrick Chamoiseau, Ousmane Sembene, Miguel Ángel Asturias, Claude McKay, Arundhati Roy, T. S. Eliot, and Melvin Tolson. It engages with theories of transnationality, diaspora, and postcoloniality, as well as world literature.

JOEL NICKELS is the author of *The Poetry of the Possible: Spontaneity, Modernism, and the Multitude* (2012).

# WORLD LITERATURE AND THE GEOGRAPHIES OF RESISTANCE

JOEL NICKELS

*University of Miami*

CAMBRIDGE
UNIVERSITY PRESS

# CAMBRIDGE
## UNIVERSITY PRESS

University Printing House, Cambridge CB2 8BS, United Kingdom

One Liberty Plaza, 20th Floor, New York, NY 10006, USA

477 Williamstown Road, Port Melbourne, VIC 3207, Australia

314–321, 3rd Floor, Plot 3, Splendor Forum, Jasola District Centre, New Delhi – 110025, India

79 Anson Road, #06-04/06, Singapore 079906

Cambridge University Press is part of the University of Cambridge.

It furthers the University's mission by disseminating knowledge in the pursuit of education, learning, and research at the highest international levels of excellence.

www.cambridge.org
Information on this title: www.cambridge.org/9781108428491
DOI: 10.1017/9781108581776

First published 2018

Printed in the United Kingdom by Clays, St Ives plc

A catalogue record for this publication is available from the British Library.

Library of Congress Cataloging-in-Publication Data
Names: Nickels, Joel author.
Title: World literature and the geographies of resistance / Joel Nickels, University of Miami.
Description: Cambridge; New York, NY: Cambridge University Press, 2018. |
Includes index. Identifiers: LCCN 2017059791 | ISBN 9781108428491 (hardback)
Subjects: LCSH: Social conflict in literature. | Social justice in literature. |
Postcolonialism in literature. | Internationalism in literature.
Classification: LCC PN56.S65.N45 2018 | DDC 809/.933552–dc23
LC record available at https://lccn.loc.gov/2017059791

ISBN 978-1-108-42849-1 Hardback

*Yeshua, my God, You make all things new!*

# Contents

# *Acknowledgments*

First, I thank you, living God of creation, You who move like a wind through our cities, healer of my heart, my guide, my counselor. In You, everything is possible!

Carrie, my wife and true friend, thank you for the countless acts of devotion and kindness you constantly perform. Thank you for the time you created for me, and for choosing me every day. You are my love and support.

Claire, daughter, joy of my heart, thank you for being you! I love you all the time.

I thank you also, Lauren Riccelli Zwicky, Paula Forteza, Alexander Gonzalez, Jennifer Vargas, Tyler Pedersen, my research assistants! What creativity and discernment you showed. Thank you for your time and the seriousness of your efforts.

I am also grateful to all of you who read and responded to this work. Thank you to those of you who engaged with me at the *ELH* Colloquium at Johns Hopkins, especially Aaron Begg, Chris Nealon, Jeanne-Marie Jackson, and Douglas Mao. I also thankfully acknowledge the support of the University of Miami Center for the Humanities, and my peers there who provided such helpful feedback on parts of this book. A University of Miami Provost Research Award also provided support for this project.

I'm grateful also for you, my friends, whose dialogue and fellowship stand behind this book. I'm talking about you, John Funchion, Joshua Clover, Jason Pearl, Nathaniel Cadle, Alexandra Perisic, Donette Francis, Brenna Munro, Tim Watson, Pam Hammons, Gema Pérez Sánchez, Liz Young, Michelle Neely, Charles Sumner, Monika Gehlawat, Jennifer Scappattone, Joseph Jeon, Ted Martin, Annie McClanahan, Jasper Bernes, Trane DeVore, Manohar Narayanamurthi, Carlos Fernandez, and Chrissy Arce. Thank you also, Ray Ryan, for your interest and support, and for making this process so easy.

Also, to my amazing sisters- and brothers-in-law, Kristen Sieh, Caitlin Sieh, Emily Watson, and Nick VanDyken – thank you for your love and friendship. What a wonderful family you are to me!

# Introduction: The Literature of Spatial Occupation – A Nonstate Research Agenda

"World literature" and "resistance" seldom appear together in the same sentence. Why is this?

Could it be because we have somehow come to consider world literature as "polite" literature – as the canon of masterpieces produced by elite networks of literary prestige?

Or could it be because we now regard world literature as what comes after the militant resistance literatures written from the 1930s to the 1970s, as if the magnificent narratives of decolonization and neocolonial agonistics that we associate with the postcolonial era have given way to a new literary dispensation – a more globalized literature perhaps, more cosmopolitan in its affinities, less committed to physical geographies of revolt?

A brief survey of the diverse texts that have been grouped together in recent discussions of world literature gives the lie to both of these explanations. No engagement with the complexities of resistance to colonial and neocolonial domination could be more searching than what we see in texts such as Zoë Wicomb's *David's Story*, Shimmer Chinodya's *Harvest of Thorns*, Édouard Glissant's *Pays rêvé, pays réel*, Horacio Castellanos Moya's *Tirana memoria*, Raúl Zurita's *La Vida Nueva*, Pramoedya Ananta Toer's *Buru Quartet*, Habib Tengour's *Traverser*, Michelle Cliff's *No Telephone to Heaven*, and Ninotchka Rosca's *State of War*. Nevertheless, the sense remains that explorations of resistance in literature belong to a past era, and that this literary dispensation has been supplanted by something altogether more urbane, more worldly – in short, by world literature.

The aim of this book is to provide a conceptual vocabulary that could begin to account for the forms of territorialized resistance on display in world literature and, in doing so, help us move beyond the false opposition between postcolonial literature (conceived primarily as a corollary of nationalist revolution) and world literature (conceived as the cosmopolitan alternative to such militant, territorialized literatures). This inert opposition has been perpetuated, I believe, because of our difficulty in identifying and theorizing forms of mass-based, territorialized resistance whose terminus is not the capture and administration of the state. If we continue to view all forms of militant, territorialized resistance through a state-centric lens, it may in fact seem that there existed a period of nationalist revolution and state-building – namely, the postcolonial period, with its postcolonial literatures – which has now been superseded by an ensemble of deterritorialized investments, whose corollary is, somehow, world literature.

What this account overlooks, however, is the host of powerful, mass-based groups that occupy territory, evict security forces, and establish mechanisms of assembly and self-government – neither in the name of the state nor in the name of cosmopolitan governance projects. Outside of the theoretical binarism we have constructed – nationalism on the one hand, cosmopolitanism on the other – there is an entire world of territorially-based struggles aimed at constructing forms of self-government outside of the state, maintaining power bases in sustained conflict with the state, or assembling organs of struggle that are state-dystonic. What about the uprisings and strikes that were conducted outside of state-centric party politics, but that were nevertheless crucial to the decolonization process, from Sholapur (1928) and Kishoreganj (1930) to Dakar (1946) and Mombasa (1947)? What about land occupations conducted extra-legally, and often in direct confrontation with state forces (Cherán, 2011 to the present; Malawi, 1994 to the present; the Philippines, 1990s; Brazil, 1995 to the present)?

What about those historical flashpoints in which workers occupy workplaces and self-manage them, not in the name of state-centric legal struggles, but as forms of mutual aid and self-defense in a conflictive relationship with the state – as occurred in Greece (2012), Argentina (2001–2003), Iran (1978–1979), Portugal (1974–1975), Jamaica (1969), Algeria (1962), Budapest (1956), Poland (1956), Java (1945–1946), Germany (1919), and Turin (1919–1920)? At moments like these, a problematic evolves that is accounted for neither by contemporary theories of statecraft nor by the deterritorialized politics of cosmopolitanism. Such nonstate formations are territorially-based networks of occupation and self-defense; they are as remote as can be from the ideas of "global cooperation" and "global financial governance" espoused by cosmopolitan theory.[1] And yet, their organizational activity takes place outside the hierarchical power structures and centralized command structure of the nation-state. They constitute forms of nonstate space whose internal workings, organizational models, and political capacities have been largely overlooked both by theorists of the nation-state and by theorists of cosmopolitanism, diaspora, and transnational migration.

This neglect is especially surprising in the field of postcolonial studies, because of the major role that such nonstate networks and strategies have played in decolonization struggles and their aftermaths. As French *Pied-Noirs* fled newly independent Algeria, for example, abandoning their fields and factories, peasants and workers seized control of them and established rank-and-file management committees to direct production, outside the aegis of the National Liberation Front (FLN) and the postcolonial state. "The spontaneous actions by the workers," writes Thomas L. Blair, "burst unexpectedly upon the post-Evian interim Provisional Executive Council, placing it in a difficult political position" *vis-à-vis* the French state, which was keen to maintain the exiting *colons'* property rights over assets that had already been expropriated by nonstate networks.[2] This kind of rank-and-file self-management, initiated and carried through by nonstate networks, was "never envisaged by FLN leaders as a form of economic organization appropriate to post-independence Algeria"[3] – in fact, it had been neither theorized nor anticipated by the militia leaders who would become the principal state actors in the newly independent Algerian state. Nevertheless, the fledgling Algerian state moved quickly to recognize these new collectives legally as *biens de l'État* – in the process doing its best to subvert their autonomy. By 1963, these nonstate spaces had been subsumed into state forms of command, with state-appointed directors enjoying de facto power over workers' management committees, and the formerly independent workers' union UGTA was nationalized and used to suppress strike activity.

In other words, the militant reorganization of the vast majority of Algeria's processes of social production during decolonization was the work of nonstate forces, external to the FLN and its state-centric methods, and these nonstate forces then had to struggle against the centralization of power that nationalist leaders began to implement.

This agon between state and nonstate forces during the decolonization process is by no means unique to Algeria. From 1925 to 1926, 200,000 workers in Canton and Hong Kong revolted against British imperialism with an astonishingly long 14-month general strike, under the direction of a nonstate body of worker delegates: the Canton–Hong Kong Strike Committee. This massive nonstate network of armed pickets and committeepeople functioned as an effective countergovernment throughout the duration of the general strike, operating outside any party structure, and even maintaining nonstate judicial operations and prison facilities. Though the strike represented a staggering blow to British commerce, the Nationalist party under Chiang Kai-shek, fearing a power network external to its own, forcibly ended it in October 1926, jailing many of the strikers and liquidating the nonstate networks that defined their activity. Once again, the initiative of nonstate networks proved essential to spearheading a crucial phase of the decolonization process, and, once again, their autonomous networks were dismantled by the centralized powers of the nationalist party.

Similar patterns would play out in Kenya, Ghana, Indonesia, and Guinea within the first months of independence, with state forces crushing and dispersing the nonstate networks that had helped bring them to power. One of the most instructive examples of this dynamic is the case of Sékou Touré, who led a massive nonstate coalition in a general strike in 1950, and helped organize the anti-metropolitan Confédération générale du travail – autonome, but who, upon achieving state power, suppressed all independent union activity and transformed Guinea into a single-party state. Here we have a figure who was crucial to the development of the nonstate labor networks that helped prepare the groundwork for the decolonization process, who, as head of state, would ban strike activity, fallaciously claiming that any strike, when "directed against an African government … affects African authority, reinforcing by this means … the authority [of the dominant power]."[4]

What all of this suggests is that to comprehend the complex geographies of the twentieth and twenty-first centuries' literatures of resistance, it is essential to understand the relationship between state space and something that has rarely been theorized in discussions of world literature – namely, nonstate space.

But what is nonstate space? Or, more precisely, where is it?

Broadly defined, "nonstate space" refers to social space that is made up of human networks, decision-making processes, and creative practices external to the nation-state and irreducible to its forms of governance. Examples of nonstate space can be found in regions where state power has fractured or disappeared, in pastoralist and nomadic societies that govern themselves in the absence of a state, as well as in nonstate networks and behaviors that exist within functioning states, as sites of contestation and counterpower.

The fact that "nonstate space" refers to any social space outside of state-centric forms of regulation means that its potential purchase is extremely broad, ranging from the self-governing peoples of the Andes, the Himalayas, and Southern Africa, to maroon and pirate communities from the sixteenth to the nineteenth centuries, to nonstate social movements and organizations of colonial and neocolonial spaces. The concept of nonstate space therefore occupies an interdisciplinary zone of engagement that has already begun to be defined by scholars such as M. Bianet Castellanos, Lourdes Gutiérrez Nájera, Arturo J. Aldama, and Maximilian C. Forte working on indigeneity from a transnational perspective, as well as scholars such as Kathryn Milun, Maia Ramnath, Elinor Ostrom, and Derek Wall, whose work engages in the nonstate configurations that belong, respectively, to land rights legislation in Australia and the Western Sahara, the Indian decolonization movement, common pool resource problems, and the history of the commons in England, Mongolia, and India.[5]

What has not been attempted yet, however, is a literary geography that explores the specific potentialities and limits that representations of nonstate social configurations exhibit, with a view to articulating how such nonstate capacities take shape differentially in divergent geopolitical contexts. One of the main contributions such a project would be in a position to make would be to delineate the tropological resources, epistemologies, and micropolitical strategies that belong to representations of political communities external to state-centric social structures, as opposed to those whose tactical horizon is defined exclusively by the conquest or reform of the state apparatus.

This book represents a first step in the direction of such a literary-historical mapping. It stages an investigation into some of the ways in which nonstate space has been represented in world literature from the early twentieth century to the present, and its main goal is to help develop a language that can account for the representation of capacities for self-government that have evolved in nonstate configurations across a wide variety of geopolitical contexts. Accordingly, this book does not attempt an exhaustive account of nonstate space in world literature so much as articulate a research agenda in the humanities that will require much more effort to define and develop itself. Nevertheless, this book's focus on territorially-based, nonstate forms of self-government points beyond some central conceptual impasses faced by transnational theory today.

Consider, for example, the oscillation in contemporary transnational theory between the image of the postcolonial state as a class-stratified, compradorized space and the image of it, in the words of Pheng Cheah, as a "necessary ... political agent for defending the peoples of the South," made all the more exigent because "transnational networks are, in and of themselves, neither mass based nor firmly politically institutionalized."[6] According to this theoretical optics, the postcolonial state may often be, in Fanon's words, little more than a "manager for Western enterprise,"[7] but, in the absence of any viable nonstate political configuration, state sovereignty is resurrected as the only realistic weapon that postcolonial populations are in a position to wield.

This theoretical caution is understandable, given the role that states have often played as defensive bulwarks against Western projects of underdevelopment. As Radhika Desai points out, "contender states … accelerate … development to contest imperial projects of dominant states" and "this politico-economic dialectic, and not the market or capitalism conceived in exclusively economic terms, is responsible for productive capacity spreading ever more widely around the world."[8] This state-sponsored combined development, she notes, "generally empowers working classes and popular sectors,"[9] and is given short shrift by cosmopolitan theories which mistakenly claim that "nation-states were not relevant to explaining the world order."[10] Gregory Jusdanis similarly argues that cosmopolitanism's dreams of global "peace and prosperity … come at the expense of small societies," and that the "utopian world of scattered diasporas, open borders, and hybrid identities" simply does not possess a political agent of sufficient force to protect vulnerable nations.[11]

Clearly, therefore, postcolonial states have, at times, implemented progressive social policy and acted to loosen the stranglehold of Western imperialism. No doubt Tariq Amin-Khan is correct when he argues that strong statist policies in the postcolonial world have kept "predatory transnational capital more or less at bay" for significant periods, strengthened the postcolonial industrial sector, and instituted the kinds of land reform that promote economic self-reliance.[12] What is being drawn attention to here, instead, is that every national liberation movement is composed of some elite actors whose power networks embody the future postcolonial state *in statu nascendi* and other, nonstate, actors whose massive productive and associational capacities must first be used to bring the postcolonial state into being, but which are, in case after case, forcibly separated from institutions of power once the state has established itself. As state theorist Göran Therborn explains, "representative politicians must establish some rapport with the population at large, but once elected … party leaders and prime ministers are usually made and unmade by parliamentary groups, rather than by extra-parliamentary bodies of their party."[13] In postcolonial states, this structural distance between state and nonstate networks is especially dangerous, given the ex-colonizer's usual capacity to intimidate and control the thin superstratum of state actors that has been set up to govern in the name of the nation as a whole.

What this means for our analysis is that nonstate space exists not merely in those movements that reject the state outright – anarchist and syndicalist movements, or the various other anti-state movements of recent history. Nonstate space also exists in struggles that take the nation itself as their zone of contention. Indeed, many of the productive and associational assemblages that are the lifeblood of nationalist revolution are nonstate assemblages of workers, peasants, and other ordinary citizens, possessing organizational networks and channels of solidarity that are separate from state-centric leaders and that often come into conflict with them.

In part, this is because of the difference between the *nation*, as a site of collective investment belonging to the inhabitants of a shared territorial space, and the *state*, as an embodiment of the political institutions, police powers, and bureaucracies that are erected to govern in the name of the nation. As Vilashini Cooppan points out, this idea of the nation, as the "projection and protection of an internal collective personality" is in no way reducible to the juridical and political institutions of the state.[14] It is not surprising, therefore, that many nationalist struggles are overwhelmingly comprised of nonstate networks and assemblages – especially in the case of anti-colonial revolutions, in which the colonizer comes to be associated with state functionality and the nation becomes a site of investment for nonstate organizational efforts. The profound importance of anarchism to Filipino nationalists like José Rizal and Isabelo de los Reyes is just one of the more striking examples of this coexistence of nationalist strategies and deeply anti-state networks and methods. As Benedict Anderson has shown, Rizal's attraction to propaganda by the deed and Isabelo's decision to "radicalize and organize the working class in Manila" had their roots in anarchist politics, which these nationalists adopted as an integral part of anti-colonialist praxis.[15]

The observation to be made here is that even within the domain of nation-based struggle, a wide variety of attitudes toward nonstate networks and organizational forms exists. In nationalist movements spearheaded by military cadres or operatives within the colonial legislative structure, nonstate spaces and networks may never enter into the public dialogue surrounding the independence struggle, except in the specter of forms of "disorder" that must supposedly be suppressed in the name of law and order. By contrast, in nationalist movements that rely heavily from the beginning on self-organized blocs of workers, peasants, and other ordinary citizens, public dialogue often enshrines such nonstate networks as the heart of the nationalist movement, to the point of projecting the state-to-be as nothing more than the self-administration of already-existing nonstate networks.

The point of this study is not to measure the success of states in making good on their promises to reflect and represent nonstate networks. Rather than draw up a balance sheet of state failure and state welfare along these lines, I choose to focus on the specific potentialities for group formation, decision-making, and self-defense that nonstate networks possess in and of themselves, regardless of whether at some point they become channelized into investments in the nation as a unit of sovereignty. I proceed in this way because in working my way through literary representations of nonstate workers' organizations, rural insurgencies, strike campaigns, mutual-aid networks, and alternative governance systems, I noticed that the literature of nonstate networks simply speaks a different language than literature focused on the internal workings of the nation-state and its protagonists. Instead of triangulating narrative primarily through a national "superaddressee" of the kind E. San Juan describes, who is supposed to personify the "close dialectical unity between the individual and the mass," such works often track disconnected processes of reciprocal self-constitution, in which nonstate actors emerge and achieve synergy without reference to centralized state leaders.[16] And instead of poetic portraiture focused on the moral agonies leaders face in distributing resources, such literature returns again and again to scenes of auto-appropriation, in which ordinary people take ownership of their workplaces and land, without the mediating presence of states, parties, or their bureaucracies.

Literary treatments of nonstate processes such as these therefore have tropological organizations all their own, which are distinct from literatures of national *Bildung*. Novels devoted to nonstate processes, such as Claude McKay's *Banjo* and Patrick Chamoiseau's *Le papillon et la lumière*, often feel plotless, since their action is not organized around the *crise de conscience* of a central, national protagonist, the aftermath of which is meant to allegorize a postcolonial national dénouement. Other novels, such as Ousmane Sembene's *Les bouts de bois de Dieu* and Arundhati Roy's *The God of Small Things* do have robust underlying plot structures, but often invest more narrative energy in diegetically undeveloped scenes of auto-appropriation and self-organization than their overall systems of characterological motivation can easily support. Similarly, the nonstate poetic imaginations I analyze here are remote from investments in individual lyric figures, using highly fractured verse forms to imagine futural nonstate constellations.

What these works bring into view through these means is technologies of association that are external to state bureaucracy and state command. The most distinctive characteristic of these technologies of association is that they project alternative governance systems, rooted in shared spaces of group-formation and decision-making. In each literary itinerary my chapters trace, I show how these nonstate networks stand in direct contrast to the structures of hierarchy and command that anticipate new state formations.

This is why I emphasize the *spatiality* of these nonstate networks and processes. This book's focus is not the "virtual electronic neighborhoods"[17] that Arjun Appadurai describes in his account of diasporic imaginaries, nor is it the nomadic, deterritorialized human flows that Gilles Deleuze imagines as the substrate of globalization. As Imre Szeman points out, this invented "'post-national' world of hybrid subjectivities" is often little more than "a political fiction whose intent is to transform the remaining spaces of the public in terms of the neoliberal logic of the private (capitalist) enterprise."[18] Within this kind of cosmopolitan optics, Weihsin Gui argues, "culture's mobility, heterogeneity, and radicalism are encompassed by globalization and become symptoms of its administration."[19]

The nonstate spaces I analyze have little in common with these cosmopolitan fictions of globalized, migratory identities, both because these deterritorialized flows are often theoretical fictions that replace the real misery of economic migration with a fantasy of global travel, and because these cosmopolitan worldscapes are really only *spaces* in the loosest sense of the term: imaginary maps of consumption patterns or migratory trajectories that often develop no mass-based forms of political agency. What if we replaced this loose, undefined spatiality – really, the abstract, agentless space of global capital – with Merleau-Ponty's definition of space as the lived schema by means of which humans project and test out their capacities for action on their environment? In this account, space is not defined as an empirical extension of matter, but as the "sense which is revealed where the paths of my various experiences intersect, and also where my own and other people's intersect and engage each other like gears."[20]

Nonstate space, in this sense, would refer to the schemata of purposive action humans acquire by virtue of traversing the shared spaces that make social reproduction outside the state possible. Conceived in this way, nonstate space could be imagined as a lived projection of the transformative actions made possible by people's relationships to the infrastructures, built environments, production processes, and associational dynamics that structure their everyday lives. It is at this level of complex, interlinked reproductive practices, I'd propose, that spaces of self-government out-side the state first become palpable – sometimes in the barricades that protect sites of nonstate medical care, food production, and community self-regulation from state interference, sometimes in the communication networks that mobilize ordinary citizens to occupy city squares, highways, ports, and industrial areas with incredible speed.

Spaces like these embody mutual-aid processes, self-defense assets, and forms of goods creation that function as real existing counterpowers to the state. And it is precisely this capacity to erect state-dystonic forms of self-government that distinguishes nonstate assemblages from other forms of grassroots political activity, whether they be reform movements, minority-party electoral drives, or lobbying efforts of various kinds. While such grassroots movements often overlap with nonstate assemblages, borrowing personnel from and voicing solidarity with them, they are nevertheless perfectly commensurable with state command functions, seeking primarily to change the existing distribution of resources within state bureaucracies. Nonstate space, by contrast, emerges only when recourse to the legal apparatuses of the state has been forcibly withheld by the authorities or collectively abandoned by nonstate actors, with struggle being reopened on the terrain on which the basic structures that make social life possible are contested – not just discursively, but by means of conflicting spatial occupations, expropriations, and relations of force.

If the term "nation" refers to the matrix of investments populations sustain with respect to language, ethnicity, and culture, nonstate space could be imagined as the entire range of lived relationships to technology, production, transport, group-formation, and ad hoc communications networks that ideologies of nationhood seek to capture and direct. This is why, while national affiliation exists as a durable psychological investiture, nonstate space is rarely made the object of conscious reflection or emo-tional cathexis – that is, until the process of "loyalty transfer" to nation-hood breaks down.[21] Indeed, nonstate space typically emerges only as a collective experience of *rupture* within the primordial fabric of social orga-nization, which opens up a space of social reproduction administered by ordinary people themselves, outside of state-centric forms of legitimation and ideological habit. *Vis-à-vis* the well-worn and constantly reinforced channels of national identification, nonstate space could be imagined as a zone of pre-predicative experience, in Husserl's sense: a world of func-tional equilibria, kinesthetic facilitations, and interhuman adjustments that function pre-rationally to distribute social space, and which rarely become thematic objects of consciousness in and of themselves, unless their smooth working is extrinsically interrupted.

What this study asks is how it is possible to imagine the resources and potentialities such nonstate spaces possess. Distributed across the intersecting skills and powers that humans acquire as a function of their socially reproductive capabilities, nonstate space nevertheless often has little ideological "support." It consists not so much in programs or ready-made affective cultures as in patterns of interaction that exist in highly variable relations to states: sometimes effectively channelized into their structures of delegation and rendered inert, sometimes forcibly liquidated by the state, and sometimes developing autonomously outside the state.

Whatever postures they maintain toward the apparatuses of the state, however, nonstate spaces are never simply the byproduct of existing ideologies of national belonging or state functionality, which means that innovative reading practices are necessary to decode the specific potentialities for self-government that nonstate spaces possess. In this study, I look to literary representations of nonstate space because works of literature are particularly adept at projecting the matrix of lived relationships within which nonstate space has its being. One of the challenges we face in picturing nonstate space is that the built environments, productive processes, and human networks that make nonstate space possible are often precisely those that are at the basis of state functionality, to such an extent that it is difficult to imagine them existing as anything other than state assets.

Reading for nonstate space therefore means remaining attentive to the "regimes of sensible intensity" that Jacques Rancière describes in *The Politics of Aesthetics*: the "trajectories between the visible and the sayable, relationships between modes of being, modes of saying and modes of doing and making" that literature renders visible.[22] Such "map[s] of the sensible," Rancière stresses, are not merely mimetic representations of existing distributions of social roles and occupations, but ways of "interfering with the functionality of gestures and rhythms adapted to the natural cycles of production, reproduction and submission" (*PA* 39). In fact, Rancière defines the function of literature itself in terms of its capacity to disrupt the existing distribution of the sensible. In contrast to scholarly history, literature "shifts the focus from great names and events to the life of the anonymous … [and] revokes the oratorical model of speech in favor of the interpretation of signs on the body of people, things, and civilizations" (*PA* 34).

No doubt, some works of literature introduce such "lines of fracture and disincorporation into imaginary collective bodies" (*PA* 39) more than others. Nevertheless, my decision to focus on literature in this study does owe much to Rancière's sense of literature's capacity to constitute "uncertain communities" (*PA* 40) at a distance from the matrix of fantasies and investments defined by the nation-state. The kind of mapping involved in this literary vocation is akin to the "cognitive mapping" described by Frederic Jameson, in that it "enable[s] a situational representation on the part of the individual subject" of "the ensemble of society's structures as a whole."[23] But Jameson's conception of cognitive mapping relies on a schematic distinction between "the phenomenological experience of the individual" and the capitalist "world space" that frames that experience without being lived or represented within its contours.[24] This perspective frames literature as that mediating space that constantly refers lived experience to its framing truth, the "unrepresentable totality" of multinational capital which, if mapped, would allow us to "regain a capacity to act and struggle which is at present neutralized by our spatial as well as our social confusion."[25]

My approach in this book flips this relational dynamic on its head, reading first and foremost for scenes in which the social functionality that multinational capital requires in order to function is revealed to operate at the level of experiential relations that involve people's capacities for reproductive, interhuman action. Rather than promoting the idea of capitalist worldspace as an "elsewhere," into whose realm literature transports the immediacies of interpersonal experience, the analytic of nonstate space emphasizes the immanent reconfigurations of interpersonal reproductive relations that the agents of capital must effect in order to perpetuate the extraction of value. The "mapping" that literature performs within this analytic is therefore not primarily cognitive, and is not imagined as part of a comprehensive epistemological project – as if the capacity to act collectively depended, first, on nonstate actors' capacity to situate themselves with respect to a global totality, navigate this abstract representational space with accuracy, and then translate this global knowledge into concrete strategic imperatives.

The cartographies I read for are to a much larger extent *relational* cartographies, in which large-scale social systems become sensible as such in and through collective action aimed at transforming them – much like Husserl's eidetic variation maps out the coordinates of a perceptual field only by experimentally altering the systems of qualitative dependency that determine its structure. This kind of relational mapping takes seriously Édouard Glissant's warning that the attempt to inscribe populations fractured by New World slavery and colonialism into "History with a capital H," far from "reinforcing a global consciousness or permitting the historical process to be established beyond the ruptures experienced," instead merely entifies the historical process, as if "history [were] simply a sequence of events" to be "conceived in terms of the list of discoverers and governors" of colonized spaces.[26] In such spaces, literature's role should not be to refer the local immediacies of colonized experience to the Eurocentric structures of capital accumulation that overarch them. Such a process of referral only reaffirms the historical narrative that so many colonized peoples have internalized anyway: that their local histories are only epiphenomena of larger processes controlled by the Global North. In "the void of an imposed nonhistory," literature should instead take shape as an "experimental mediation" – a process that Glissant describes in terms of relational constructs in which "analytic thought is led to construct unities whose interdependent variances jointly piece together the interactive totality."[27]

This conception of a social totality that is composed not just of an awesomely unapproachable exchange process, but also of the networked, interhuman processes that animate it, exceed it, and contest it, is central to the literary works I analyze in this book. To demonstrate literature's capacity to extrude, from the everyday texture of relational life, the nonstate capacities hidden within the regimes of capitalist work and leisure, this book stages three literary-geographical itineraries in each of its three main chapters.

The first chapter examines literature devoted to one of the most adaptable and potent examples of nonstate space: the general strike. Taking up the challenge Gayatri Spivak has recently articulated to account for the differential "reterritorializations" of the general strike phenomenon on a global scale,[28] I address literary representations of three general strikes of the colonial and postcolonial world: Patrick Chamoiseau's representations of the political activity surrounding the 2009 general strike in the French Antilles in *Les neuf consciences du Malfini* and *Le papillon et la lumière*; Ousmane Sembene's representation of the Dakar–Niger Railway Strike of 1947–1948 in *Les bouts de bois de Dieu*; and Miguel Ángel Asturias' representation of the Guatemalan General Strike of 1944 in *Los ojos de los enterrados*.

My argument is that in each of these very different cultural and political milieux, the general strike allows the implementation of forms of coordination, delegation, and executive action that are irreducible to the vertical concentrations of power intrinsic to the state form. Chamoiseau draws on the ad hoc, local methods of social organization and emergency production surrounding the 2009 French Antillean General Strike to imagine

"l'horizontale plénitude du vivant" outside state-sponsored forms of capital realization.[29] Sembene shows how the 1947–1948 Dakar–Niger Railway
Strike resurrects traditional Bambara ceremonies and legal discourse, and
how the strikers rearticulate these cultural forms within contemporary modes
of community self-regulation, which include the shaping participation of
women and proletarian subjects in altogether new ways. Asturias describes
the uneasy interpersonal dynamics among a network of plantation workers,
railway workers, teachers, professionals, students, and soldiers that combined
to make possible the 1944 Guatemalan General Strike, which led to the overthrow of the Ubico dictatorship and precipitated democratic elections several
months later.

Analyzing these divergent and locally evolved forms of nonstate space
allows me to articulate a new theory of anti-colonial agency, which is based
less on strategies of reappropriation than on what I call "eidetic rupture":
the redeployment of nonstate organizational practices and forms of knowledge as modern technologies of self-government.

The second chapter of this book is devoted to authors who imagine
how such forms of nonstate self-government could constitute the basis
of alternative forms of internationalism. I begin by placing debates about
nonstate internationalism in the context of the anti-globalization and
Occupy movements, which have struggled to articulate how nonstate
practices could become institutionalized on anything more than a local
scale. I then turn to the work of Arundhati Roy and Claude McKay,
whose literary works suggest modes of nonstate internationalism outside
of both statist communism and the capitalist nation-state. Roy's nonstate
internationalism is visible in her treatment of the Naxalite movement
in her 2011 *Walking with the Comrades* and her 1997 *The God of Small
Things*. Reading these works together helps make it clear that *The God of
Small Things'* symbolic layerings of Naxalite activists, Untouchable factory workers, and the "failed developmental bourgeoisie" are an attempt
to imagine a nonstate development project that could somehow borrow
elements from rural insurgency programs, proletarian internationalism,
and decentralized development initiatives such as those undertaken in
Kerala in the late 1960s.

Claude McKay offers similarly complex socio-political superpositions
in his 1929 novel *Banjo*, as well as in nonfiction works such as *The Negroes
in America* and *Harlem: Negro Metropolis* and in his recently rediscovered
novel manuscript *Amiable with Big Teeth: A Novel Concerning the Love
Affair between the Communists and the Black Sheep of Harlem*. McKay's idea
of a Negro Bund, modeled on the General Jewish Labor Bund, as well as

his many overlapping images of alternative exchange economies and self-organized communities, make clear his ambition to discover mechanisms of economic mutual aid and local self-rule that could "go global" even in the absence of party, state, and interstate mechanisms.

My final chapter focuses on literature that speculates about "nonstate futures" – specifically, about the ways that cultural identity and transnational exchange would have to be rethought in a future world governed by nonstate processes. The chapter focuses on Melvin Tolson, whose poems "E. & O. E.," *Libretto for the Republic of Liberia*, and *Harlem Gallery* imagine a nonstate and specifically black internationalism, and T. S. Eliot, the ambivalent internationalist whose models of poetic agency Tolson restages and writes against. The chapter recovers the surprising anti-colonial critique that Eliot articulates in *Notes towards the Definition of Culture* and analyzes passages from "The Waste Land" as attempts to imagine a world culture based on a federation of postcolonial nations – Lithuania, Bosnia, Ireland, and India standing as sites of anti-colonial agency in the poem. Tolson's critique of Eliot targets the covertly Eurocentric "placelessness" of Eliot's imagined world culture, and proposes an entirely different model of nonstate cultural exchange based on local structures of self-government. This political vision, I argue, takes as its starting point the Non-Aligned Movement of Nehru, Nasser, Nkrumah, and Sukarno, but it also contains a critique of the class hierarchies that often stubbornly persist within decolonizing states. His method, therefore, is to use the resources of modernist abstraction to project a future world-system in which these fundamentally state-based forms of anti-colonial agency come up against the limits of capitalist development and make visible new forms of nonstate internationalism. Tolson's nonstate poetics therefore embodies a form of nonstate ideation with a scope and allusiveness rivaling Eliot's, but which is rooted in non-hierarchical modes of self-government of global reach.

All in all, then, this book develops a theoretical method that renders visible imaginations of nonstate forms of organization, production, and cultural negotiation. The literary geographies with which it engages extend from the early twentieth century to the very recent present, and construct an alternative genealogy of transnational writing that spans the modern/postmodern, center/periphery, and postcolonial/world literature divides.[30]

Mapping out the transnational connections between these twentieth- and twenty-first-century struggles is an urgent critical project because examining the ways in which nonstate space has metastasized in different locales can help us understand how and why nonstate space can emerge, even in geographies that appear to be dominated by state power. In social worlds where the military resources and logistical and surveillance capabilities of the state seem to incorporate all aspects of life under the aegis of state space, it can be difficult to imagine how nonstate space can emerge. In recent theory, such ruptures have proved exceptionally difficult to conceptualize, often being represented as an unaccountable force, or even an aporia.

This book offers a new kind of literary geography in response to these challenges – the challenge of thinking a lived rupture with state space, the challenge of imagining an internationalism rooted in nonstate political configurations, and the challenge of imagining global noncapitalist futures. In each chapter, I show how the speculative resources of literature offer ways to move beyond some of the conceptual impasses that confront the humanities today. What literature can offer us is new stories, new images, that relate to the ways that capacities for self-government are born, out of places from which, to an outsider, they might seem least likely to emerge. This process is a qualitative at least as much as a quantitative one. It inheres in the way people transform themselves, their relationships, and their lived environments on the most fundamental level; it therefore unfolds in a domain of experience whose richness and many-sidedness literature is preeminently able to evoke.

This does not mean, however, that I seek to delineate some universal history of nonstate processes in this book or that the texts I focus on are drawn from a canon of world literature classics. According to the method I pursue, "world literature" does not refer to Pascale Casanova's idea of a "world literary space" composed of intellectual networks and forms of prestige that circulate on a global scale. Evocative as this idea is, it centers on forms of canonization and elite literary milieux that marginalized literary figures such as Melvin Tolson and Miguel Ángel Asturias were never able to leverage so as to secure the "literary legitimacy" that Casanova sees as the ultimate desideratum of the World Republic of Letters.[31] Placing comparatively peripheral writers such as these next to acknowledged "greats" such as T. S. Eliot and Arundhati Roy is therefore an act of "cultural parataxis," in Susan Stanford Friedman's sense – a way of reading for "multiple centers, agencies, and subjectivities," rather than assuming "a single center from which power flows unidirectionally."[32]

Such a mode of reading proposes that what counts as "world literature" can be defined as a *product* of the critical itinerary constructed in order to answer problems of global scope, as opposed to a canon, however broad, of works that have achieved world literary status by virtue of real networks of cultural prestige or canons of aesthetic merit.[33] This approach agrees with Franco Moretti's idea that "world literature is not an object, it's a *problem*" – an experiment that proceeds by defining "a unit of analysis … and then follow[ing] its metamorphoses in a variety of environments."[34] Like Rebecca Walkowitz, however, I seek to avoid "separat[ing] the analysis of literary circulation from the analysis of literary production" in the way that Moretti's model of distant reading encourages, instead deploying both reading at a distance and forms of close reading attentive to the way literary works emerge as part of a "network of peripheries that are irreducible both to nation and to globe."[35]

An approach such as this is able to register how a poet like Melvin Tolson, whose work never circulated with the kind of breadth canonical modernist texts enjoyed, nevertheless contributes to world literary ideation – the literary thinking of global problematics – even more powerfully than a poet of the stature of T. S. Eliot. It is also able to register how an early-twentieth-century black radical like Claude McKay might contribute powerfully to questions raised in the work of an author as culturally and historically removed from him as Arundhati Roy. This way of critically constructing a world literature itinerary is able to avoid not only the pitfall of "presentism" that David Damrosch mentions in *What Is World Literature?*[36] and the "Eurochronology problem" evoked by Christopher Prendergast and Arjun Appadurai,[37] but also the drive to "encyclopedic mastery and scholarly ecumenicalism" whose legacy Emily Apter interrogates in *Against World Literature*.[38] As Apter argues, the "ethic of liberal inclusiveness" such an approach to world literature promotes, as well as the "formal structures of cultural similitude" it strives to uncover, can obstruct political critique and too often accompany a "reflexive endorsement of cultural equivalence and substitutability."[39]

What if, instead of this, world literature were redefined as a matrix of creative ideation that is not captured by the state-form, its optics, or its "ethics." The literary-historical "scale enlargement" Wai Chee Dimock recommends in *Through Other Continents* is a potent gesture in this direction, as is Matthew Hart's analysis of the literary linking of "local forms of belonging and political action to a 'deterritorializing' refusal to take the relationship among a people, a state, and a language as a settled object of value."[40] What I add to this conversation is a focus on spatial occupations and practices of self-government that offer themselves as alternatives to the vertical power structures of the state – not just by virtue of nomadic dispersion or transnational tastes or affects, but as part of a nonstate politico-economic project that each author I examine brings partially into view.

Approaching world literature in this way means reassessing the meanings of the words "world" and "literature" as they have been deployed in recent scholarship. This is because, as the Warwick Research Collective (WReC) points out, the "world" in world literature risks projecting the fiction of "a 'level playing field,' a more or less free space in which texts from around the globe can circulate, intersect and converse with one another."[41] Such a concept of literary sharing ignores the stark inequalities in the world-system that the privileged realm of literary worldedness traverses in an ideal form. The fact that only some, privileged, largely Euro-American publishers dominate this field leads to the awkward conclusion that world literature, in principle, includes works produced everywhere, but, in practice, is restricted to the small number of authors and ideas that have access to the infrastructures of global publishing.

To avoid this embarrassment, it is tempting to redefine world literature along the lines suggested by WReC itself: as "literature that registers the (modern capitalist) world-system."[42] Such an approach has the merit of dispensing with the concept of literature as an autonomous realm of ethical exchange and placing literature, instead, squarely in the middle of global contestations that result from "the imposition of capitalism on cultures and societies hitherto un- or only sectorally capitalised."[43] My own analyses borrow this perspective, viewing Arundhati Roy's Kerala in terms of the United States' underdevelopment agenda in the subcontinent and Patrick Chamoiseau's Martinique in terms of the French metropole's neocolonialist designs on its overseas departments and regions. But also crucial to my concept of world literature is what Pheng Cheah refers to as the process of *worlding* that is an integral part of literature's experiential structure: that is, its capacity to project "the totality of meaningful relations that is the ontological condition for the production of values and norms."[44] In Cheah's account, world literature should not be defined simply as literature that *registers* the process of global capitalist expansion, in the language of WReC, but as literature that embodies the imaginative vocation to "remake the world against capitalist globalization" (*WIW* 2).

Unfortunately, Cheah's language of normativity remains within the ethico-discursive orbit of Habermasian communicative action, and his approach as a whole maintains allegiance to a quixotic, Derridean account of social change, as being awarded through an unaccountable "gift of time." Nevertheless, his definition of world literature as involving a fundamental "self-determining plasticity of human existence" (*WIW* 199) that can imaginatively remake social space on a global scale discloses an essential horizon of world literature that I take up in this book. It is a concept of world literature that I define not in terms of a currently existing theater of transnational friendship and understanding, but in terms of the relational technologies, interhuman logistics, and tactical approaches that world literature archives, and which can be used to construct imaginations of postcapitalist worldhood that have, in a sense, always been implied by the conception of world literature as a space of free self-activity, equally available to all. World literature, in other words, is taken up as an incomplete, futural project in my analyses – one geared toward imaginations of governance complexes and micropolitical strategies that could remake worlds against or beyond capitalist spaces of accumulation.

World literature as an inexistent, or as a futural conjecture, but one undergirded by very real structures of globalized dependency and struggle: this is the proposition I explore in this book – one which seeks to animate our reading practices not through the touristic injunction simply to understand other cultures, but rather through the imperative to assemble culturally divergent strategies of encounter, affective sutures, and interpersonal postures, to ask which of them are context-bound and which might be reinvented or metamorphosed to operate within cultures of struggle that possess, or could possess, cognates in real or imaginable social struggles of global scope.

As Cheah puts it in *What Is a World?*, "Global capitalist economic activity with its single division of labor thrives best in the absence of a corresponding global unified political structure" (*WIW* 78). Instead of positing global literary circulation as a guilty, partial compensation for this lack of governance complexes of the scale and pervasiveness of the capitalist world-system, why not imagine world literature as the disciplinary project that reads both for the social pathogens created by the globalization of capital and for literary traces that point toward a (partial, fragmentary, or altogether inexistent) globalization of dissent, recomposition, and self-government?

In this book, I look for proleptic traces of these forms of worlding in literary works that document both real and imagined complexes of nonstate self-rule – rooted in local systems of mutual aid, decision-making, and reproduction, but networked globally outside the aegis of state and interstate forces. That such nonstate complexes often become most lucidly visible through works of literature could be viewed as something like a scandal if we remain attached to the idea of literature as a zone of authenticity opposed to geopolitical ideation – what Chris Nealon describes as literature's status as an object to be mined for its "ethical value as a vulnerable tissue of fragments."[45] But what if we took seriously the proposition that literature can itself be a potent force of social ideation, helping to transform theoretical knowledge by encouraging us to imagine the politically unimaginable?

This is the proposition I explore in this book. In doing so, I advance a theory of social transformation that is not primarily a theory of transformed sign-systems or forms of reappropriation, but rather a theory of transformation based on populations' lived relationships to their social environments, a theory of new spatial choreographies that give rise to new habits of thought and new relations of force.

How do such new configurations come into being? How do they organize nonstate phenomenologies and modes of intercourse?

To understand this, let's first gain a deeper understanding of what is meant by nonstate space and how it differs from state space.

## Nonstate Space

Nonstate space is easiest to visualize in social groups that have rejected the state wholesale, such as the self-governing hill dwellers of Southeast Asia that James C. Scott describes in *The Art of Not Being Governed*. "The economic, political, and cultural organization of such people is," he explains, "in large part, a strategic adaptation to avoid incorporation in state structures."[46] Existing outside the "space of appropriation" defined by the state, and employing state-evasive productive forms and modes of organization, such societies exhibit "a social structure that can be both disaggregated and re-assembled" efficiently (*ANB* 211).

If states promote legible, appropriable, measurable social spaces, nonstate societies such as these inhabit regions remote from state control, evolve decision-making practices that are difficult to coopt, and produce crops (such as root vegetables) that cannot be easily quantified, appropriated, or transported by state forces. Whereas modern cadestral maps are designed to streamline the process of state appropriation, nonstate forms of measure "construct the landscape according to units of work and yield, type of soil, accessibility, and ability to provide subsistence, none of which would necessarily accord with surface area" (*ANB* 27). In the European context, the *journal* and the *morgen* are good examples of this: they are units of measure corresponding to the number of days required to work a given plot of land – a variable that could vary dramatically "depending on the strength of local draftpower and the crops sown, and ... as technology (plow tips, yokes, harnesses) affected the work a man could accomplish in a day" (*ANB* 26).

The nonstate forms of knowledge encoded in such forms of reckoning embody competencies that are irreducible to state control, and which exhibit astonishing levels of sophistication. The nonstate Russian village committees Scott analyzes, for example, "ke[pt] records for allocating allotment lands, organiz[ed] communal plow teams [and] fix[ed] grazing schedules" (*ANB* 207) in the absence of any official government bureaucracy.

The state, in Scott's terminology, is "parasitic" on informal, nonstate processes such as these, which have often predated the state by hundreds of years. Possessing no productive apparatus of its own, the state can therefore be seen, fundamentally, as a power of annexation, which folds existing forms of largely autonomous production into itself, transforming these context-sensitive forms of nonstate knowledge into "State-Accessible Product."[47] Nonstate space is a way of designating social networks that have succeeded in reclaiming these creative processes and managing them outside the aegis of the state.

Maroon communities of escaped slaves, nomadic and other self-governing peoples, and the peasantries of Europe until the eighteenth century all furnish examples of this kind of nonstate space. But what about complex, industrial societies inhabited by millions, rather than hundreds or, at most, thousands, of people? Is it really possible to speak of nonstate space in a modern, industrial world which has all but obliterated craft production and the autonomous forms of work and mutual aid that were its social corollaries? In such industrially-developed spaces, work processes and their attendant modes of social reproduction are, in a much more direct way, the *product* of state-sponsored economic development. How could nonstate space exist in a social landscape that appears to be determined through and through by state power?

In his accounts of contemporary anti-state social movements, Raúl Zibechi describes the capacity of nonstate networks to "open spaces or gaps in the dominant system, physical and symbolic spaces of resistance that became spaces of survival."[48] Zibechi's account of Aymara neighborhood councils in El Alto, Bolivia, for example, focuses on the ways in which horizontally-organized groups mount collective works projects, control market stalls, regulate education, and even impose fines through a Federation of Neighborhood Councils – in short, "fulfill the functions of a state," but in such a way that the community's capacity to "defend itself, impart justice and meet basic needs" is not institutionally ossified in "separate bodies" removed from the populace itself (*TR* 30, 31). In the October 2003 revolt against the cheap export of natural gas to the United States, these nonstate powers mobilized 500,000 people to blockade roads, dig deep trenches, and create networks of committees to organize food supply and factors of self-defense, without any organizational structure outside that provided by the neighborhood councils, exhibiting a "type of collective, rotating, and decentralized leadership" that avoided vertical concentrations of power (*TR* 43).

In Zibechi's account, this "nonstate orientation of political action" is characteristic not just of Bolivia's organizers, but also of the landless movement in Brazil, indigenous Ecuadoran activists, neo-Zapatistas, and Argentine workers who occupied and self-managed factories in the wake of the massive capital flight of 2001 (*TR* 83). These various movements share several characteristics, according to Zibechi: they seek "autonomy from the state as well as from political parties," an autonomy that is rooted in their creation of self-managed forms of production and political cohesion; they are organized around "accomplish[ing] tasks previously overseen by the state," whether it be in the self-managed schools of Brazil's landless movement or the Zapatista *casas de salud* that provide health care outside the aegis of the Mexican state; they view "land, factories, and settlements as spaces in which to produce without bosses or foremen," characterized by "a minimal division of labor and based on new techniques of production that do not generate alienation or destroy the environment"; and they are rooted in "family and community daily life, often taking the form of territorially-based self-organizing networks," as opposed to hierarchical forms of organization based on separations "between those who direct and execute … in which the leaders are separated from the bases" (*TR* 16, 21, 17, 17, 18, 18).

Nonstate space, in this context, refers not just to forms of state evasion practiced by pastoralist and nomadic societies, but to a recapturing and territorializing of spaces within the nominal orbit of modern capitalist states, in a way that severs them from state forms of accumulation and command. The difference between this kind of nonstate space and state evasion is that the former does not just seek an enclave of nonstate self-administration, but presents itself as an organizational process that could become generalized within the matrix of modern relations of production and exchange, and views the factory, the city, and the masses not as enemies, but as a landscape of relationships that could be self-organized.

An increasingly large amount of theoretical attention is being devoted to such twenty-first-century forms of nonstate self-organization. Paul Mason sees post-2008 forms of global protest as embodying new forms of revolt, "led by fragmented and precarious people" and characterized by networked action, swarm tactics, and liberated spaces of "experimental, shared community."[49] Alain Badiou, as well, sees the events of the Arab Spring as part of a "rebirth of history" under way in the first decades of the twentieth century, in which "the advent of a different world" is palpable.[50] Even Slavoj Žižek, more well-known for his lionizing of the party as a "strong body able to reach quick decisions," celebrated the spirit of "popular self-organization" in the Greek protest movement and "the crowd in Tahrir square … that embodied the true *volonté générale.*"[51]

This theoretical turn toward nonstate-oriented forms of social organization represents something crucial in the geopolitical landscape of popular struggle: a turn away from the capture of state bureaucracies, and a turn toward self-organization. In Tahrir Square, for example, hundreds of thousands of protestors not only overwhelmed and neutralized state security forces, but also set up field hospitals and a ring of checkpoints around Tahrir Square, imposing nonstate forms of regulation on a space formerly dominated by the largest police establishment in the country. Similarly, in 2012, in the General Hospital of Kilkis, Greece, health workers occupied the building and reopened it under workers' control, issuing a statement that it "will henceforth be self-governed and the only legitimate means of administrative decision making will be the General Assembly of its workers."[52] Related forms of nonstate organization were also visible in Tunisia, where, in mass meetings, citizens elected nonstate provisional councils to organize logistics and sanitation, and workers at Tunisie Télécom, Société nationale de distribution des pétroles, Banque Nationale Agricole, and Société Tunisienne d'Assurances et de Réassurances took control of their workplaces, forcibly removing their CEOs from their offices.

But twenty-first-century social movements do not possess a premium on nonstate tactics and organizational modes. How do today's occupied squares and workplaces compare with the Iranian *shuras* of 1978–1979, which instituted nonstate, nonparty worker control of factories, farms, schools, and the military, extending even to the sourcing of raw materials and the coordination of sales on a large scale?[53] How do they compare with the Portuguese *comissões de trabalhadores* of 1974–1975, which established nonstate, nonparty worker control over 4,000 workplaces in the country and organized – jointly with land workers – the military, popular clinics, cultural centers, and residents' commissions, which coordinated the occupation of vacant housing?[54] How do they compare with the nonstate *cordones industriales* of Chile in 1972 and 1973, the *assemblee autonome operaie* of Italy in the 1970s, the *autogestionnaires* of Algeria in 1962, or the earlier experiences of nonstate counsel, armed self-regulation, and production-in-common pioneered by workers in Russia (1917), Germany (1919), Italy (1919–1920) Spain (1936–1939), Indonesia (1945–1946), and Hungary (1956)?

In this book, I argue that there are fundamental connections between these twentieth-century forms of nonstate space and those we have seen in the first years of the new century. Both historical moments are character-ized by massive mobilizations of nonstate actors which must contend with state forces that seek to undermine, channelize, or suppress them. In the process, an immense number of diverse nonstate actors have attempted to consolidate operational strategies, tactical networks, and micropolitical forms to combat state power. In certain cases, nonstate actors have established shifting, agonistic alliances with state actors to institutionalize the social forms they have developed (Algeria [1962], Argentina [1973 and 2001–2003], Venezuela [2002–2003]), in other cases, formidable hostility to the state is maintained (West Bengal, Andhra Pradesh, Bihar, Madhya Pradesh, Uttar Pradesh, and other "Naxalite-affected" areas [1967 to the present], Chiapas [1994 to the present], Bolivia [2000 and 2003]). But whatever the vicissitudes of nonstate actors and methods, their struggles constitute a body of strategies, tactics, forms, and knowledge that are in urgent communication with each other, sometimes consciously, some-times unconsciously.

The historical continuities between these twentieth- and twenty-first-century forms of nonstate space have often been overlooked in favor of forms of "epochal thinking" that stress a division between early-twentieth-century forms of workers' struggle and more recent struggles. The theoret-ical cooperative Théorie Communiste, for example, sees twentieth-century workers' struggles as hopelessly mired in the logic of production: "as long as struggles remained attached to the workplace," the French theorists argue, "they could only express themselves as a defense of the condition of the working class," as opposed to a self-abolition of the working class itself.[55] In other words, the ideals of self-management, of "extending the condition of work to everyone … and rewarding labor with its rightful share of the value it produces (through various schemes of labor-accounting)" just keep alive the regime of industrial value-production that should instead be super-seded by a complete "abolition of work."[56] More recent "riots, lootings and strikes without demands" supposedly reflect a more radical refusal of work in its entirety, and mark a shift away from the older workers' movements' ambitions to take control of production and gear it toward human need.[57]

Raúl Zibechi, despite the power of his analysis, sometimes falls into a similar line of argument. The old labor movement, he claims, "saw the state as the point of reference, object and target of their action," and shared its "unitary, centralizing logic," using "strikes and demonstrations" that were intended merely to "increase their bargaining power," whereas the "self-affirming forms of action" of the new social movements "tend to replace the older forms, such as the strike" (*TR* 63, 63, 18).

Claims such as these are perplexing, first, because Zibechi himself highlights the crucial role that strikes, factory occupations, and forms of self-management – inherited from early-twentieth-century struggles – play in the new social movements, and second, because such claims ignore the vast diversity of nonstate strategies that have emerged globally, and span the twentieth and twenty-first centuries, outside reform-oriented models of labor activism: the hartals, bandhs, general strikes, and "stayaway" campaigns that link early- and mid-twentieth-century Indian, Ghanaian, and Chinese decolonization to post-1970s militancy in Zimbabwe and South Africa; the role of factory occupation in early-twentieth-century Italy and decolonizing Algeria, resurrected in Uruguay (1973), Chicago, United States (2008 and 2012), Pyeongtaek, South Korea (2009), Isle of Wight, UK (2009), Helwan, Egypt (2013), Thessaloniki, Greece (2013), Priverno, Italy (2014), Amiens, France (2014), and Dandenong, Australia (2015); and the development of organs of racial self-defense within larger workers' movements, from the Jewish Bund, beginning in the 1890s, to the African Blood Brotherhood, active in the 1910s and 1920s, to the League of Revolutionary Black Workers, the Revolutionary Action Movement, The Black Panther Party for Self-Defense, and the Black Liberation Army.

How might our theories of postcolonial agency and global social movements shift if they fully registered the importance of these continuities?

One shift we could envision would be to begin regarding *the nonstate* not simply as a space of autotelic revolt or sectarian lifestyle practices, but as the real, networked productive capacity of society, awakened into concerted action through its self-separation from the state. This would mean taking seriously the ambitions of twentieth- and twenty-first-century nonstate actors to devise methods of decision-making and production external to party and state structures, but still capable of facilitating social exchange on a scale that could rival state and interstate apparatuses.

Far from representing a perpetuation of the logic of capital and the subordinate position of the working class, this ambition represents one of the most direct and comprehensive threats to the capitalist state that has yet been devised. This is because, despite common parlance ("state infrastructure," "state health care"), the state has no productive capabilities of its own, but is constituted instead as a mechanism for the vertical transfer of wealth and power away from its generative source in nonstate reproductive networks. Only the collective self-direction of socially useful activity outside of state structures reveals this bizarre nakedness of the state for all to see, while at the same time displaying the kinds of profound interpersonal transformation that become possible when the state's powers of annexation are suspended.

Admittedly, without stories and images of these kinds of transformation, it can be difficult to imagine how production in common and decision-making about supplies, logistics, and techniques could be conducted outside of the production regimes of the capitalist state – difficult to imagine how all production and decision-making doesn't somehow ultimately *belong* to the state. This is where the qualitative resources of literature can offer a corrective to theoretical arrogance about the intellectual "limitations" of workers, or their tendency to reproduce only the capitalist productive regimes that they know.

Possessing an adequate theory of the state also helps. Only by fully grasping the functional relationships embodied in the state can we understand the magnitude of the transformation that is ventured in nonstate mechanisms of production and exchange.

## Autogestion

In his study *De l'État*, Henri Lefebvre offers a theory of the state that helps open up some crucial questions about the distinctions and relationships between state and nonstate social configurations. In the fourth volume of this lapidary work, he describes the state as "binding" itself to space: "L'État se lie à l'espace."[58] This image of the state linking or attaching itself to something external to itself is crucial, as it contains the first inkling of a theory of nonstate space as a socially generative basis of state functions. But in this chapter, and in many of his other writings on the topic, Lefebvre has great difficulty defining this other space, this space beyond the state: is it "l'espace économique préexistant (preexistent economic space)" or "le territoire dit national (the so-called national territory)"?[59] Perhaps it is what Lefebvre describes as the "sociopolitical constitution" of society[60] or, at an even greater level of abstractness, its "differential space"?[61]

As historians of the state remind us, it is a mistake to imagine the modern state, with its bureaucracies, regulatory apparatuses, and personnel, simply grafting itself onto a "natural" economic order that precedes it. Whether it be in nineteenth-century Prussia, where the state embodied a *rapprochement* between junkerdom and the Rhenish bourgeoisie, or in Meiji Japan, where it represented a strategic alliance between the anti-*bakufu daimyō* and the merchant houses of Osaka and Kyoto, the modern state emerges as a politico-economic compromise between the controllers of social wealth.[62] As such, the state is not external to "the economic" except insofar as it serves a mediating role to coordinate economic functions that are in the interests of all ruling elites, but that could not be performed satisfactorily by any particular ruling elite.

This is why Nicos Poulantzas describes the state as a "factor of *political organization* of the dominant classes" who "left to themselves ... are not only exhausted by internal conflicts but, more often than not, founder in contradictions which make them incapable of governing politically."[63] Because of the "profound division of the bourgeois class into antagonistic fractions" and the fact that this "isolation ... is not compensated by anything, as it is by 'collective labor' on the side of the wage-earning workers of the working class," the state emerges as precisely that compromise between self-seeking "private capitalists" that enforces the interests of the class as a whole, as opposed to any individual class fraction.[64]

As Lefebvre notes, this regularization of economic relations reconfigures social space under the aegis of *l'espace étatique* – state space – which homogenizes and controls processes of production, exchange, surveillance, and organized violence which no individual capitalist could effectively coordinate him- or herself. In the third volume of *De l'État*, Lefebvre even goes so far as to refer to *le mode de production étatique*, in which the state emerges "comme forme la plus générale – forme des formes – de la société (as the most general form – the form of forms – of society)."[65]

The economy, in general, then, or the market, according to the fantasies of neoliberal authors, is not the location of nonstate space. On the contrary, "state" and "economy" refer simply to overlapping networks of power that continually share personnel and condition one another. According to this view, the state is structured as a mechanism of wealth transfer: it ensures the conditions whereby wealth can be transferred from a massive body of producers to a small, networked class which disposes of this wealth, and reproduces these inequalities of production and direction of wealth on a world scale.

Nonstate space, accordingly, is not a liberation of the economy from the state, as if the former consisted in organic economic activity which the latter arrived belatedly to arrogate and distort. The form of appropriation the state represents is already determined by the requirements of the economy with which it emerged historically: a form which ensures, through its police apparatuses and other forms of legalized violence, that property in common, direct appropriation of wealth by producers, and democratic decision-making rooted in the workplace have no standing and can be met with violence.

What this ultimately means for Lefebvre is that nonstate space emerges, as such, not through purely economic forces, but through an active, politico-economic process of *autogestion* – that is, a process in which those who produce social life assert a federative and mutual control over the productive process itself. As he explains, this vision has its origins in Proudhonian anarchism, and specifically in Proudhon's idea of industrial democracy, which "eliminate[s] the role of employers in factories and in the State" and institutes "workers' associations, the seats of the social constitution, as constitutive elements and reference points."[66] The radical thesis behind this idea is that ordinary people – coworkers, producers, the "rank and file" – have the capacity not just to organize their own production processes, but to coordinate the exchange of goods and services collectively on a large scale, deploying the "modalities of autogestion ... at all levels of social practice, including the agencies of coordination."[67] Only through autogestion, Lefebvre concludes, are humans in a position "to harness the organization of everydayness, to appropriate for themselves their own proper social life, by abolishing the discrepancy between the technical control of the outside world and the stagnation of practical relations."[68]

According to this formulation, nonstate space is not an inert, and purely economic, "outside" of the state, but rather an active process of subsuming economic relations under the control of the producers of social wealth, allowing "the members of a free association [to] take control over their own life, in such a way that it becomes their work [*œuvre*]."[69]

This proposition, that ordinary workers could organize their own productive and exchange practices on a large scale, is so far removed from the everyday experiences made possible under capitalism that it sometimes requires a complete change of perspective to weigh its implications. The case of Argentina's *fábricas ocupadas* is instructive in this respect. In response to the major capital flight that occurred in 2001 upon Argentina defaulting on its national debt, workers began occupying their factories and reopening them under their own direction. They established decision-making bodies, sales mechanisms, and structures of remuneration, and liaised with self-organized neighborhood councils; ultimately more than 300 factories in Argentina were under workers' control by 2008.[70] They also helped organize factory-sponsored community centers, libraries, medical clinics, bakeries, dining facilities, lectures, and classes.[71]

Nevertheless, the initial response of one worker in the Buenos Aires Grissinopoli factory to self-management is representative: "lo que más lo costó (the hardest thing he had to face)," he remembered, "fue convencer a sus compañeros de que ellos estaban perfectamente capacitados para poner la fábrica a producir (was convincing his coworkers that they were perfectly capable of running the factory themselves)." Before they instituted self-management, he recounts, "creían que estaba loco (they thought I was crazy)."[72]

Throughout such narratives of nonstate organizational practices, therefore, one point is articulated again and again: that the process of *horizontalidad* involved its participants in a massive transformation of their senses of self and their capacities, and that spatial occupation was at the center of this transformation.

No doubt, over the past fifteen years, members of the *fábricas ocupadas* movement have fought for state recognition of their worker-recovered workplaces, and currently the Ministry of Labor, through its "Self-Managed Labor Program," keeps records on over 300 recovered workplaces throughout Argentina, many of which receive municipal, provincial, or national subsidies. The tense and contradictory relationship between state and nonstate forces that this legal codification of recovered factories embodies is an important element of the nonstate problematic as I analyze it in this book.

A focal point of the 2009 French Caribbean General Strike, for example, was the list of demands the Liyannaj Kont Pwofitasyon (LKP) issued to the French State in its "120 Propositions" – many of which France agreed to meet as part of the Jacques Binot Accord of March 4th. Similarly, one of the major accomplishments of the Guatemalan General Strike and Revolution was the forcing of democratic state elections in December 1944, which broke the stranglehold that the US-backed dictator Jorge Ubico had on the Guatemalan state.

But not all such détentes between state and nonstate actors prove durable, even in the short term. By May 2009, the French state had made clear its intention to avoid implementing some of the most important parts of the Jacques Binot Accord, which led to further mass demonstrations on the part of the nonstate networks organized under the heading of the LKP. Likewise, the Arévalo regime in Guatemala refused to implement the large-scale land reform supported by the nonstate networks that had broken the power of Ubico, and repeatedly used military force to crush strikes in the countryside. Only after years of nonstate political mobilization and strike activity was the radical economic initiative formulated by the Guatemalan railway union implemented by Jacobo Árbenz.

What these examples teach us is that state reforms, often attributed to the genius or benevolence of individual institutional actors, are frequently compelled by the activity of nonstate protagonists, whose narratives have been lost to history. Such state actions often make possible land reform, anti-poverty campaigns, and legal protections for ethnic minorities and women – social initiatives that demonstrate the substantive progressive changes states are in a position to make. The state actors who take responsibility for these initiatives are well-documented; they are part of "History with a capital H," in Glissant's formulation. But what about the nonstate processes, struggles, and capacities that so often undergird state actions of this kind?

Chamoiseau's fables, by focusing on the evolution of new capacities and powers in networks that exist close to the ground, evoke processes of precisely this kind – the moments in which ordinary people, with all their limitations, prejudices, egoisms, and fears, existing within narrow spatial circuits and narrower realms of capacitation, suddenly evolve decision-making powers, directive capacities, and interpersonal technologies beyond everything that seemed possible just hours before. Asturias' attention to the micropolitics of the nonstate forces that propelled the Guatemalan General Strike similarly makes visible forms of affect, tactical sensitivity, and collective resistance that are remote from a state-centric optics.

What theoretical resources do we have to understand such moments of comprehensive human transformation? Psychology, phenomenology, sociology, philosophy, or economics alone cannot grasp this transformation adequately, as it is an interhuman process that involves a complex interchange among all these areas of social ontology, and that produces something rarely glimpsed by any of them.

This moment, this process, is what I refer to as eidetic rupture, and to understand it we have to draw on all the resources with which theory, and especially literature, provide us.

### Eidetic Rupture

In the language of phenomenology, *eidos* refers to the general form or structure that governs the appearance of the perceptible world. In *Experience and Judgement*, Husserl defines this structuring background to experience as "pre-predicative experience" – that is, a "passive pregivenness" that precedes and conditions every act of conscious intention.[73] "Passive," though, is actually not the best word, since, as Merleau-Ponty points out, *eidos* is, more than anything, a lived sense of the possibilities for action that an experiential arena elicits – an "inner framework of Being" that is "like the jointures of phenomena that the non-figurative painting represents by a cross or a 'flexuous line.'"[74] The best way to imagine this eidetic realm is as a deep "operative intentionality" that "produces the natural and antepredicative unity of the world and of our life, being apparent in our desires, our evaluations and in the landscape we see ... and furnishing the text which our knowledge tries to translate into precise language."[75]

What's still so useful about this theoretical model is that it opens upon a realm of pre-rational codes and types that condition conscious experience, but which do not belong strictly to the regime of "linguistic construction," or "discourse," in general.[76] The eidetic sphere is the sphere of spatial relationships, physical exigencies – what Husserl describes at one point as "correlative multiplicities of kinesthetic processes" – and also, by extension, the sphere of pre-cognitive patterns that concrete work relationships, class stratifications, and differential forms of resource allocation define.[77]

Merleau-Ponty is especially deft at illustrating how these realms of spatial practice simultaneously populate our sensorium with pre-linguistic spatial codes and establish the coordinates along which possibilities for social transformation are foreclosed and facilitated. On one hand, "vision is already inhabited by a meaning (*sens*) which gives it a function in the spectacle of the world and in our existence" – Merleau-Ponty's most striking examples of this are that "a wooden wheel placed on the ground is not, *for sight*, the same thing as a wheel bearing a load," and "a body at rest because no force is being exerted upon it is again for sight not the same thing as a body in which opposing forces are in equilibrium."[78] Spatial givens such as these, precisely because they are not consciously operative, form a vast operative intentionality which alone makes purposive action possible, and which constitutes a "core of primary meaning round which ... acts of naming and expression take shape" (*PP* xv).

But, on the other hand, spatial relationships inaugurated through historically variable forms of social domination also shape this operative intentionality. "Suppose that I work as a day-laborer," Merleau-Ponty offers, "having no farm of my own, no tools, going from one farm to another hiring myself out at harvest time; in that case I have the feeling that there is some anonymous power hovering over me and making a nomad of me, even though I want to settle into a regular job" (*PP* 444). This lived sense of concrete exigencies and limits constitutes an eidetic field, in which different workers "feel alike, not in virtue of some comparison, as if each one of us lived primarily within himself, but on the basis of our tasks and gestures" (*PP* 444).

Nevertheless, this shared eidetic field does not automatically produce struggle in common – if a "worker learns that other workers in a different trade have, after striking, obtained a wage-increase, and notices that subsequently wages have gone up in his own factory," he may or may not perceive that "his life is synchronized with the life of the town laborers and that all share a common lot" (*PP* 444). If he does experience this synchronicity, moreover, it has as little to do with "decid[ing] to become a revolutionary" (*PP* 444) in an intellectualistic way as it does with mechanically responding to economic shifts. If a transformation occurs, it occurs because "social space begins to acquire a magnetic field and … the connection objectively existing between the sections of the proletariat … is finally experienced in perception as a common obstacle to the existence of each and every one" – a process, Merleau-Ponty stresses, that "becomes clearly discernible beyond ideologies and various occupations" (*PP* 445).

This theory of social transformation is fundamentally different from theories of semiotic slippage or discursive reinscription, because its object of analysis is not just linguistic systems, but an eidetic sphere composed of spatial relationships, concrete practices, shared needs, and patterns of social facilitation and limitation. This is not to say that linguistic representation is alien to the eidetic realm – by the time of *The Crisis of European Sciences*, Husserl would stress that *eidos* is substructed through "built-up levels of validity acquired" and that linguistic and other cultural factors are built into this process, to the extent that "even what is straightforwardly perceptual is communalized."[79] What phenomenology stresses in this connection, however, is the tension that exists between linguistic sign-systems and concrete, spatial exigencies that constitute an experiential fabric intertwined with them – a plenum that is present to the speaker as a "folding over within him of the visible and the lived experience upon language, and of language upon the visible and the lived experience."[80] It is not a question of denying that ideology mediates even the "immediacies" of sense experience; this insight is inescapable, and is as old as Hegel's critique of sense-experience in the *Phenomenology of Spirit*. It is a question, rather, of asking what forces could possibly disrupt the seamless processing of lived experience according to one regime of eidetic *Sinngebung* and provide direction for the birth of something new.

It doesn't seem accidental that Merleau-Ponty chose the strike as a point of rupture that allows a reconfiguring of eidetic space. The deliberate with-drawal of labor power is, ultimately, not simply a linguistic maneuver, but a spatial act that disrupts the smooth functioning of material and imma-terial production systems on the most fundamental levels. This is because strikes, no matter how modest their scope or goals, always introduce a rift in social space between those who produce goods, services, knowledge, images, and experiences and those who produce nothing, other than the regime according to which those productions are made the property of another. The rupture that a strike produces is thus generated from within the quotidian distributions of work and wealth that constitute a given eidetic field, but opens upon a completely different mode of spatial orga-nization, made available through the centering of organizational activity within the body of workers themselves – an act which, however tempo-rarily, renders perceptible the actual function of managerial "organization," namely, the concentration of executive functions outside the control of workers themselves.

Sociological literature is filled with desperate insistences that such forms of managerial hierarchy are necessary. Weber's "complexity thesis" itself belongs to this tradition: "the more complicated and specialized modern culture becomes, the more its external supporting apparatus demands the personally detached and strictly objective *expert*."[81] "The ruled," therefore, "cannot dispense with or replace the bureaucratic apparatus once it exists, for it rests upon expert training, a functional specialization of work, and an attitude set on habitual virtuosity in the mastery of single yet methodically integrated functions."[82] Our own internalization of this sense of things, our underestimation of our own organizational capacities, belongs to a particular, shared feel for situations, a particular eidetic regime. If *eidos* is defined as a virtual "integration of nascent movements" – an intuitive pro-jection of a body's capacity for action – it is defined just as much by socially inaccessible spaces as it is by those available to be moved in.[83] The kines-theses that define eidetic experience are composed of flinches, avoidances, and a sense of the unlawful just as much as they are of spatial facilitations and appropriations.

Spatial occupations – whether they be strikes or other kinds of coor-dinated action – rupture this eidetic regime, because they fundamentally alter the lived schemata of one's capacity for purposive action. This can occur, on the most basic level, as an expanded prehension of what can be accomplished in large groups, as opposed to alone: "Der Zug von etwa zweitausend Personen vor dem Gendarmeriegebäude ankam (The column of about two thousand people arrived in front of the police station)," Max Hoelz writes in his narrative of the 1919 German Revolution, "viele gaben ihre Waffen freiwillig, den anderen wurden sie mit Gewalt abgenommen … Die Gendarmen wurden gefangengesetzt und mußten mit uns nach einem günstig gelegenen Lokal marschieren, das ich für Verteidigungszwecke bestimmt hatte (many gave up their arms voluntarily, the others had to be forced to do so … We arrested the policemen and forced them to march with us to a well-positioned building that I had chosen for defensive purposes)."[84]

At a higher level of complexity are the forms of eidetic rupture specific to the mass strike itself. In her 1905 pamphlet "The Mass Strike," Rosa Luxemburg describes the mass strike as "a gigantic, many-colored picture of a general arrangement of labor and capital that reflects all the complexity of social organization."[85] Luxemburg uses this bold language because what is at issue in a mass strike such as the 1905 general strike in Russia is nothing short of the mechanisms by which society organizes the production of its necessities and its distributions of labor and decision-making authority. In 1905, workers not only mobilized a strike force of two million, paralyzing economic life in the Empire, but also constituted workers' councils that hoped to position themselves as organs of self-management and political coordination on a national scale. Luxemburg's image of the "intellectual, cultural growth of the proletariat" under these complex conditions is unforgettable (*ERL* 134). She describes how "the same bakers and shoemakers, engineers, and printers of Warsaw and Lodz, who in June 1905 stood on the barricades and in December only awaited the word from Petersburg to begin street fighting, find time and are eager, between one mass strike and another, between prison and lockout, and under the conditions of a siege, to go into their trade-union statutes and discuss them earnestly," noting that they even "severely reprimanded their leaders and threatened them with withdrawal from the party because the unlucky trade-union membership cards could not be printed quickly enough – in secret printing works under incessant police persecution" (*ERL* 137).

Though she intends some humor in the image of "these barricade fighters of yesterday and tomorrow" placing such passionate importance on "statutes, printed membership cards, adhesive stamps, etc.," Luxemburg is attempting to convey how workers were learning to become self-governing, to insist on their place in the new scheme of things, and on the details of self-management (*ERL* 136). It is an image of the mass strike as a "living political school," which gives birth to unprecedented skills, passions, and needs, and which stages a rupture with a previous eidetic regime, in which democracy was conducted in an elite stratum, far removed from workers' interests or directive control (*ERL* 130).

Eidetic ruptures such as these are difficult to capture in works of theory, as they involve the process whereby the means of decision-making, as well as the social production process as a whole, suddenly becomes available to spatial intuition. In other words, they involve a qualitative shift, in which the social process of reproduction is suddenly imagined as a spatial field that can be experientially traversed.

In his novel *Der Kaiser ging, die Generäle blieben*, Theodor Plievier captures one such moment in the cogitations of Sült, an electrical engineer active in the 1919 German Revolution. Disaffected by the betrayals of the unions and aware of the limited scope of covert organization, Sült suddenly visualizes the extent of the electrical workers' socially constitutive potency. As the firemen regulate the fires and carbon monoxide content of their boilers and the steam is converted into current, Sült perceives how "der Strom rollt die mit Arbeitern beladenen Straßenbahnen den Fabriken, eine Stunde später die Angestellten, Stenotypistinnen und Verkäuferinnen den Büros und den Warenhäusern zu (the current drives the trams, laden with workers, to the factories; an hour later the clerks, stenographers and shop girls to the offices and stores)."[86] His vision extends even further: "Der Strom treibt Maschinen, Kräne, die Lifts in den Hotels, er füllt die Telephon- und Telegraphendrähte mit surrendem Leben (the current drives engines, cranes, hotel elevators; it fills the telephone and telegraph wires with humming life)."[87] Finally, he observes, "Die Turbinen und Stromnetze der Elektrizitätswerke, die Maschinen, Drehbänke und Dampfhammer in den Fabriken: die Arbeitskraft, die alles treibt, ist die Grundlage des kapitalistischen Systems (The turbines and supply systems of the power stations, the engines, lathes and steam hammers in the workshops: this, the power which drives everything, is the foundation of the capitalist system)."[88] Without it, "alles andere – Regierung, Parlament, Militärgewalt" (everything else –government, parliament, military power)" must needs collapse, as Sült imagines it will, should the general strike last but eight days – an eventuality which, he hopes, will allow the workers themselves to regulate production and gear it toward "die tatsächlichen Bedürfnisse der Gesellschaft" (the actual needs of society)."[89]

What is the social logic that informs the culturally distinct, geographically differential – but nevertheless recognizable – reappearance of this ruptural mode of apperception in a work such as Asturias' 1960 *Los ojos de los enterrados*? In the tense lead-up to the 1944 Guatemalan Revolution, the government is ready, the main agitator in the novel explains, "con sus tropas, sus policías, sus periódicos, con la fuerza, la represión, y la propaganda, para repeler a los que alteraran el orden en las formas conocidas, golpes de Estado, revueltas, atentados, pero no en la forma en que ahora se les plantea: ¡dejando de hacer! …, eh …, eh … (with their troops, their police, their newspapers, with force, repression, and propaganda to put down those who want to change the order of things in the familiar way, coups, uprisings, assassinations, but not in the way in which it's put up to them now: not doing anything! … heh … heh …)"[90]

Just as the organizer Rámila argued to the fruit-haulers of Tiquisate that without their hands "la Compañía se queda con las manos vacías, con sus trenes y barcos sin fruta (the Company is left with its hands empty, with its trains and ships without fruit)" (*OE* 326/*EI* 463), Tabío San asks what the government will do if "le desorganizan hospitales, escuelas, tribunales, por falta de practicantes, mestros y pasantes de derecho, y si, como se espera, médicos jefes de salas y abogados jueces y magistrados, secundan la huelga (hospitals, schools, and courts break down for a lack of practitioners, teachers, and law clerks, and if, as is hoped, doctors in charge of wards and lawyers who are judges and magistrates back the strike" (*OE* 401/*EI* 572). As in Sült's image of superstructural collapse, this vision of *el edificio* of the state being undermined makes it possible to imagine the governing class being left "bajo sus escombros, con todo y sus policías, y sus bancos, y sus jueces, y su presidente, y su comandantes, y sus generales (under the ruins with their police and everything, their banks, their judges, their president, their commandants, and their generals" (*OE* 325/*EI* 463). And this is not all. Tabío San sees the general strike as just the beginning of "la marcha de campesinos y obreros hacia el poder (the march toward power of workers and peasants)," into a reality that is beyond "todo lo imaginado (everything that was imagined)" – "un *tiempo de ficción* (a *time of fiction*)" (*OE* 393/*EI* 562, 561), in the sense that its potentialities exceed everything that is imaginable within the current eidetic regime.

A similar eidetic rupture occurs in Sembene's *Les bouts de bois de Dieu*, in which the workers' capacity to regulate their activity on a massive scale first becomes imaginable only when the doors of the railway cars that they have abandoned "s'ouvraient soudain sous la poussée du vent comme des gueules béantes (open suddenly, like gaping mouths, under the pressure of the wind)"[91] – revealing both the social space vacated by the workers and the unarticulated capacity for recombination they embody. And, finally, listen to Patrick Chamoiseau's account of the 2009 French Caribbean General Strike:

> C'était paradoxal de voir un ordre économique et politique brusquement pétrifié; les zones industrielles et les temples de la consommation interdits et éteints; une trâlée d'institutions évidées, immobiles, et cet ensemble autrefois essentiel servant d'écrin à quoi? À un plus de vie et de passion. Comme un cimetière qui soudain se révèle sous l'irruption d'une jouvence de biodiversité ... Comment alors ne pas comprendre que nous n'étions pas en face d'une «crise-pouvoir-d'achat-vie-chère» qui demandait qu'on la résolve, mais que nous allions vers ces tressaillements obscurs qui peuvent ouvrir à mutation ou à métamorphose.
>
> (It was ironic to see an economic and political order suddenly paralyzed; industrial areas and the temples of consumption barred and lifeless; a slew of emptied, inert institutions, and this once essential ensemble serving as a backdrop to what? To more life and passion. Like a cemetery that suddenly reveals itself as an explosion of youthful biodiversity ... How, then, do we not grasp that we were not facing a "crisis of the high cost of living" that must be resolved, but that we are on the cusp of the kind of fantastic convulsions that can precipitate a mutation or a metamorphosis.)[92]

The political metamorphosis that Chamoiseau describes here, which takes shape only when the mechanisms of the prevailing eidetic regime are brought to a standstill, is imagined, fittingly, as a discourse between two moths in his novel *Le papillon et la lumière*. As these aerial beings traverse social space, inserting themselves among shops, banks, and a McDonald's restaurant left abandoned by the general strike, Chamoiseau figures the powers of mutual counsel and horizontal exchange that were awakened out of the ruptural site of the French Antillean General Strike.

Eidetic rupture, then, refers to a lived sense of socially recombinative potency that exceeds an existing distribution of executive and reproductive capabilities, and that in doing so creates, practically and imaginatively, new spatial practices. As the above examples show, eidetic ruptures occur with reference to the socially creative capabilities of the population at large – in other words, society's capacity to create goods, services, practices, and decision-making infrastructures separate from and irrespective of state systems of governance and control. These socially creative capabilities take shape around potentialities that are conditioned to the core by differential cultural, economic, and geopolitical circumstances. But what they share is their power to reproduce, enrich, and facilitate directive communication throughout the social body, even in the absence of state resources.

General strikes render this socially creative capability palpable precisely by *dismantling it* in a highly organized way, such that very little of what previously counted as social space exists, except for the very organizational structure that has deliberately negated it. According to this logistical paradox, in which the recombinative potency of social creators is felt precisely in their active suspension of everything that makes social life possible, the general strike creates a negative image of the plenitude of nonstate space. Meanwhile, the exigencies of existence that persist in this social void make necessary the creation of complex nonstate logistical networks – the food distribution relays and water task forces represented in *Les bouts de bois de Dieu*, the underground communication systems represented in *Los ojos de los enterrados*, and the local production networks that inform Chamoiseau's representations of the political stakes of the French Antillean General Strike.

It is important to dwell on details such as these, because theorists have often had so much difficulty imagining the resources nonstate actors possess, outside of their capacity to rearticulate the "master text" of state-sponsored ideologies in tendentious, but often practically indeterminate, ways. I hasten to add that such "master texts" are often at issue in eidetic ruptures; Tiémoko's creative engagement with André Malraux's *La Condition humaine* in *Les bouts de bois de Dieu* is a remarkable example of this – seizing upon this orientalist, semi-Stalinist French text for examples of decentralized political activity is a way of reading against the grain that has immediate practical consequences. What he sees in the novel has more to do with the Chinese workers who established nonparty militias and judicature during the 1925–1926 Hong Kong General Strike than it does with the hierarchical party politicking the novel dwells on.

But eidetic ruptures are not just ways of redeploying or reappropriating master texts. Instead, they stage an intervention into the real relations of force that perpetuate a given eidetic regime. In creating a new balance of forces, they have the capacity to "postdate" master texts, and often do so virtually overnight, as the ideological force of the once naturalized eidetic regime suddenly applies to nothing currently sensible.

C. L. R. James offers a memorable example of this kind of maneuver in his account of the 1950 Gold Coast General Strike. The colonial master text in this case involved the tirelessly repeated racist cant that Africans are "organically incapable of self-government." To this myth is added another, namely that "the British government has by and large aimed at bringing [African] peoples to the stage where they would be able to exercise self-government, despite certain lapses from principle to which all nations, all peoples and all individuals are of course subject, human nature being what it is."[93] In James' account, this myth forms "the unconscious premise" and "instinctive basis" of African subjects themselves, and the process of "ma[king] adaptations" and "discard[ing] some elements of the myth" and "add[ing] others" does nothing to undermine its basic premises, just as Greek myths were not undermined by being "continually organized and reorganized to suit new situations" (*NGR* 29).

So what *is* capable of undermining such a myth? Just days after the Colonial Secretary summoned Kwame Nkrumah to inform him that Africans would never succeed in carrying out a general strike, due to their "backwardness, primitiveness [and] instability," all economic life in the country came to a halt (*NGR* 132). "The response," James emphasizes, "was complete": "all employed workers stayed at home and employers, including the government, the biggest employer of all, closed down" (*NGR* 133). Faced with losing 50 million pounds in revenue every day the general strike continued, the colonial government acted quickly, declaring a state of emergency and arresting many of the leaders of the Convention People's Party. After twelve days, "the government was certain that it had defeated the general strike." But for James the reality was exactly the inverse: "the general strike had defeated the government" (*NGR* 139).

In what sense? James explains: "In the general strike, [the people] had learnt their own power, their own incredible solidarity, had seen themselves mobilized under a leadership of their own choosing against the alien government and seen that, despite all appearances, they were masters in their own country" (*NGR* 138–9). Ever since the 1948 riots in Accra, the "heterogeneous collection of chiefs, government officials, merchants and lawyers" had been trying to use the threat of lawlessness to impose on the government "the necessity of sharing the power with themselves" (*NGR* 46). But, according to James, it was precisely this middle stratum of society that was behaving "lawlessly": "they were lawless because the laws that they were trying to administer had been rejected by the people and they had no force with which to enforce them" (*NGR* 46). The people, by contrast, acted as a "disciplined community obeying its own laws," engaging itself in "politics in the Greek-city sense of the word" – a process that "embraced the whole man, symbolized the beginning of a new stage of existence" (*NGR* 46, 84).

This all-embracing and self-organized transformation is precisely that of eidetic rupture. It is fundamentally different from coups d'état, palace intrigues, and purely electoral shifts, in that it operates by depriving the state of the socially reproductive processes it needs to exercise its power, and it does so through a broad-based application of force. The capacity of subject peoples for self-government is announced not just through sly reappropriations of the colonist's vocabulary, but through a demonstration of their monopoly of socially creative potency. As seen in the 1996–1997 South Korean General Strike, the 2006 Guinean General Strike, and the 2007 South African General strike, among others, it is impossible for the state to staff with its security forces the docks, railways, schools, hospitals, and essential businesses that even a minimal condition of social functionality would require, try as it might to do so. Mass strikes confront the state with its nakedness in this respect, its resourcelessness in the face of what is sometimes called mass "non-cooperation," but which can, in actuality, transform itself into a lethal assault on the bases of state-functionality themselves. The myth of "organic incapacity" is thus shattered through the population's proving itself – to use a Hegelian phrase – as the reproductive basis of all social organization, and grasping itself as such.

### Self-Government outside the State

Formulations such as these broach the question of what the political horizon of eidetic rupture is – a question of scale, but also a question of institutional longevity. If the general strike is a punctual assertion of potentially state-lethal forms of organization, how is it possible to imagine the institutionalization of this social form? The 1919 Seattle General Strike, the 1919 German General Strike, the 1920 Turin General Strike, the 1973 Chilean General Strike, and the 1978 Iranian General Strike all offer examples of industries reopening on a mass scale under workers' control, as do more recent forms of workers' self-management in Brazil, India, Venezuela, Mexico, Uruguay, and Greece.[94] But can we imagine these local forms of autogestion elaborating themselves into transnational forms of self-government, without seeing their functions alienated into the politburos, central committees, and dictatorial populisms which were so rife during the twentieth century? This question is especially pressing for the ethnic minorities and other marginalized populations who have so often found themselves sidelined by historical workers' movements and postcolonial state-formations. Is there any way to imagine local nonstate activity that could "go global" without threatening to subsume the identities and cultural practices of these groups?

This question is at the heart of the forms of nonstate internationalism I analyze in the second chapter of this book. Moving on from the question of the mass strike and the eidetic ruptures associated with it that I explore in my first chapter, this second chapter focuses on two authors – Arundhati Roy and Claude McKay – whose writing bears the imprint of the "double betrayal" of the internationalist idea: the betrayal of the Communist International, which in 1934 McKay was already able to perceive as a "stuffed carcass," and the betrayal of the liberal internationalism of interstate institutions such as the United Nations and multilateral Non-Governmental Organizations (NGOs).[95]

Growing up in Kerala in the 1960s, Roy watched as the United States used the United Nations' World Food Programme and other NGOs to implement Public Law 480, crippling India's food autonomy and sabotaging agricultural modernization in the subcontinent. At the same time, she witnessed what she describes as the "cocktail revolution" of the institutional communists who came to power in Kerala in 1967 – communists in name only, who "never overtly questioned the traditional values of a caste-ridden, extremely traditional community."[96] It is this double betrayal that forms the background context of her 2011 *Walking with the Comrades* as well as her 1997 *The God of Small Things* – two works that speculate about forms of nonstate mobilization that embody elements of an alternative internationalism.

The 1967 revolt of peasant sharecroppers in Naxalbari, and the more recent revival of "Naxalism" among adivasi communities resisting the destruction of their ancestral lands, become the focal point of Roy's nonstate imagination, but not because she sees in them anything like a socio-political ideal. On the contrary, she expresses anxiety about the Naxalites' "single-minded, grim military imagination" and even said in an interview that if they ever came to power the first person they would hang would probably be her![97] The Naxalites become an important agential nexus in Roy's writings, instead, because they embody a principle of nonstate territorial occupation that operates outside both institutional communism and liberal internationalism. In the same year that Indira Gandhi began implementing the agro-imperialist "Green Revolution" and Marxist-led governments in Kerala and West Bengal hesitated, once again, to institute land reform in the countryside, a network of largely indigenous peasants formed armed peasants' committees in every village of Naxalbari, occupied land, and set up a nonstate "parallel administration to look after villages."[98]

As several historians have pointed out, the United States- and United Nations-backed "Green Revolution," which channeled fertilizer, machinery, and genetically modified seeds into the Indian countryside, was in reality a form of agricultural anti-modernization, as only the wealthiest farmers could afford these inputs – a fact that resulted in "economic polarization in rural areas" due to increased rents, the displacement of rural workers, and the limited applicability of these new technologies.[99] In addition to this failure of United Nations-style internationalism, Indian peasants confronted a communist officialdom that maintained its "subservience to the control of the rural elite," refusing to undertake desegregation for Untouchables or institute meaningful land reform.[100]

In this context, and in the more recent adivasi insurgencies against mining multinationals, Naxalism represents a direct form of spatial occupation that effects nonstate community self-government in regions neglected for decades by the state. At the same time, through the complex symbolic layerings Roy effects in *Walking with the Comrades* and *The God of Small Things*, these nonstate occupations come to represent engines of global engagement far more extensive than what their enclaves of armed opposition seem equipped to provide. In my reading of Roy's novel, these nonstate spaces are the incommunicable, unacknowledged *complement* of the modernization project Chacko, that sad factory owner, represents. As we learn from economists such as D. Narayana and Raman Mahadevan, in those Indian regions where more people have benefited from land reforms, "agricultural growth and agrarian surpluses were channelized into non-farm enterprises, thus spawning a unique pattern of entrepreneurial development and modern industrialization."[101] Mahadevan explains this as follows: "the commercialization process as reflected in the spawning of agro- and plantation-based industries provided space for the growth of sections of indigenous capital."[102]

This developmental path, however, which is based on the "emergence of agrarian surplus as a source of commercial and industrial development," has been highly uneven in postcolonial India, in large part due to the systematic colonial dismantling both of this modernization dynamic and of the "artisanal route" to industrialization that is so often its corollary.[103] As my readings of Roy's novel suggest, Chacko is the emblem of precisely this failure of the Indian "developmental bourgeoisie" to advance the modernization project Narayana and Mahadevan describe – a failure that has its roots in the stalled land reforms and caste-based forms of social ossification that the Naxalites in Roy's novel are combating. What Roy's deft symbolic layerings suggest is that Chacko's cosmopolitan dream – of entering the "world market," of contributing to international material and cultural exchange from a position of strength – may, paradoxically, depend upon exactly the kind of betrayals that the Naxalite character in the novel embodies. That is to say, *The God of Small Things* proposes what, from the point of view of its characters, could only be viewed as an impossible solution to India's postcolonial underdevelopment, e.g., a process of social development linked not to the forms of state-sponsored trade liberalization instituted in the 1960s and radicalized after 1991, but to nonstate forms of territorial occupation, forcible land redistribution, and revolutionary self-government.

It is a solution based not so much on the Chinese model of state-based redistribution and surplus accumulation (which is, nevertheless, a crucial subtext to Roy's novel) as on some almost unimaginable process whereby nonstate reappropriation in the countryside migrates into areas marked by small-scale factory production, becoming a bottom-up force of social development in spaces abandoned by a fluid middle class. It is the kind of solution that is often articulated most provocatively in profoundly imaginative literature: counterfactual, almost inconceivable, and yet capturing the passion of generations of Indian students, peasants, intellectuals, and professionals, for whom Naxalism represented not just an isolated peasant insurgency, but a wholesale rejection of failed state-centric programs, and a nonstate vehicle of social development and internationalist politics.

Claude McKay's vision of nonstate internationalism is just as ambitious as Roy's, and like hers it invites us to reconsider many of our theoretical presuppositions about self-government and internationalism. McKay's *Banjo* has long been viewed as a narrative of cosmopolitan flexibility, and Brent Edwards' analysis of the novel as a document of "vagabond internationalism" frames it brilliantly as "an internationalism of the defective: the unregistered, the undocumented, untracked – an ab-nationalism, as it were, of all the 'Doubtful.' "[104] Similarly, Michelle Ann Stephens describes *Banjo* as a chronicle of "the black male's 'freedom in flight' and 'freedom to love' outside the paradigms and narratives of the nation-state."[105] But both of these critics pick up on something else that is crucial about McKay's novel – that, on some level, it also offers itself as a heuristic of protopolitical associational activity among the diasporic Africans whose lives it represents. Edwards describes Banjo's desire to find in his band "a model of the social, a way to ... institutionalize a vision of black internationalism,"[106] and Stephens sees in *Banjo* a departure from Garveyite nationalism and an attempt to imagine "other forms of black collective organization that could counter the powerful myth of nationhood."[107]

Allowing for the fact that McKay's method in *Banjo* is not systematic political argument, is there nevertheless a way to account for the complex politics of this nonstate internationalism – a way to make sense of what Edwards and Stephens describe, surprisingly yet correctly, as the novel's emphasis on institutionalization and group organization?

A conversation between Leon Trotsky and McKay that appeared in *Pravda* and *Izvestia* and was reprinted in McKay's 1923 *The Negroes in America* helps bring this question into focus. Trotsky asks McKay "What are the most expedient organizing forms for a North American Negro movement?"[108] McKay responds by describing the political dialogue that he helped establish between black soldiers in London and the communist International Club he was part of in 1919 and 1920. McKay then continues in the rest of his book to refer to the Friends of Negro Freedom, the African Blood Brotherhood, and the Jewish Bund as organizations from which his own vision of black internationalism borrows, as well as the anarcho-syndicalist Industrial Workers of the World (IWW), which he describes as a "revolutionary union in which not the slightest distinction is made on the basis of race, nationality, or skin color."[109] He even includes a lengthy (four-page!) quote by IWW organizer Bill Haywood in which he claims "We were workers 'outside the law,' and therefore enjoyed the sympathy of Negroes who represent a *race* 'outside the law.' "[110]

This assortment of different organizational models may seem impossibly heterogeneous, but it actually contains several crucial through lines that can help us understand the specific character of McKay's nonstate imagination. The Friends of Negro Freedom, for example, was a black-led, working-class organization that promoted black mutual aid, union organization, and economic association. In explicit contrast to Marcus Garvey's Universal Negro Improvement Association (UNIA), it was a socialist organization conceived as a means to help black workers become union organizers. McKay even describes the organization's co-founder, A. Philip Randolph, as a "socialist of the Debs school," highlighting the importance of the IWW to his perspective.[111] The Friends of Negro Freedom, then, was external both to the American Communist Party and to UNIA. Accordingly, it stood outside these two templates of internationalism. This was a characteristic it shared with the African Blood Brotherhood, which was a self-organized organ of armed, racial self-defense that emerged out of the racial violence of the summer of 1919.

The kind of internationalism that McKay outlines in *The Negroes in America*, then, has as little to do with the leadership cults and state-centrism of Garveyism as it does with the entrenched hierarchies and rigid centralism of institutional communism. Instead, it is an internationalism that is rooted in local, race-based forms of mutual aid, labor agitation, and self-defense. This is why the Jewish Bund is an important organizational model for McKay. Since its emergence in the 1890s, the General Jewish Labor Bund existed simultaneously as an organ of racial self-defense and as an agent of socialist internationalism, leading strikes in multiple cities during the 1905 Revolution and becoming an important, dissident bloc within the patchwork revolutionary democracy forged in the early Soviet Union. In *The Negroes in America*, then, what McKay is stressing is a form of nonstate internationalism comprised of community-level hubs of horizontal decision-making that would be led by rank-and-file black workers, as opposed to being directed from on high either by charismatic leaders or by a bureaucratic elite. McKay's interest in the IWW makes perfect sense in this context. By insisting that rank-and-file delegates from workplace committees could take over all the functions of state and international governing bodies, the IWW offered an organizational form in which all political decision-making would have its roots in spokespeople who were answerable to and recallable by the local communities for whom they speak.

So the image McKay shares with Trotsky – of his back-and-forth movement between the club for black soldiers and the communist International Club – is a way of imagining how race-based forms of organizational consciousness could emerge as part of an internationalist political culture. Crucially, McKay does not present himself as an agitator deployed by the International Club to "relate to" the black soldiers. In fact, in *A Long Way from Home*, he describes his membership in the black soldiers' club as a precondition for his being able to tolerate life in London: "I went often and listened to the soldiers telling tales of their war experiences in France, Egypt, and Arabia. Many were interested in what American Negroes were thinking and writing. And so I brought to the club copies of American Negro magazines and newspapers."[112]

This is exactly the kind of scene we find related in *Banjo* – an ad hoc exchange of ideas, debate, and fraternization between black men from "the West Indies and Africa, with a few colored Americans, East Indians, and Egyptians among them."[113] To an outside observer, such associational activity may seem apolitical. It has no legible executive apparatus and exhibits no party structure. But precisely because of this, the scene is for

McKay the best imaginable template of black organizational life – indeed, in his exchange with no less an organizational thinker than Trotsky, it is the one image of political association that McKay chooses to share. But why?

The principle McKay is illustrating has everything to do with where the impulse to political organization originates – within bureaucratic centers remote from the diasporic associational life McKay documents, or from within the lateral dynamics of this group life itself. Already in 1922, McKay was voicing concern about "the silly rot about Negroes in general that sometimes gets printed in the radical press" and warns that the "white radical … often loses his keen perceptions when he approaches the Negro question."[114] Similarly, in his recently rediscovered 1941 novel *Amiable with Big Teeth: A Novel Concerning the Love Affair between the Communists and the Black Sheep of Harlem*, McKay explains that the main black characters of the novel reject orthodox Marxists who "advocated that Aframericans should surrender the right to think and act as a group to their 'white friends.'"[115]

All the same, McKay admits in his letter to Trotsky that "little has been done" on the part of "progressive Negroes" to conduct "large-scale communist propaganda among their race."[116] Accordingly, *Banjo* should be read not as a turn away from black proletarian politics, but rather as a map of the discursive rhythms and group dynamics from which a black proletarian politics would have to emerge. One of McKay's points in the novel is that a centralized apparatus of political representation could never effectively graft itself onto the systems of mutual aid and black expressive culture that the beach dwellers in *Banjo* embody – that the forms of life delineated by these black diasporans have their own political logic and organizational coherence.

This is why, even in *Harlem: Negro Metropolis*, published eleven years after *Banjo* and eighteen years after his exchange with Trotsky, McKay is still advocating for locally organized independent black unions like Randolph's Pullman Porters, the Harlem Labor Union, and the Afro-American Federation of Labor, and lamenting the fact that "Negroes in the trade unions have never had any group organization to protect their special interests."[117] In fact *Harlem: Negro Metropolis,* as a whole, is an attempt to map out "the mass movements of Harlem" so as to "yield an indication of the trend and direction of the group as a whole," in order to combat the impression that the diverse diasporic blacks of Harlem are "doomed to remain an unwieldy, inert, and invertebrate mass."[118] The fact that the black political culture of Harlem merges seamlessly with its religious movements, its musical life, and its mutual aid systems does not detract from its organizational potential, according to McKay. On the contrary, it suggests that we must forge a different kind of political optics to understand its potentialities – one attuned to the internal logic of unplanned group dynamics as opposed to top-down bureaucratic structures. McKay even suggests that Harlem's "patchwork of humanity," which "did not evolve from any blueprint of interracial and international adjustment" had "something of the quality of the Vieux Port of Marseilles" – precisely the area whose inhabitants McKay chronicles in *Banjo*.[119]

Far from tracing a major shift in McKay's politics from the early 1920s to the early 1940s, my chapter on his work stresses the continuities of vision that can be seen throughout his work, both in his rejection of authoritarian communism and in his search for organizational forms that could emerge from the sophisticated transnational currents of black life that he chronicles in his novels and nonfiction. By focusing on the nonstate spaces whose internal logic McKay so carefully records, I show that, though he does celebrate the dynamic lifestyle of his beach-dwelling characters, he is also offering a micropolitical portrait of the affective politics and mutual-aid dynamics that he believed must subtend any effective nonstate black internationalism.

My final chapter focuses on literature that speculates about futural forms of nonstate space that could emerge as part of geopolitical processes of planetary scope. I concentrate on T. S. Eliot and Melvin Tolson in this chapter because both authors use non-narrative, highly fragmented poetry to imagine nonstate itineraries that it is difficult to imagine any complex of fictional characters traversing. At the same time, though, both authors offer up templates of cosmopolitan affect in the poetic personae that populate their works. They do so, however, not to promote the forms of transnationalism associated with these cosmopolitan personae, but to highlight them as *obstacles* to the forms of nonstate internationalism they presage. In other words, both Eliot and Tolson use modernist techniques of juxtaposition and abstraction to interrupt the cosmopolitan affect on display in their poems, while simultaneously "panning out" to make visible planetary forms of nonstate political organization external to cosmopolitan worldscapes.

In "The Waste Land" Eliot does this by setting up Countess Marie as a prototype of cosmopolitan affect, then revealing her transnational sympathies for what they are: an affective bridge meant to create a sense of commonality between subject peoples and the imperialist powers that dominate them. This is the kind of cosmopolitanism Eliot saw at work in the wars of position that occurred before, during, and after World War I, and which he uses "The Waste Land" to expose. Counterintuitive though it may be, my argument is that the forms of geopolitical cognition at work in "The Waste Land" still have immense contemporary relevance, first, because many of the same forms of affective bridging are still being used to enlist subject peoples into a cosmopolitan project sponsored and directed by predatory nations and NGOs, and second, because Eliot's poetic mode in "The Waste Land" was organized around vitiating these forms of cosmopolitan affect and finding alternatives to them. In my analysis of Eliot's work, I discover templates of anti-colonial revolt and affective intransigency that may appear very un-Eliotic indeed, but that emerge as part of his attempts to imagine a nonstate internationalism external to the forms of Wilsonian democracy Eliot witnessed in the early twentieth century.

I pair Tolson with Eliot in this chapter for two main reasons. First, Tolson takes Eliot's vision of a nonstate internationalism capable of defending subject peoples and expands it exponentially, developing an entirely new vision of nonstate space based on his encounters with black internationalism, anti-Stalinist communism, and the Non-Aligned Movement of African and Asian peoples. Like Eliot, he uses the resources of literary modernism to imagine the futural geopolitical structures that would make a nonstate internationalism on this scale possible. But, writing in the period of early globalization and decolonization, Tolson approaches the economic and political issues such a nonstate project would face with a rigor and thoroughness altogether beyond Eliot's scope. What Tolson explores in works like "E. & O. E.," *Libretto for the Republic of Liberia*, and *Harlem Gallery* is the proposition that only transnational alliances originating in the Global South and based in nonstate forms of economic and political self-assertion can be imagined as alternatives to the various affectively-charged cosmopolitanisms of the neocolonial core.

The forms of anti-colonial self-assertion Tolson imagines in his poetry are fundamentally different from Eliot's as well, and this is the second reason for pairing these two modernist poets. In fact, Tolson stages an explicit critique of the placelessness of Eliot's model of anti-colonial agency. Aligning it with Hamlet's strangely impersonal musings about death, Tolson sees in Eliot's work an aestheticized model of nonstate agency that is ultimately modeled on the predatory self-exteriorization of capital in the age of imperialism. To counter this model of nonstate internationalism, which still relies upon a racialized zone of "free play" that it simultaneously creates and abjects, Tolson evolves an entirely different model of internationalism, born of capitalist crisis and composed of a transnational body of subject peoples brought together in the nonstate space of a very un-Eliotic death by water. The internationalism that is forged in this critical moment is not the unimaginable internationalism of Eliot, tacitly rooted in the Global North and relying on a contextless murder/suicide that seems in some ways to belong to the involutions of global capitalism itself. Instead, it is a futural vision that is inspired by the fundamentally state-based developmental agendas of the Non-Aligned Movement, but that extrapolates from them, to imagine the forms of nonstate self-government that could become possible as a consequence of world-systemic shifts that capitalist crisis precipitates.

The vision of nonstate space that this poetic strategy unfolds is breathtaking in its scope and power. Not only does Tolson evolve a model of South–South economic and cultural exchange to replace the watery language of "tolerance" that is attendant upon many neo-imperial forms of cosmopolitan discourse, but also he projects this exchange outside of the elite superstrata of the postcolonial nation-state, framing it as a nonstate movement of peoples, rooted in local forms of mutual aid and self-government. Such nonstate images appear only in micro-examples that populate Tolson's work – as in all the authors I examine, nonstate space emerges here not as a *fait accompli* or a detailed program, but in imagined interpersonal trajectories that elicit strategies of micro-reading and critical futurology. My aim in this book is to isolate these brief moments when nonstate ideation emerges as the almost unrepresentable structural precondition for the more local aporias of a text, and to display them as micro-examples of spatial configurations that exist beyond the false binaries of nationalism and cosmopolitanism or developmentalism and mass agency.

Viewed in this context, the abstraction and allusiveness of Tolson's poetry can be seen for what they are. Neither the product of political disengagement nor some decontextualized drive to "imitate" high modernism, as is sometimes claimed, they are attempts to figure something that is still almost impossible to bring into view in the language of "sensible" political argumentation: the motivations, internal workings, and conditions of possibility of an internationalist politics founded not on cosmopolitan tastes, crypto-imperialist wars of position, or an abstract discourse of human rights, but rather on nonstate networks and peoples' movements brought together on a global scale as a result of capitalist crisis.

In recent years, attempts have been made in the theoretical realm to conceptualize nonstate forms of political association on the kind of scale that Tolson and the other authors I consider in this book imagine. In *Other Asias* and *Who Sings the Nation-State*, Gayatri Spivak views alliances between Asian regions – South Asia or West Asia, for example – as offering the possibility of a "new continentalism"[120] whose "regional cross hatchings" might be capable of "producing something other than nation-statism,"[121] and she mentions the Non-Aligned Movement of the 1960s as a possible precedent for such nonstate positionalities. But her model of continentalism still retains an irreducible role for the state as a "porous abstract structure," which could serve as a transnational body of redistribution as well as an administrative center of "shared health, education, and welfare structures."[122]

Walter Mignolo also strikes a balance between state and nonstate forces in his attempts to imagine alternatives to cosmopolitanism. On the one hand, he sees nonstate peoples' movements such as the Ejército Zapatista de Liberación Nacional as staging a decolonial break with Western epistemologies and reviving forms of praxis better suited to indigenous values and folkways. On the other, he sees states such as China, India, and Brazil as posing a challenge to Western accumulations of power and epistemological dominance, to such an extent that he too invokes the Non-Aligned Movement of decolonizing countries as a model for what these dewesternizing states may yet accomplish. At his most optimistic, he imagines the possibility of state and nonstate forces collaborating, to make possible "decolonial horizons in the domain of the state"[123] – Evo Morales' presidency, and in particular his rapprochement with the nonstate organization Comuna, being the most suggestive example of the kind of synergy he proposes.

It's noteworthy that both Spivak's and Mignolo's imaginations of nonstate futures are oriented toward countries of the Global South whose economies and emerging power blocs constitute a challenge to the geopolitical dominance of today's imperial hegemons. This, in itself, stages a significant departure from cosmopolitan rhetorics geared toward ideas of understanding or "openness" between developed and underdeveloped countries, as opposed to the more direct economic and political forms of self-assertion postcolonial powers are beginning to exercise. But the question of how such alternative hegemons and trade blocs could open up nonstate potentialities or devolve into a condition of nonstateness is for the most part an open one in these theorists' works. No doubt Spivak's harkening back to Pan-Africanism as a possible model of nonstate political organization is a fascinating gesture in this direction, but it is a gesture that is unaccompanied by a theory of how a transition from interstate alliances to nonstate ontologies could be accomplished.

In our own time, it remains almost impossible to imagine a nonstate organization of trade, decision-making, and social life. Cosmopolitanism's panoply of NGOs and "nonstate groups" – so often proxies of state and interstate forces – could, in this sense, be interpreted as a colossal failure of our capacity to imagine the nonstate as such. Could it be that nonstate organization is precisely the figure that lies outside contemporary distributions of the sensible – that it is the insensible of the cosmopolitan imagination?

This book explores modalities of nonstate thinking in an attempt to begin remedying this insensibility, and with the hope of finding some paths out of the theoretical deadlocks it has created. To do so, it examines manifestos, histories, theoretical works, publications of the World Bank and the Organisation for Economic Co-operation and Development (OECD), and preeminently, world literature. This is because the question of the nonstate is simultaneously a geopolitical and an aesthetic one, in Rancière's sense: a matter of what can be brought into view within a given distribution of the sensible.

Taking this proposition seriously – that what is socially imaginable depends at least in part on the regimes of sensuous particularity within reach – I look to world literature for the resources it affords us in thinking through the nonstate as a global regime of politics and aesthesis. As films such as Sembene's astonishing *Emitaï* and *Ceddo* demonstrate, the written word does not have a monopoly on the representation of such collective ruptures – such films powerfully capture exactly the kind of "heroism of the everyday" that is involved in the substruction of nonstate space. In our world of screens and memes, however, I find it useful to focus on the written word to demonstrate the power it has to capture the transhuman internalities that are key to the concept of nonstate space. After all, nonstate space is not simply defined by physical extension, as might be supposed, but announces itself through transformed capacities for relation that are akin to a "shared interiority." Such capacities are, in a sense, inexistent, since they are only partially captured by visible material practices. I turn to the resources of the written word, then, as an inventory of the partially ostensible, partially invisible social affects, relational modalities, psychic forms, and epistemological strategies that world literature mobilizes. They are a record of the interpersonal capacities and interior forms which alone can transform state space into nonstate space.

Nonstate space is neither a metaphysical preexistent, nor an economic *Tatsache*, nor an inert "outside" of the state. It is an interpersonal creation, which unfolds with astonishing complexity, and from within the differential cultural, material, and spiritual resources that belong to different places, times, and peoples. Learning how to read for these resources, how to detect their incipiencies, their points of capacitation, and their vulnerabilities, is the practice that I pursue in this book – a practice that is necessarily global in scope, given the global compass, and global project, of nonstate space itself.

**Notes**

1  See, respectively, Jack Crittenden, *Wide As the World: Cosmopolitan Identity, Integral Politics, and Democratic Dialogue* (Lanham: Lexington Books, 2011), 3; and David Held, *Cosmopolitanism: Ideals and Realities* (Cambridge: Polity, 2010), 206.

2  Thomas L. Blair, *The Land to Those Who Work It: Algeria's Experiment in Workers' Management* (New York: Doubleday, 1970), 40.

3  Immanuel Ness and Dario Azzellini, eds., *Ours to Master and to Own: Workers' Control from the Commune to the Present* (Chicago: Haymarket Books, 2011), 228.

4  See Frederick Cooper, "The Dialectics of Decolonization: Nationalism and Labor Movements in Postwar French Africa," in Frederick Cooper and Ann Laura Stoler, eds., *Tension of Empire: Colonial Cultures in a Bourgeois World* (Berkeley: University of California Press, 1997), 423.

5  See M. Bianet Castellanos, Lourdes Gutiérrez Nájera, and Arturo J. Aldama, eds., *Comparative Indigeneities of the Américas: Toward a Hemispheric Approach* (Tucson: University of Arizona Press, 2012); Maximilian C. Forte, ed., *Who Is an Indian?: Race, Place, and the Politics of Indigeneity in the Americas* (Toronto: University of Toronto Press, 2013); Kathryn Milun, *The Political Uncommons: The Cross-Cultural Logic of the Global Commons* (New York: Ashgate, 2011); Maia Ramnath, *Decolonizing Anarchism: An Antiauthoritarian History of India's Liberation Struggle* (Oakland: AK Press, 2011); Elinor Ostrom, *Governing the Commons: The Evolution of Institutions for Collective Action* (Cambridge: Cambridge University Press, 1990); and Derek Wall, *The Commons in History: Culture, Conflict, and Ecology* (Cambridge: MIT Press, 2014).

6  Pheng Cheah, "Given Culture: Rethinking Cosmopolitical Freedom in Transnationalism," in Pheng Cheah and Bruce Robbins, eds., *Cosmopolitics: Thinking and Feeling beyond the Nation* (Minneapolis: University of Minnesota Press, 1998), 300, 312

7  Frantz Fanon, *The Wretched of the Earth*, trans. Constance Farrington (New York: Grove, 1963), 154.

8 Radhika Desai, *Geopolitical Economy: After US Hegemony, Globalization and Empire* (London: Pluto, 2013), 2–3.

9 *Ibid.*, 12.

10 *Ibid.*, 1.

11 Gregory Jusdanis, *The Necessary Nation* (Princeton: Princeton University Press, 2001), 42, 3. See also Bob Jessop, who makes the important point that "state power is a form-determined, institutionally mediated effect of the balance among all forces in a given situation" – an observation that allows us to recognize important differences between different states, some of which can be "reorgani[zed] ... in order to redefine their accessibility" (Bob Jessop, *The Capitalist State* [New York: New York University Press, 1982], 225, 224).

12 Tariq Amin-Khan, *The Post-Colonial State in the Era of Capitalist Globalization: Historical, Political and Theoretical Approaches to State Formation* (New York: Routledge, 2012), 104.

13 Göran Therborn, *What Does the Ruling Class Do When It Rules?: State Apparatuses and State Power under Feudalism, Capitalism and Socialism* (London: NLB, 1978), 106.

14 Vilashini Cooppan, *Worlds Within: National Narratives and Global Connections in Postcolonial Writing* (Stanford: Stanford University Press, 2009), 1.

15 Benedict Anderson, *Under Three Flags: Anarchism and the Anti-colonial Imagination* (London: Verso, 2005), 227.

16 E. San Juan, Jr., *Beyond Postcolonial Theory* (New York: St. Martin's Press, 1999), 214.

17 Arjun Appadurai, *Modernity at Large: Cultural Dimensions of Globalization* (Minneapolis: University of Minnesota Press, 1996), 197.

18 Imre Szeman, *Zones of Instability: Literature, Postcolonialism, and the Nation* (Baltimore: Johns Hopkins University Press, 2003), 28.

19 Weihsin Gui, *National Consciousness and Literary Cosmopolitics: Postcolonial Literature in a Global Moment* (Columbus: Ohio State University Press, 2013), 6.

20 Maurice Merleau-Ponty, *Phenomenology of Perception*, trans. Colin Smith (London: Routledge, 1996), xx.

21 See Gregory Jusdanis on the psychological dynamics that govern "the transfer of a person's loyalties to the nation" (*The Necessary Nation*, 30).

22 Jacques Rancière, *The Politics of Aesthetics,* trans. Gabriel Rockhill (London: Continuum, 2008), 39. Hereafter cited as *PA*.

23 Frederic Jameson, *Postmodernism, or, the Cultural Logic of Late Capitalism* (Durham: Duke University Press, 1991), 51.

24 Frederic Jameson, "Cognitive Mapping," in Cary Nelson and Lawrence Grossberg, eds., *Marxism and the Interpretation of Culture* (Bloomington: University of Illinois Press, 1990), 349.

25 *Postmodernism*, 54.

26 Édouard Glissant, *Caribbean Discourse: Selected Essays,* trans. J. Michael Dash (Charlottesville: University Press of Virginia, 1999), 248, 61, 70, 73.

27 Édouard Glissant, *Poetics of Relation*, trans. Betsy Wing (Ann Arbor: University of Michigan Press, 1997), 65, 137, 92–3.

28 Gayatri Spivak, "General Strike," *Rethinking Marxism* 26:1 (2014), 13.

29 Patrick Chamoiseau, *Les neuf consciences du Malfini* (Paris: Gallimard, 2009), 229.

30 Susan Stanford Friedman's work mounts a similar, and extremely powerful, challenge to what she calls the "center/periphery and diffusionist frameworks still prevailing in the field across the disciplines" (Susan Stanford Friedman, *Planetary Modernisms: Provocations on Modernity across Time* [New York: Columbia University Press, 2015], x), as do works such as Steven S. Lee's *The Ethnic Avant-Garde: Minority Cultures and World Revolution* (New York: Columbia University Press, 2015), John Marx's *Geopolitics and the Anglophone Novel, 1890–2011* (Cambridge: Cambridge University Press, 2012), and Weihsin Gui's *National Consciousness and Literary Cosmopolitics: Postcolonial Literature in a Global Moment*. What I add to these efforts is a new way of constructing a non-Eurocentric network of texts around nonstate spatial occupations and forms of self-government.

31 Pascale Casanova, *The World Republic of Letters*, trans. M. B. DeBevoise (Cambridge: Harvard University Press, 2004), 40.

32 Susan Stanford Friedman, "Cultural Parataxis and Transnational Landscapes of Reading: Toward a Locational Modernist Studies," in Astradur Eysteinsson and Vivian Liska, eds., *Modernism*, vol. I (Amsterdam: John Benjamins, 2007), 38.

33 Like Paul K. Saint-Amour in his study of literary encyclopedism, then, I lay out "not a canon but a heuristic" (Paul K. Saint-Amour, *Tense Future: Modernism, Total War, Encyclopedic Form* [Oxford: Oxford University Press, 2015], 10) – what Biman Basu explores, in a different vein, by way of "affective assemblages that span geographical regions" (Biman Basu, "Postcolonial World Literature: Forster–Roy–Morrison," *The Comparatist*, 38 (October 2014), 159.

34 Franco Moretti, *Distant Reading* (London: Verso, 2013), 46, 53–4.

35 Rebecca Walkowitz, *Born Translated: The Contemporary Novel in an Age of World Literature* (New York: Columbia University Press, 2015), 86, 91.

36 David Damrosch, *What Is World Literature?* (Princeton: Princeton University Press, 2003), 17.

37 Christopher Prendergast, "The World Republic of Letters," in Christopher Prendergast, ed., *Debating World Literature* (London: Verso, 2004), 6. Prendergast cites Arjun Appadurai in this connection, specifically *Modernity at Large: Cultural Dimensions of Globalization* (Minneapolis: University of Minnesota Press, 1996), 30.

38 Emily Apter, *Against World Literature: On the Politics of Untranslatability* (London: Verso, 2013), 41.

39 *Ibid.*, 41, 2.

40 Matthew Hart, *Nations of Nothing But Poetry: Modernism, Transnationalism, and Synthetic Vernacular Writing* (Oxford: Oxford University Press, 2010), 40.

See also Wai Chee Dimock, *Through Other Continents: American Literature across Deep Time* (Princeton: Princeton University Press, 2006). See also in this connection Jed Esty and Colleen Lye, "Peripheral Realisms Now," *Modern Language Quarterly,* 73:3 (2012), 269–88 – especially their focus on "thinking relationally across different kinds of subordinated positions on different scales" (272).

41  The Warwick Research Collective, *Combined and Uneven Development: Towards a New Theory of World-Literature* (Liverpool: Liverpool University Press, 2015), 22.

42  *Ibid.*, 20.

43  *Ibid.*, 19.

44  Pheng Cheah, *What Is a World?: On Postcolonial Literature As World Literature* (Durham: Duke University Press, 2016), 10. Herafter cited as *WIW*.

45  Chris Nealon, "The Prynne Reflex," *The Claudius App* 4 (February 2013): online at http://theclaudiusapp.com/4-nealon.html.

46  James C. Scott, *The Art of Not Being Governed: An Anarchist History of Upland Southeast Asia* (New Haven: Yale University Press, 2010), 39. Hereafter cited as *ANB*.

47  James C. Scott, *Seeing Like a State: How Certain Schemes to Improve the Human Condition Have Failed* (New Haven: Yale University Press, 1999), 6.

48  Raúl Zibechi, *Territories in Resistance: A Cartography of Latin American Social Movements*, trans. Ramor Ryan (Oakland: AK Press, 2012), 40. Hereafter cited as *TR*.

49  Paul Mason, *Why It's Still Kicking Off Everywhere: The New Global Revolutions* (London: Verso 2013), 81, 84.

50  Alain Badiou, *The Rebirth of History*, trans. Gregory Elliott (London: Verso, 2012), 1.

51  Slavoj Žižek, *The Year of Dreaming Dangerously* (London: Verso, 2012), 82, 81, 88.

52  "Greek Health Workers Take Over Control of Hospital," *In Defence of Marxism*, February 6, 2012. www.marxist.com/kilkis-hospital-workers-control.htm.

53  For a book-length treatment of Iranian workers during the revolution, see Assef Bayat, *Workers and Revolution in Iran* (London: Zed Books, 1987).

54  See Immanuel Ness and Dario Azzellini, eds., *Ours to Master and to Own: Workers' Control from the Commune to the Present* (Chicago: Haymarket Books, 2011), 263–81; and John Hammond, *Building Popular Power: Workers' and Neighborhood Movements in the Portuguese Revolution* (New York: Monthly Review Press, 1988).

55  Théorie Communiste, "Bring out Your Dead," *Endnotes* 1 (October 2008), upg. http://endnotes.org.uk/issues/1/en/endnotes-bring-out-your-dead.

56  *Ibid.*

57  Théorie Communiste, "Much Ado about Nothing," *Endnotes* 1 (October 2008), upg. http://endnotes.org.uk/issues/1/en/theorie-communiste-much-ado-about-nothing.

58  Henri Lefebvre, *De l'État, Tome IV: Les contradictions de l'État moderne* (Paris: Union Générale d'Éditions, 1978), 259. English translation: Henri Lefebvre,

"Space and the State," in Neil Brenner, Bob Jessop, Martin Jones, and Gordon MacLeod, eds., *State/Space: A Reader* (Malden: Blackwell, 2003), 84.

59 *De l'État, Tome IV*, 262, 261–2. *State/Space* 85.

60 Henri Lefebvre, *State, Space, World: Selected Essays,* trans. Gerald Moore, Neil Brenner, and Stuart Elden, ed. Neil Brenner and Stuart Elden (Minneapolis: University of Minnesota Press, 2009), 142.

61 Henri Lefebvre, *The Production of Space*, trans. Donald Nicholson-Smith (Oxford: Blackwell, 1991), 52.

62 See, for example, Perry Anderson, *Lineages of the Absolutist State* (London: New Left Books, 1974), 273–8; and E. H. Norman, *Origins of the Modern Japanese State: Selected Writings of E. H. Norman*, ed. John W. Dower (New York: Pantheon, 1975), 110–210.

63 Nicos Poulantzas, *Political Power and Social Classes*, trans. Timothy O'Hagan (London: NLB, 1973), 298.

64 *Ibid.*

65 Henri Lefebvre, *De l'État, Tome III: Le mode de production étatique* (Paris: Union Générale d'Éditions 1977), 179. Translation mine.

66 *State, Space, World*, 142.

67 *Ibid.*, 148.

68 *Ibid.*, 146.

69 *Ibid.*, 150.

70 See John Restakis, *Humanizing the Economy: Co-operatives in the Age of Capital* (Gabriola Island, British Columbia: New Society Publishers, 2010), 214.

71 On the links between neighborhood assemblies and *fábricas recuperadas* see Maristella Svampa and Damiá Corral, "Political Mobilization in the Neighborhood Assemblies: The Cases of Villa Crespo and Palermo," in Edward Epstein and David Pion-Berlin, eds., *Broken Promises?: The Argentine Crisis and Argentine Democracy* (Lanham: Lexington Books, 2006), esp. 132–3.

72 Cooperativa de Trabajo Lavaca, *Sin Patrón: Fábricas y empresas recuperadas por sus trabajadores. Una historia, una guía* (Buenos Aires: Lacava Editora, 2004), 25. English translation: The Lavaca Collective, *Sin Patrón: Stories from Argentina's Worker-Run Factories*, trans. Katherine Kohlstedt (Chicago: Haymarket Books, 2004), 43.

73 Edmund Husserl, *Experience and Judgment: Investigations in a Genealogy of Logic*, trans. James S. Churchill and Karl Ameriks (London: Routledge, 1973), 30.

74 Maurice Merleau-Ponty, *The Merleau-Ponty Reader*, trans. Leonard Lawlor, ed. Ted Toadvine and Leonard Lawlor (Evanston: Northwestern University Press, 2007), 445.

75 *Ibid.*, viii.

76 Nicholas Brown demonstrates the continuing power such a phenomeno-logical orientation can lend to analyses of global capitalism in his concept of the "eidaesthetic project" of twentieth-century literature – its capacity to

stage a "mutilated but real striving after the utopian representation of the absent totality" (Nicholas Brown, *Utopian Generations: The Political Horizon of Twentieth-Century Literature* [Princeton: Princeton University Press, 2005], 22). His analysis bears on Jean-Luc Nancy and Philippe Lacoue-Labarthe's account of the way the aesthetic comes to be freighted with an impossible responsibility: that of "overcoming contradictions produced by capitalism itself" by "philosophically resolving antinomies whose origin lies outside philosophy" (*Utopian Generations*, 14) – the *eidos* he invokes is therefore not identical to the more Husserlian idea of *eidos* I invoke here. But it's similar enough, especially in the sense in which *eidos* rescripts larger dynamics of capital accumulation, that Brown's account should be named as a powerful precursor to my own.

77 Edmund Husserl, *The Crisis of European Sciences and Transcendental Phenomenology*, trans. David Carr (Evanston: Northwestern University Press, 1970), 161.

78 Maurice Merleau-Ponty, *Phenomenology of Perception*, trans. Colin Smith (London: Routledge, 1996), 52. Hereafter cited as *PP*.

79 Husserl, *The Crisis of European Sciences and Transcendental Phenomenology*, 33, 163.

80 Maurice Merleau-Ponty, *The Visible and the Invisible,* trans. Alphonso Lingis (Evanston: Northwestern University Press, 1968), 126.

81 Max Weber, *Economy and Society: An Outline of Interpretive Sociology*, vol. II, trans. Ephraim Fischoff *et al.*, ed. Guenther Roth and Claus Wittich (Berkeley: University of California Press, 1978), 975.

82 *Ibid.*, 988.

83 *The Merleau-Ponty Reader*, 445.

84 Max Hoelz, *Vom „weißen Kreuz" zur roten Fahne: Jugend-, Kampf- und Zuchthauserlebnisse* (Berlin: Malik-Verlag 1929), 88. My translation.

85 Rosa Luxemburg, *The Essential Rosa Luxemburg: Reform or Revolution and the Mass Strike,* ed. Helen Scott (Chicago: Haymarket Books, 2007), 128. Hereafter cited as *ERL*.

86 Theodor Plievier, *Der Kaiser ging, die Generäle blieben* (Frankfurt am Main: Fischer Taschenbuch Verlag, 1932), 105. English translation: *The Kaiser Goes: the Generals Remain*, trans. A. W. Wheen (New York: Macmillan, 1933), 92. Translation slightly altered.

87 *Der Kaiser ging*, 105. *The Kaiser Goes*, 92. Translation slightly altered.

88 *Der Kaiser ging*, 103. *The Kaiser Goes*, 90. Translation slightly altered.

89 *Der Kaiser ging*, 103–4. *The Kaiser Goes*, 90–1. Translation slightly altered.

90 Miguel Ángel Asturias, *Los ojos de los enterrados* (Buenos Aires: Editorial Losada S.A., 1960), 401. Hereafter cited as *OE*. English translation: Miguel Ángel Asturias, *The Eyes of the Interred*, trans. Gregory Rabassa (New York: Delacorte Press, 1973), 572. Hereafter cited as *EI*.

91 Ousmane Sembene, *Les bouts de bois de Dieu* (Paris: Le Livre Contemporain, 1960), 128. My translation.

92 Patrick Chamoiseau, "Les 'états généraux' ne sont pas à la hauteur de la dynamique à l'œuvre." *Le Monde.* March 14, 2009. My translation.

93 C. L. R. James, *Nkrumah and the Ghana Revolution* (Westport: Lawrence Hill, 1978), 30. Hereafter cited as *NGR.*

94 See Dario Azzellini, *An Alternative Labour History: Worker Control and Workplace Democracy* (London: Zed Books, 2015).

95 Claude McKay, *The Passion of Claude McKay: Selected Poetry and Prose, 1912–1948,* ed. Wayne F. Cooper (New York: Schocken Books, 1973), 198.

96 Arundhati Roy, *The God of Small Things* (New York: Harper, 1997), 64.

97 Arundhati Roy, *Walking with the Comrades* (New York: Penguin, 2011), 208.

98 Sumanta Banerjee, *In the Wake of Naxalbari: A History of the Naxalite Movement in India* (Calcutta: Subarnarekha, 1980), 111.

99 *Ibid.,* 15. See Vandana Shiva, *The Violence of Green Revolution: Third World Agriculture, Ecology and Politics* (London: Zed Books, 1991); and Nick Cullather, *The Hungry World* (Cambridge: Harvard University Press, 2011).

100 Ross Mallick, *Indian Communism: Opposition, Collaboration and Institutionalization* (Oxford: Oxford University Press, 1994), 15.

101 D. Narayan and Raman Mahadevan, "Introduction," in D. Narayan and Raman Mahadevan, eds., *Shaping India: Economic Change in Historical Perspective* (London: Routledge, 2011), 12.

102 Raman Mahadevan, "Revisiting Indian Capitalists in Colonial India: Some Critical Reflections," in D. Narayan and Raman Mahadevan, eds., *Shaping India: Economic Change in Historical Perspective* (London: Routledge, 2011), 138–9.

103 *Ibid.,* 138.

104 Brent Hayes Edwards, *The Practice of Diaspora: Literature, Translation, and the Rise of Black Internationalism* (Cambridge: Harvard University Press, 2003), 239.

105 Michelle Ann Stephens, *Black Empire: The Masculine Global Imaginary of Caribbean Intellectuals in the United States, 1914–1962* (Durham: Duke University Press, 2005), 203.

106 *The Practice of Diaspora,* 219–20.

107 *Black Empire,* 157.

108 Claude McKay, *The Negroes in America,* trans. Robert J. Winter (Port Washington: National University Publications, 1979), 8.

109 *Ibid.,* 35.

110 *Ibid.,* 32.

111 Claude McKay, *Harlem: Negro Metropolis* (New York: E. P. Dutton, 1940), 221.

112 Claude McKay, *A Long Way from Home* (San Diego: Harvest, 1970), 67.

113 *Ibid.,* 67.

114 Claude McKay, *The Passion of Claude McKay: Selected Poetry and Prose, 1912–1948,* ed. Wayne F. Cooper (New York: Schocken Books, 1970), 74.

115 Claude McKay, *Amiable with Big Teeth*, ed. Jean-Christophe Cloutier and Brent Hayes Edwards (London: Penguin Classics, 2017), 136.

116 *The Negroes in America*, 10.

117 *Harlem: Negro Metropolis*, 183.

118 *Ibid.*, 30.

119 *Harlem: Negro Metropolis*, 29.

120 Gayatri Chakravorty Spivak, *Other Asias* (Oxford: Blackwell, 2008), 213.

121 Gayatri Spivak and Judith Butler, *Who Sings the Nation-State?: Language, Politics, Belonging* (Kolkata: Seagull Books, 2011), 91.

122 *Ibid.*, 245.

123 Walter Mignolo, *The Darker Side of Western Modernity: Global Futures, Decolonial Options* (Durham: Duke University Press, 2011), 33.

# CHAPTER I

# The General Strike in the Literature of Decolonization: Ousmane Sembene / Miguel Ángel Asturias / Patrick Chamoiseau

In January 2009, a general strike spread across Guadeloupe, completely paralyzing economic activity in the French Antillean region for forty-four days and leading to the largest political mobilization in its history. The strike was organized by an alliance of dozens of trade unions and political and cultural organizations, known as the Liyannaj Kont Pwofitasyon (LKP) – roughly translated, the Alliance Against Profiteering. By the first week of February, the general strike had spread to Martinique, shutting down supermarket chains, gas stations, and small businesses on the island, which also saw blockades of its capital city's center and industrial areas.[1] Then, in March, a general strike broke out in the French Indian Ocean territory Réunion, which saw roadblocks and massive protests similar to those in the French Antilles.

In the two years before 2009, general strikes had spread through South Africa, Guinea, Swaziland, Nigeria, Zimbabwe, Egypt, Lebanon, Greece, Argentina, Portugal, France, and the Dominican Republic, many of them involving mass protests and clashes with security forces. Then, in 2012, a transnational general strike against austerity was carried out in Spain, Portugal, Greece, France, Italy, and Belgium.[2] In Spain, Greece, and Italy, these strikes were particularly incendiary, involving street battles with police and paralyzing commercial traffic and urban centers.

What are we to make of this widespread use of mass strikes in twenty-first-century political struggles? How do they relate to the mass strikes of the twentieth century in terms of their strategies, aims, and epistemologies? Is their position in the political and literary imagination of today's geographies of struggle comparable to their position in those of the twentieth century? Why or why not?

Far from being merely a question of tactical orientation, this question cuts to the heart of contemporary theories of global capitalism and its cultures of political organization. Some theorists, such as Raúl Zibechi, argue that the strike is fundamentally a twentieth-century political weapon, which has been superseded by the neighborhood council, the general assembly, and new forms of territorial occupation.[3] From a different perspective, Eugene W. Holland suggests that direct confrontations with the state and capital should be avoided, in favor of a "slow-motion general strike," in which individuals and groups "walk away from dependence on capital and the State, one step, one stratum, at a time," while simultaneously evolving "other forms of self-organization and self-provisioning."[4]

Comparing the function of the twenty-first-century general strike to that of the previous century's means taking a position on these debates about the status of work, citizenship, and the role of the state in contemporary globalized capitalism. It also means examining the fantasies, transformative experiences, and interpersonal microdynamics that are mobilized in mass strikes occurring in this century and the last. In examining the literature and political geography of a few pivotal general strikes of the twentieth and twenty-first centuries, I seek to highlight several key points.

First, I argue that it's a mistake to see the general strike as an obsolete tactic, belonging strictly to twentieth-century strategic orientations. One of the paradoxes of contemporary globalized capitalism is that while information and capital are relayed rapidly across the globe via ever new technologies and instruments, commodities themselves are still largely produced and circulated according to the rhythms of nineteenth- and early-twentieth-century technologies: factories, ships, ports, warehouses, and rail lines. It is true that neoliberal capital has had great success in diverting much factory production to spaces where workers are politically isolated and face extreme state violence should they attempt to organize. But this does not reflect a global decline in manufacturing – which accounts for 30.5 percent of Gross World Product[5] – let alone shipping, which is responsible for 90 percent of all world trade by volume.[6] By contrast, that emblem of postmodern mobility, the airplane, accounts for only 0.5 percent of world trade by volume.[7]

Reports of the death of industrial labor have been similarly exaggerated. According to the 2014 World of Work Report, more than one in five people who works for a living on our planet is an industrial worker.[8] This means that factories, ships, ports, warehouses, and rail lines constitute massive bottlenecks of contemporary global capitalism, which are extremely vulnerable to spatial occupation, blockade, and the self-subtraction of labor. The three strikes I examine in detail – the Antillean General Strike of 2009, the Dakar–Niger Railway Strike of 1947–1948, and the Guatemalan General Strike of 1944 – all exploit this vulnerability of global capital in similar ways, bringing economic life to a virtual standstill and opening up spaces of collective organization and decision-making remote from state institutions and processes.

My second point is that mass strikes, precisely because of the potentially lethal threat they pose to the state, encourage the expansion of such nonstate decision-making apparatuses at an almost unbelievable rate. In the context of a mass strike, nonstate actors who have never been called upon to play a shaping role in their social life are suddenly prompted to develop organizational capacities and tactical sensitivities that must vie with the combined organizational intelligence and coercive force of the state. The fact that these newly-developed nonstate capacities often exceed those of the state, crippling even its capacity to mobilize deadly force, often triggers a fundamental shift in nonstate actors' perception of their social power and creative initiative. I refer to this moment as one of "eidetic rupture," because it shatters the *eidos*, or basic, unconscious, meaning-giving structure of nonstate actors, and gives rise to a sense of their creative capacities as forces that have an existence outside of the capital relation, and which possess the virtual power to organize themselves and sustain human life in its absence. In this sense, the general strike can be viewed as a form of collective proprioception, in which nonstate space is mapped out and realized.

However, in contrast to Holland's calls for a titrated, collective exit from the spaces and apparatuses of capitalist production, these eidetic ruptures occur only as part of an occupation and repurposing of workplaces and networks of commodity exchange. Nonstate space and nonstate organizational capacities therefore emerge directly out of the confrontation mass strikes stage *vis-à-vis* the state and capital, not as privileged autonomous zones marked off by small groups. This is essential, because it invites us to view nonstate space not simply as a space of retreat, but as an assemblage of production practices and coordinative abilities whose competencies rival those of the state both in scale and in executive focus.

My third point is that the characterization of the mass strike as a merely economic form of struggle, which is secluded from the political, social, and cultural dynamics of the population at large, ignores the multiple ways in which economic, political, social, and cultural forces are inextricably linked in mass strikes of the twentieth and twenty-first centuries. Because they arrest the machinery of the state so fully, opening a social void where once the regulatory power of the state had license to assert itself, mass strikes throw nonstate actors back on whatever resources they have, stimulating forms of mutual aid, strategic planning, and debate about communities' needs and aspirations, all of which are rooted in the political, social, and cultural capabilities of nonstate actors.

My final point is that approaching such nonstate capabilities as sites of political self-assertion allows us to reassess the forms of agency that are available to nonstate actors, especially in spaces marked by the predatory history of colonialism and neocolonialism. Rather than focusing on strategies of reappropriation, in which nonstate actors absorb and resignify the ideologies, languages, and cultures of the oppressor in oppositional ways, this approach invites us to consider moments in which the colonial presence as a whole is suddenly perceived as a horrifying, grotesque imposition, unnecessary to the reproduction of social life, and standing as the main obstacle to the development of nonstate actors' rich cultural resources. The colonial and neocolonial mass strike provides an especially bountiful archive of such forms of agency, since it confronts the colonizer not just with forms of moral suasion or symbolic rearticulation, but with a comprehensive negation of the machinery of empire, a dismantling of empire's economic raison d'être, and a voiding of empire's capacity to carry out its material and ideological itinerary.

In this sense, colonial and neocolonial mass strikes are an interrogation not of the colonizer, but of the colonized themselves – of their capacities for self-direction, cultural creation, and organization. The void created by the mass strike becomes a stage on which nonstate capabilities suppressed by the colonial and neocolonial state are rediscovered and exercised, in dialogue with exigencies and structures of feeling that are often remote from the cultural armature of the oppressor. These nonstate capabilities and cultural forms often make only a fleeting appearance on the stage of history, as they are coopted, demobilized, or crushed by comprador states and neo-imperial social forms. But attending to the eidetic ruptures and oppositional cultures of the colonial and neocolonial world will give us a glimpse of the formidable nonstate resources that exist beneath the vertical concentrations of power in the colonial and neocolonial state.

In its broad outlines, this research agenda isn't entirely new. In many ways, it's a continuation of the project of Subaltern Studies to write a "history from below" "from the distinct and separate point of view of the masses ... using unconventional or neglected sources in popular memory [and] oral discourse."[9] But my focus on mass strikes in the colonial and neocolonial world, and on the literature devoted to these phenomena, requires a few shifts of emphasis and theoretical innovations.

This is the case for a few reasons. To begin with, mass strikes in the colonial and neocolonial world, though often accompanied by protest movements, peasant insurgencies, and other forms of armed opposition, possess a social logic and noematic structure that is distinct from these other modes of struggle. The principal reason for this is that the main weapon deployed in a mass strike is complete *withdrawal* from the material processes that make empire possible. The comprehensiveness of this threat to empire is staggering to contemplate: depriving the colonizer of the ability to produce and transport fuel, food, and other necessities of life, shutting down the colonizer's ports and means of transportation, robbing empire of its capacity to transport even its military by sea or rail – the mass strike expresses, as its ultimate horizon, a will to starve, immobilize, and economically ruin the colonizer. More than this, confronted by the vast negation of vital processes they have accomplished, nonstate actors often come to perceive themselves as a general social force, not dependent on empire for its social potency, and able to organize and nourish life in the absence of the state.

Equally important is the fact that general strikes rely for their cohesiveness and potency on a vast number of horizontal decision-making processes, logistical innovations, and mutual-aid structures. The organizational logic and executive structure at work in these phenomena are distinct from the vertical command structures so often seen in nationalist armies, just as they are distinct from the forms of retaliatory action analyzed so brilliantly in Ranajit Guha's *Elementary Aspects of Peasant Insurgency in Colonial India*. No doubt colonial and neocolonial mass strikes often revive customary forms of assembly, self-defense, and mutual aid, which is why Guha's insistence on the deliberate, politically charged, and non-spontaneous "consultative process" involved in peasant revolts is especially relevant to the social ontology of mass strikes.[10] But, precisely because the decentralized, vernacular political processes involved in mass strikes aim at a dissolution of the total life process of empire, they imply – objectively, as part of the strategic leverage they exert – something in excess of the symbolic reversals and acts of revenge Guha analyzes. They imply the existence of a regulative counterpower, robust in its capacity for self-government, and, ultimately, the possibility of a reconstitution of the world, outside of colonial and neocolonial social logics.

This process has a different organizational style, cultural language, and level of comprehensiveness in every mass strike. The 2009 Antillean General Strike saw port closures, the shutdown of Pointe-à-Pitre International Airport, the closure of most big retailers, and a language of revolt that focused on persistent racial divisions in the *départements et régions d'outre-mer*, the need to develop the regions' capacity to provide for their own basic needs, and the imperative to curtail the stream of French imports that keeps its Caribbean territories in a state of neocolonial dependence. The Dakar–Niger Railway Strike was in some ways less comprehensive, involving only railway workers and dockers. However, the transnational nature of the strike, involving cities in Senegal and French Sudan, and its immobilization of the French empire's only means of efficiently transporting food, manufactured goods, and manpower into the African interior, lent it a political heft that terrorized the colonial power.[11] Organizing a network of 19,000 workers along the 1,287 kilometers of the Dakar–Niger line, the strike focused in large part on pay equity between black and white employees, and was a major milestone in Senegal's path to independence, even though this demand was not a principal driving force behind the strike itself.[12]

The 1944 Guatemalan General Strike involved agricultural workers of Tiquisate and Bananera, railway workers, sectors of the urban proletariat, students, teachers, and elements of the Guatemalan professional classes. The strike paralyzed the country's massive banana industry and made Guatemala City effectively ungovernable, with students and military officers conducting armed struggle with forces loyal to the country's dictator, Jorge Ubico. The strike, protests, and armed struggle resulted in democratic elections being held within twenty-four weeks – a process that resulted in the election, first, of the reluctant populist Juan José Arévalo Bermejo, and then of Jacobo Árbenz, who instituted some of the most significant land reform measures to benefit indigenous peasants in the history of Latin America.

As these examples show, there is no "universal history" of mass strikes that somehow plays out an identical social script in such widely disparate cultures and historical periods. In the French Antilles and French West Africa, for example, racial inequalities were at the center of the mass strike movements – in the former, the LKP constantly stressed that a handful of *béké* families, many of them having acquired their wealth in the time of slavery, controlled the vast majority of industries in the French overseas departments, while whites were given preferential treatment in government jobs. This led to a tactical alliance among union workers, independence activists, and small businesspeople, the latter of whom were perceived to be part of an Antillean project of economic self-reliance. Though the dangers of cross-class alliances like these were clear to those in leadership roles – Élie Domota, for example, stressed that "notre organisation est anticapitaliste (our organization is anti-capitalist)" and that "la lutte des classes ne peut être subordonnée à la lutte de libération nationale (the class struggle must not be subordinated to the national liberation struggle)"[13] – employers' syndicates such as the Syndicat des transporteurs de marchandises de Guadeloupe and the Union des transporteurs de voyageurs were welcomed in the Union générale des travailleurs de Guadeloupe (UGTG) in its fight against the neoliberal destruction of local transport enterprises, and the LKP stressed the need to build up local businesses in its communiqués during the 2009 General Strike.

By contrast, during the Dakar–Niger Railway strike, the struggle against longstanding racial inequalities led to no comparable alliance between striking workers and sectors of the black West African bourgeoisie. On the contrary, local imams, comprador politicians, and African business owners assembled a redoubtable class unity against the strikers, attempting simultaneously to starve, beat, and cajole them into submission. On the other hand, the Guatemalan General Strike, though not organized around racial inequalities, as the majority of its protagonists perceived themselves to be of Ladino ancestry, did see an alliance between elements of the bourgeoisie and the working class, in large part because of the restriction of opportunities experienced by sectors of the middle class. Additionally, women played a major role in spearheading the strike in Guatemala, because of the extreme tactical importance rural teachers had in connecting rural and urban workers. This is similar to the recent experience in the Antilles, in which women workers played a major role in the general strike movement, whereas in the Dakar–Niger Railway Strike, women played an essential role precisely because of their central importance to the mutual aid networks and forms of protest developed outside the union struggle proper.

These different strikes thus unfold along extremely complex vectors of race, class, and gender. No unitary theory of mass strikes or nonstate space "in general" could do justice to these specificities in the absence of a careful examination of such differential socio-political realities. Each mass strike, and each form of nonstate space to which it gives rise, emerges from a specific history, engages specific cultural energies and tensions, and involves culturally specific ambitions, grievances, and epistemologies of struggle. And yet, the fact that nonstate actors of such different backgrounds, life experiences, and historical moments all combine and organize mass strikes, forming different nonstate communication networks, striking forces, and oppositional epistemologies in the process, is truly remarkable, and might seem like nothing short of a miracle, in the absence of a careful socio-political examination of each site of struggle. It is to combat this sense that the appearance of oppositional struggle, and its points of overlap with other sites of struggle, is somehow miraculous or unaccountable that I bring together movements and literatures that are so geographically, temporally, and culturally remote from one another.

At the same time, the remarkable points of overlap these works share invite us to rethink some of the ways we cordon off pre-war and post-war literature, postcolonial literature, and modernist and postmodernist literature. If nonstate space, eidetic ruptures, and general strikes interweave a polyphonic language of tactical sensitivities and organizational modes throughout literatures belonging to each of these categories, perhaps the forms of periodization and canon-formation we're used to conceal deeper irrigations and blockages that new forms of literary geography can explore with greater suppleness. One of the virtues of performing such a literary geography with a focus on the mass strike in particular is that it is a phenomenon that returns us to a basic, structural fact that all societies subsumed by capital share: that without workers producing, a society ceases to function.

As we will see in Sembene's novel *Les bouts de bois de Dieu*, this fact overshadows the complex weave of postcolonial nationalisms, comprador politicians, and union bureaucracies whose interactions the novel chronicles. Without help from their elected politicians or even the radical Confédération générale du travail (CGT), workers are represented as having to create their own organs of nonstate self-government. Similarly, in *Los ojos de los enterrados*, strikers must organize in a country where opposition parties are illegal. Yet again, in Guadeloupe and Martinique, political organizers continually highlight "l'apathie morale de l'État (the moral apathy of the state)," "qui n'a pas su exercer son rôle de régulateur ... et qui se révèle être une véritable faillite (which has failed to exercise its role as a regulator ... and which has proven itself to be utterly bankrupt)."[14] Accordingly, the LKP refuses to negotiate with mediators, and instead develops highly flexible nonstate organizational methods which forced a direct confrontation between the strikers and the French state.

In all of these cases, the mass strike highlights the non-representative quality of colonial and neocolonial political actors. Even in cases where party-aligned forces are a component of the struggle, as in the 2009 Antillean General Strike, strikers must develop forms of mutual aid and organization outside the state and beyond the logic of the party form. Labor unions play a central role in all three of these mass strikes: in Senegal, the independent railway union orchestrated strike activity in its entirety; in Guatemala, railway and agricultural workers' unions were crucial to the organization of the mass strike; and in the French Caribbean, the UGTG was a major organizational force. But each of these unions became a mass directive organ precisely by opening up spaces of struggle outside of legislatively focused state politicking. In the case of the Dakar–Niger Railway Strike, this meant forming a new labor organization, outside of the Stalinist and white-dominated CGT, which at the time maintained that African struggles should be subordinated to those conducted in the French metropole. In Guatemala, it meant constituting "mutual benefit associations"[15] during a time when unions had been abolished, and even the words "strike" and "worker" had been proscribed.[16] In the French Caribbean, it meant employing forms of labor action dating back to the 1952 Guadeloupe General Strike within the context of a broad-based nonstate struggle that included both unions and other political and community organizations.

Nonstate social organisms such as these, which develop the extra-legal capacities of both well-established labor organizations and newer social forces, construct an alternative history at the same time as they anticipate an open question: how to imagine, beneath independence parties, permanent political elites, and comprador proxies, the horizontal organization of political life, the autogestion of the masses. This open question runs throughout the twentieth and twenty-first centuries, beneath the statist solutions of Maoism, Sovietism, and postcolonial capitalism. Every so often, it is reopened – not according to some ineluctable historical logic, but in spaces where the misery of capitalist underdevelopment, new cultures of resistance, and deep-rooted traditions of mutual aid achieve a tension that cannot be defused by conventional crisis-management techniques.

These spaces have been communicating with one another for more than a century. They reach out to one another for completion. They restart their covert history in surprising, unpredictable places.

Is there a way to "periodize," to unpack, to trace the becoming of this history – not in a linear fashion, or according to ethnocentric phases, but according to local, shifting topographies of exploitation and resistance that have been resulting in unpredictable explosions, here, there, for over a hundred years?

Patrick Chamoiseau provides one of the most recent internal cartographies of this kind of nonstate space, assembled out of the recent experiences to which the General Strike in the French Antilles gave rise. Let's begin with this twenty-first-century general strike and see what it has to teach us about the relevance of two general strikes dating from the era of colonialism.

## La profusion inattendue des émergences

Patrick Chamoiseau is best known for his extraordinary 1992 novel *Texaco*, which narrates the prehistory and contemporary life of a shantytown outside Fort-de-France. The novel is a chronicle of nonstate space *in extremis*; the shantytown it depicts is populated by rural workers displaced by the collapse of the Martinican sugar industry in the 1950s, by other unemployed workers migrating from the city itself, and by older generations of ex-slaves who fled from a precarious life on the hillsides. The nonstate space these migrants construct is a social structure of last resort for a population that has been ravaged by colonial slavery, free-trade imperialism, and state-sponsored violence and displacement. The forms of resistance and mutual aid its characters develop testify to the ingenuity, collective intelligence, and constructive capacity of such squatter populations. However, the forms of collective self-assertion in Texaco are primarily focused on defending the shantytown against the city council, which plans to raze it. The civil engineer who has been sent for this purpose, but who is won over by Texaco's residents, therefore becomes a political focal point by the novel's end, to the extent of being referred to as "the Christ," after he halts the destruction of the settlement and helps ensure that electricity is brought to its residents.[17]

What is the relationship of these forms of nonstate space to more broad-based forms of protest in Martinique and the Caribbean generally? What forms of political self-assertion have groups like Texaco's inhabitants developed since the publication of Chamoiseau's novel in 1992, and how do they relate to the General Strike of 2009? Is the impact of these recent developments visible in any way in his more recent works?

In a 2009 manifesto, entitled *Manifeste pour les "produits" de haute nécessité*, Chamoiseau, along with Édouard Glissant and another seven cosignatories, linked the 2009 General Strike to "une absurdité coloniale (a colonial absurdity)" that subtends the conflicts surrounding high prices and low wages in the French overseas departments. Inscribed within "le labyrinthe obscur et indémêlable des prix (marges, sous-marges, commissions occultes et profits indécents) (the dark and hopelessly entangled labyrinth of prices [margins, sub-margins, kickbacks, and profiteering])" is the fact that the populations of Guadeloupe and Martinique were "détournés de notre manger-pays, de notre environnement proche et de nos réalités culturelles (estranged from our native food, from our immediate environment, and from our cultural realities)," "pour nous livrer sans pantalon et sans jardins-bokay aux modes alimentaires européens (to be delivered over, trouserless and without *bokay* gardens, to European eating patterns)."[18]

In this context, negotiating with the French state for price controls, subsidies, and so on, "peut certes améliorer quelque souffrance dans l'immédiat (may certainly mitigate some suffering for the moment)" but "l'illusoire bien-faisance de ces accords sera vite balayée par le principe du 'Marché' (the illusory benefits of these accords will be quickly swept away by the principle of 'the Market')."[19] What is of fundamental necessity, then, is the following: "de jeter les bases d'une société non économique, où l'idée de développement à croissance continuelle serait écartée au profit de celle d'épanouissement; où emploi, salaire, consommation et production serait des lieux de création de soi et de parachèvement de l'humain (to lay the foundation for a noneconomic society, where the idea of continually expanding development would be rejected in favor of that of fulfillment – where wages, salaries, consumption, and production would be places of self-creation and the actualization of humanity)."[20]

At the level of realpolitik, Chamoiseau and his collaborators stress, this demand is completely commensurable with those issued by the LKP, such as a minimum wage based on the actual cost of living in Guadeloupe, a stoppage of foreclosures, and the creation of an adequate public bureau of vocational training – in short, with solutions that remain within the orbit of state-based action.[21] What they seek to point out is simply that beneath *le prosaïque* of social programs and benefits lies *le poétique*: "l'aspiration à un épanouissement de soi, là où la nourriture est de dignité, d'honneur, de musique, de chants, de sports, de danses, de lectures, de philosophie, de spiritualité, d'amour, de temps libre affecté à l'accomplissement du grand désir intime (the aspiration to self-fulfillment, nourished by dignity, honor, music, songs, sports, dance, readings, philosophy, spirituality, love, free time devoted to the satisfaction of our innermost desires)."[22]

Within the regime of *le prosaïque*, it is necessary to develop local, Caribbean sources for vital imports, and to promote food and energy self-sufficiency. But what this opens within the regime of poetic value is, quite simply, "tout ce qui fait que la vie vaut la peine d'être vécue (everything that makes life worth living)": "autorégénération et autoréorganisation … une amplification de l'imaginaire, une stimulation des facultés cognitives, une mise en créativité de tous, un déboulé sans manman de l'esprit (self-regeneration and self-reorganization … an expansion of the imagination, a stimulation of the cognitive faculties, a blooming of creativity for all, an untutored acceleration of the spirit)."[23] For the manifesto's authors, this ultimately opens upon a vision of the near future: "Petits pays, soudain au cœur nouveau du monde, soudain immenses d'être les premiers exemples de sociétés postcapitalistes, capables de mettre en œuvre un épanouissement humain qui s'inscrit dans l'horizontale plénitude du vivant (small countries, suddenly at the new heart of the world, suddenly immense in being the first examples of postcapitalist societies, capable of implementing a human fulfillment which is inscribed within the horizontal plenitude of the living)."[24]

What is extraordinary about these formulations is not just their vision of creative capacities unfolding, but their positing of the coexistence of this self-creative poesis with the practical political logistics of the 2009 General Strike. Far from downplaying the economic dimension of the strike in favor of its more properly political, social, and spiritual dimensions, the authors of the manifesto insist on the inseparability of the economic, the political, the social, and the spiritual. It is in the context of the General Strike, in fact, that demands on the state for wage increases, job opportunities, and training can be seen for what they are: the practical dimension of a fight for human fulfillment, for the time to develop one's human capacities and forms of relation on a larger scale.

This insistence on the inseparability of poetic value and the prose of struggle can be seen in the organizational and rhetorical currents of the strike movement itself. Though the LKP derived a good part of its membership from the UGTG – Guadeloupe's largest union – it was not simply a union organization, but an alliance of over forty political, labor, and community organizations, ranging from environmental activists to associations of Carnival groups. The "120 Propositions" issued by the LKP reflect this diversity of outlook: demands for adequate public transport and protections for union organizing exist side by side with demands for the creation of a craft and agricultural nursery that would showcase local products, for the revitalization of living areas for the economic development of local activities (e.g., agro-processing and fishing), for the involvement of representatives of cultural associations in media devoted to Guadeloupian language and culture, and for the establishment of security measures to protect people from the pesticide chlordecone.[25]

What emerges out of these propositions is a rethinking of social life as a whole – an animation of creative capacities that have to do not just with wage earning, but with the creative construction of human spaces of life. As Chamoiseau noted in a 2009 interview, however, this comprehensive reckoning of human potentialities required an equally comprehensive break with a host of internalized thought-habits, ideologemes, and identifications that linked the peoples of the French Antilles to neoliberal ideologies and "l'esprit colonial (the colonial spirit)" of the metropole.[26] The general strike that ended just a few days before Chamoiseau's interview occurred, according to Chamoiseau, "en ces temps où l'économie est devenue une religion sectaire, où le pouvoir d'achat télécommande notre âme, où le sens de notre vie a sombré dans la consommation (at a time when the economy has become a sectarian religion, when purchasing power 'remote controls' our soul, when the meaning of our life is sunk in consumption)" ("J"). In such a context, the general strike necessarily "déclenche désordres et incertitudes (triggers disorder and uncertainty)" ("J"). Emerging with the disruptive force of a natural phenomenon, the strike, like an eruption, cyclone, or earthquake, is governed by "une réalité omni-dimensionnelle, laquelle devrait d'abord nous initier à fixer l'impensable (an omni-dimensional reality, which must first teach us to confront the inconceivable)" ("J").

This double-movement of disruption and newly thinkable possibilities is central to what I call "eidetic rupture" – the moment, ubiquitous in narratives involving general strikes, in which a basic, non-conscious structuring experiential logic is fractured, in a way that expands one's lived sense of creative possibilities. The forms that eidetic rupture takes are as varied as the cultures, lifeworlds, and political conflicts that are implicated in general strikes carried out in different societies. But all eidetic ruptures involve a fundamental fissure in one's sense of personal and collective capabilities: a break with customary operational modes that is often shocking.

Central to the eidetic rupture Chamoiseau describes is the break with a certain understanding of Martinique's and Guadeloupe's relationship with the French state. "Ce que l'on appelle DOM-TOM (quelle honte!) sont des archaïsmes coloniaux (What are referred to as DOM-TOM [what shame!] are colonial archaisms" according to Chamoiseau – archaisms that are fostered by the belief that Martinique and Guadeloupe could not survive politically or economically except "dans une complicité plus ou moins active, plus ou moins passive, avec les survivances coloniales (in collusion, more or less active, more or less passive, with colonial relics)" ("J").

These archaisms, Chamoiseau continues, "se sont maintenus car ils sont en nous, nous les avons intériorisés (have survived because they are in us, we have internalized them)" in the form of "un 'esprit colonial' incapable de concevoir entre la République et ses ultimes colonies une relation autre que la sujétion assistée ou la menace de rupture méprisante (a 'colonial spirit' unable to conceive a relation between the Republic and its last colonies other than that of remaining dependent subjects or the threat of a contemptuous break)" ("J"). Chamoiseau concludes as follows: "Il faut dépêcher grand congé aux religieux de l'économique, aux industrieux de l'esprit colonial, aux réflexes d'Empire (We must give the religion of the economy, the industriousness of the colonial spirit, the reflexes of Empire a permanent send-off)"; in doing so, "on éprouvera le sentiment d'abord d'un nettoyage, ensuite d'un renouveau, et on vivra la profusion inattendue des émergences (we will experience, first, a feeling of cleansing, then of renewal, and of embracing an unexpected profusion of beginnings)" ("J").

But how to imagine "giving a send-off" to such comprehensive experiential frameworks, such *mentalités unanimes* – senses of the self and the community that have worked their way into the texture of our social habits? According to Chamoiseau, the General Strike made possible such an eidetic rupture: "un brouillard d'archaïsmes qui persistent dans notre rapport à la France, et dans notre rapport à nous-mêmes (a fog of archaisms that persist in our relationship with France, and in our relationship with ourselves)," he stated, just after the 2009 strike, "va s'effondrer et peut-être disparaître dans les semaines qui viennent (will collapse, and may disappear in the coming weeks)" ("J").

So, what are the mechanisms of this collapse? How might we visualize the cognitive, spiritual, and interpersonal transformations that occur amidst the "prose" of a mass strike?

This is, preeminently, a question belonging to the sphere of literature ...

### Auto-mimesis

The fictional works Chamoiseau published in 2009 and 2011 both take shape around the experience of eidetic rupture and the forms of nonstate space that become imaginable within its complex temporality. One might expect a social upheaval as weighty as the Antillean General Strike to reawaken the forms of realist, historical narrative Chamoiseau deploys so virtuosically in *Texaco*. But something very different happened. *Les neuf consciences du Malfini* (2009) and *Le papillon et la lumière* (2011) are highly conceptual, metaphysically dense fables that combine the conventions of the Creole folktale, the prose poem, and the philosophical essay. And yet, it is within these highly abstract confabulations that the social transformations surrounding the 2009 General Strike are captured with the greatest exactitude.

*Les neuf consciences du Malfini*, written during the period of strikes, factory occupations, and heightened political focus that anticipated the 2009 General Strike, takes shape in its entirety as a slow-motion eidetic rupture. Written in the first person from the perspective of a hawk, the novel describes the numerous, painful cognitive jolts experienced by the bird as he realizes that his predatory outlook and modus vivendi separate him from the common life belonging to the flora and fauna of Rabuchon. Most of these cognitive disruptions, which are audible in the unpleasant hiccups that interrupt his narrative, occur as he observes the improvisatory, local existence of a hummingbird, whom he calls "Foufou" (the Creole name for the Antillean Crested Hummingbird). Most birds, Malfini observes, possess their own ethos, their own guiding principles, "mais pour le Foufou … *Hinnk* … je sombrais dans l'incompréhension … Elle m'apparaissait composée de plusieurs courants d'exigences qui se tressaient, s'éloignaient pour se rejoindre dans une sorte de mélange dissocié ou d'impureté instable, comme à la confluence de multiples mémoires ou de nombreuses lignées (but when it came to Foufou … *Hic* … I was drowning in confusion … To me, he seemed composed of several currents of exigency which were woven together, separating and rejoining in a sort of dissociated mélange or unstable impurity, as at the confluence of multiple memories or of many lines of descent)."[27]

In Malfini's philosophical vocabulary, Foufou lacks a singular "Ayala": a term from the Upanishads that refers to an all-encompassing, foundational consciousness, which exists beneath the seven other modalities of sense-consciousness. According to Malfini's limited imagination, "Ayala" corresponds only to the inherited beliefs and existential modes that render a species singular, unquestioning, and identical to itself. That Foufou's Ayala appears to be "incertaine, bifide, trouble, même discordante (uncertain, bifurcated, muddled, even discordant" (*M* 38) is therefore a shock to Malfini's system. But Foufou's "disponibilité infinie (infinite receptivity)" (*M* 34) becomes a source of incredible strength near the end of the novel.

When another predatory bird called Le Féroce ravages Rabuchon, going so far as to destroy the flowers that nourish the lower organisms of the quarter, Foufou accomplishes a trick that repulses the ravager, but not before the elected leader of the hummingbirds is killed. To make matters worse, a blight, known to the creatures of Rabuchon as "la mort lente," is simultaneously decimating the plant life of the region. In the face of this crisis, Foufou goes to work, spreading the pollen of all flower species far and wide, "mélangeant les poussières comme s'il avait voulu que ces vies immobiles relayent leurs dissemblances (mixing the particles as if he had wanted these immobile lives to relay their dissimilarities)" (*M* 203). Finding themselves without a leader and flying "sans système, dans une poésie de labyrinthe (without system, in a labyrinthine poetry" (*M* 205), two or three young hummingbirds begin to imitate Foufou, then, "par contamination (by way of contamination)" (*M* 205), dozens follow suit, along with all the other species of the quarter.

Soon, "ce qui n'était qu'un vrac d'imitations particulières devint une structure collective, chaotique toujours, indéfinissable et incertaine, mais intense et réelle (that which had been nothing but a jumble of individual imitations became a collective structure, chaotic no doubt, indefinable and uncertain, but intense and real)" (*M* 206). As a result of this common effort, "l'existence de l'un côtoyait celle de l'autre, l'application de l'un renforçait celle de l'autre, l'énergie de tous soutenait celle de chacun (the being of one flanked that of the other, the effort of one reinforced that of the other, the energy of all sustained that of each)" (*M* 206–7), and "Rabuchon n'était plus un territoire, ni même un embrouillement de territoires, c'était une *intention* (Rabuchon was no longer a land, nor even a tangle of lands; it was an *intention*)" (*M* 207). Having endured the tears and pain of an eidetic rupture that distances him from his Ayala, Malfini comes to believe that "la vie tenait à une infinie réorganisation de ce qui lui était donné et qu'elle transmuait en don (life stems from an endless reorganization of that which has been given to it and which it returns as a gift" (*M* 173) – and by the end of the novel he is doing his best to help, spreading seeds far and wide to assist in the effort of cross-fertilization.

What does this complex, lengthy fable have to do with recent political developments in the French Antilles? And why would Chamoiseau choose to represent these developments so abstractly? To begin with, the fable-structure of *Les neuf consciences du Malfini* allows Chamoiseau to represent the internally divided consciousness of the Martinican population as a multifaceted and changing phenomenological ecosystem. Malfini, who hails from abroad and describes himself as "une force inscrite aux violences impassibles qui régentent le vivant (a force inscribed in the inexorable violence which rules over the living)" (*M* 21), is clearly the mental representative of French imperialism – the "colonial spirit" fostered by French assimilationism, which encourages the Martinican population to view itself as the beneficiary of a "proud" imperial legacy.

In the political economy of this fable, a hummingbird named Colibri governs in the name of this imperial power. He issues edicts, expels immigrants, and controls his territory with bureaucratic passion. Foufou, by contrast, lives in a desolate corner of Rabuchon, among "insect squatters" – "de microscopiques existences qui drivaillaient en nuées compactes pour assaillir les pourritures, les excréments, les fruits tombés ou les choses mortes (microscopic existences that swarm in compact clouds to attack anything rotting, excrement, windfalls, or dead things)"

(*M* 77). The various living beings in Chamoiseau's story thus encode overlapping subject-positions and modes of self-perception that belong to the Martinican population: the "colonial spirit," as an abstract system of belief, the comprador bureaucracy, and marginalized, squatter populations of the kind Chamoiseau represented in *Texaco*.

In *Les neuf consciences du Malfini*, the capacity to create nonstate space is identified with these marginalized populations; however, unlike in *Texaco*, they are not fighting a primarily defensive struggle, but are endowed with capacities for social creation, renovation, and communication whose purchase extends across the social body as a whole. In what do these capabilities consist? Foufou's interactions with the other species of Rabuchon suggest that what is at issue is a form of creative auto-mimesis capable of constructing and sustaining nonstate space. Foufou is described as "imitant des créatures très différentes de lui: sucriers ababas, mouches bébêtes, guêpes idiotes, libellules et papillons débiles, toutes bestioles mal dégrossies qui fréquentaient toutes qualités de fleurs et menaient avec elles de mystérieux commerces (imitating creatures quite different from him: gaga sparrows, silly flies, idiotic wasps, moronic dragonflies and butterflies, all the sketchy critters that frequent flowers of every description and carry on mysterious commerce with them)" (*M* 41).

This form of omniversal mimesis is a source of incredible power in the asymmetric engagements Foufou confronts. When faced with a formidable bird called Le Moqueur that terrifies Rabuchon, Foufou mobilizes his imitative capacity and "se mit à imiter le monstre imitateur, à reproduire ses sons bâtards, ses cris sans vérité, ses chants de seconde main, à relayer dans Rabuchon cette cacophonie railleuse (begins to imitate the monstrous imitator, to reproduce his bastard sounds, his untruthful cries, his second-hand songs, to relay throughout Rabuchon this cacophony of raillery)" (*M* 49). When attacking an eagle that descends upon Rabuchon, Foufou assaults him with tactics belonging to a swarm of various species: "d'oiseaux-plongeurs, de merles fous, de crabiers invisibles, moustiques, saute relles, guêpes et vonvons … une sarabande de manières de voler, de techniques d'approche, de cris, de chants, de frappes et virevoltes qui appartenaient à des espèces diverses (divers, crazy blackbirds, invisible crab fishers, mosquitoes, grasshoppers, wasps, and bumblebees … a saraband of flying styles, techniques of approach, cries, songs, taps, and twirls that belonged to different species)" (*M* 199).

Unpredictability, speed, adaptability, receptivity, and, above all, "mimétisme" – these qualities, in combination with Foufou's seemingly infinite attention to particularities and differences, and his

ability to "relay" them, are the components of the political potentiality Chamoiseau is outlining in his fable. The power of what Édouard
Glissant calls "creolization" is clearly visible in this political capacity.
"The mutual mutations generated by [an] interplay of relations"[28] are
central to the kinds of Caribbean political actors Chamoiseau is trying
to evoke. In *Texaco*, this appeared in the vision of the squatter settlement
"comme un éco-système, tout en équilibres et en interactions … rien
que le tournoiement hasardeux du vivant (as an ecosystem, made up of
equilibriums and interactions … nothing but the haphazard whirls of
the living)."[29] But, in *Les neuf consciences du Malfini*, this becomes a force
active over the entirety of the population – a positive political force, with
an offensive capacity as great as its capacity for inclusion, differentiation,
and mutation.

Most importantly, it is a vision of political agency in which Foufou
is not part of an institutional leadership structure. Even when others
begin to imitate his life-sustaining activity, "Le Foufou ignora cette fièvre
mimétique (Foufou ignored this mimetic fever)" (*M* 205) rather than
positioning himself as a central, directive force. The entire emphasis of
Chamoiseau's political fable, then, is on the development of nonstate forms
of creative initiative, whose fundamental structure is a form of collective
auto-mimesis, in which the life-sustaining powers of nonstate actors are
imagined as a flexible process of transformative evolution remote from
centralized systems of political power.

That this nonstate power belongs simultaneously to the French Antilles'
lineages of anti-colonial struggle and to its current battles against French
neocolonialism is suggested by the role of the hummingbird in Martinican
folklore. As Richard Watts notes, Aimé Césaire and René Ménil link the
hummingbird, by way of a popular Martinican folktale, to the "marrons,"
the runaway slave communities, of Martinique: it is their struggles against
the colonizer that are evoked in the folktale that pits the hummingbird
"against all manner of creature."[30] The protean, nonstate capabilities of
Foufou thus represent "an improvisatorial, adaptive ruse in face of the negative forces of colonization," in the words of Wendy Knepper – but, more
than this, they represent a departure from exactly the statist solutions bro-
kered by Césaire which frustrate Chamoiseau so intensely.[31] If, as Stella
Vincenot points out, Césaire's support of departmentalization "meant
more political and social assimilation into mainland France," Chamoiseau's
image of an unpredictable, leaderless, nonstate combatant is meant to
evoke the forms of networked anti-neocolonial resistance embodied in the
2009 General Strike.[32]

As Chamoiseau expresses it in the quasi-manifesto with which he concludes his tale, "Le vivant n'est et ne peut se concevoir que dans son horizontale plénitude qui suppose tous les possible en relation sans aucune hiérarchie (Life is only and can only be conceived in its horizontal pleni-tude, which implies all possible relationships without any hierarchy)" (*M* 231). He continues as follows: "Aucune culture, aucune civilisation, aucun nécessité économique ou sociale ne saurait s'arroger, pour quelque raison que ce soit, le droit d'une atteinte à la perspective de l'horizontale plénitude (No culture, no civilization, no economic or social necessity is capable of arrogating, for whatever reason, the power belonging to the perspective of horizontal plenitude" (*M* 231–2).

Written in the aftermath of the 2009 General Strike, *Le papillon et la lumière* radicalizes this vision of horizontality and nonstate space. Gone is the pseudo-transcendent perspective of internalized empire, gone is the narrative of "learning from below" whereby predatory instincts are slowly and painfully dismantled. Instead, *Le papillon et la lumière* takes place in the very midst of an eidetic rupture, in which the reflexes of empire have been voided, leaving the social body strangely suspended, testing out its fledgling capabilities for nonstate social agency. These nonstate capacities are evoked in the vagaries of moths, which populate a social space that has been voided of its customary affirmations and exists as a crepuscular space of untested collective powers.

This nighttime space is the scene of a battle that is "totale et … sans pitié (total and without pity)": the "lampes, guirlandes, projecteurs et sunlights, spots de sécurité, lasers de boîtes de nuit et grands faisceaux pour patrimoines, combattent pied à pied contre des peuples d'ombres (the lamps, fairy lights, searchlights, and "sunlights," security spotlights, nightclub lasers, and floodlights for heritage buildings fight toe to toe with the people of the shadows)."[33] At the meeting space of these nighttime populations and the lights which seek to control, surveil, and entice them, "il y a de l'invisible, du pas vraiment visible, et ce pas-vu-visible que l'on voit sans rien voir (there is the invisible, the not-really-visible, and the not-seen-visible that one sees without seeing)" (*PL* 15). In these contested spaces, "dans les movances de l'ombre, une vie fiévreuse s'affole et se maintient intense, et puis explose en toutes sortes d'insectes et grandes volées de papillons sans couleurs apparentes (in these shadow movements, a feverish life careens, concentrates, and then explodes into all kinds of insects and large flutters of moths without apparent colors)" (*PL* 15).

The main action of the story involves one young moth who manages to free himself of the deadly fixation most moths have for the lights of nighttime. He seeks out a reclusive, old moth who serves as his mentor, and who helps him understand, for example, that attempting to instruct the other, mesmerized moths about their false consciousness is a mistake. Instead of pointing out the danger of the lights, he should "signaler la vie dans son ensemble (attest to life in its entirety)" by embodying a beauty which "bouleverse, éveille, réveille (disrupts, wakens, rouses)" (*PL* 59, 65).

This may seem like an apolitical pedagogy on the part of the old moth, but the context of the story makes it clear that just the opposite is true. The sites where these moths converse all explicitly evoke the 2009 General Strike, with its roadblocks, store closings, and rebellion against the signifiers and institutions of foreign capital. A damaged McDonald's sign, raining sparks and eventually fluttering off, a traffic light above a deserted intersection, a supermarket cart abandoned in a parking lot, a bank ATM which two men are attempting to unfasten and make off with – these are the locations where the moths' discourses on beauty and *l'action juste* take place. It is a social space that has already been marked by social rebellion and a refusal of capitalist exploitation, and in which nonstate actors have demonstrated their ability to bring all economic activity to a halt. The moths thus represent forms of self-creative power that could emerge in the midst of this general suspension.

In this context, Chamoiseau employs a fable, as opposed to the more realist style he deploys in *Texaco*, to extend the action of the 2009 General Strike imaginatively in a way that accounts for its potentialities as well as its actualities. The actual institutions and alliances of the General Strike achieve a high level of horizontal organizational coherence, but never manage to pervade social space with the flexibility and autopoetic quality of the moths in *Le papillon et la lumière*, and it would be difficult to represent them as doing so in literature without doing violence to the actual record of struggle in the French Caribbean – that is, unless a clearly counterfactual narrative were able to draw out the auto-generative powers that are suspended within the collective body of the strike. This is precisely how Chamoiseau uses the fable-structure in his narrative: it is a method that allows him to personify the capacities the general population possesses for nonstate coordination, and to imagine how these capacities could serve as a comprehensive socially mediating force in ways that become apprehensible in the context of the General Strike.

The fable, in other words, becomes an index of capacities for self-organization that become palpable as such only when they are divorced from the everyday operations of state space. This moment, in which the withdrawal of socially sustaining powers from the circuit of capital realization highlights their purposive variability, their flexible modes of application, is precisely the moment of eidetic rupture which Chamoiseau's fable chronicles. In this context, the moths' discourse is not about whether to act politically or not, but rather, *how* to act politically: as a vanguardist force, attempting to raise consciousness through detached polemic, or through forms of auto-creation that inspire the kind of collective auto-mimesis described in *Les neuf consciences du Malfini.*

These forms of collective emergence were everywhere on display in Martinique and Guadeloupe during the General Strike. With the big supermarkets and retail establishments closed, "residents turned to local fishermen, small-scale farmers, impromptu fruit vendors, and their own 'creole' gardens to supplement their meals ... realizing that they could live without the French imports they had grown accustomed to."[34] With political parties ensnared in disagreements on the question of independence – a rift the French state hoped to exploit and deepen by calling for a referendum on the question in the middle of the strike – the LKP brilliantly sidestepped the issue by insisting that their movement had to do with the populace's ability to survive and prosper, not, for the moment, the issue of independence. "L'UGTG est favorable à l'indépendance (The UGTG favors independence)," said Élie Domota:

> en revanche, le LKP est une coalition englobant des organisations dont certaines n'ont pas d'opinion sur l'indépendance, ou y sont hostiles. En tant que porte-parole du LKP, j'ai respecté mon mandat en ne soulevant pas cette question. À l'époque, la ministre de l'Outre-Mer, Marie-Luce Penchard, a néanmoins cherché à diviser le LKP en le taxant d'indépendantisme. Nous avons évité de tomber dans le piège, et recadré les choses en lui disant: «Nous conduisons un mouvement de revendications qui appellent bien évidemment des réponses politiques.» (however, the LKP is a coalition of organizations including some that do not have an opinion on independence, or are opposed to it. As a spokesman for the LKP, I respected my mandate by not raising this issue. At the time, the Minister for Overseas Territories, Marie-Luce Penchard, nevertheless sought to divide the LKP by accusing it of being pro-independence. We avoided falling into the trap, and reframed things, saying "We are conducting a protest movement which obviously requires a political response.")[35]

Similar rifts could have opened between service workers, industrial workers, and agricultural workers in the strike movement, yet the LKP developed an analysis that framed the productive activities of all sectors of society as essential, fighting against the construction of a deep-water port which would "ruine les petits et empêche tout développement productif local (ruin small producers and prevent local productive development)," demanding aid for farmers, a youth training plan in new fishing techniques and technologies, and "maintien et aménagement du foncier agricole (eau d'irrigation, voiries, téléphone, électricité) afin de créer des entités de production viables et en constante recherche d'autonomie (the maintenance and development of agricultural land [irrigation, roads, telephone, electricity] in order to create viable production entities and in a constant search for self-sufficiency)."[36]

Even before the strike itself, the UGTG placed the emphasis on local initiative and control: "Notre démarche vise à pousser les travailleurs à s'approprier les entreprises fonctionnelles et que les patrons ferment (Our approach aims to encourage workers to take over working businesses and those that employers close)," said UGTG representative Serge Apatout, going on to enumerate the construction, food processing, and transport companies that had already been taken over and managed by workers.[37]

The 2009 French Antillean General Strike was thus marked by the creation of nonstate space on a mass scale, not just in the roadblocks, closed ports, and barricaded airport runways that were part of the upheaval, but in the development of innovative forms of production, networked action, and cooperation that were synonymous with the movement. The fact that the spokespeople of the strike made a host of demands upon the French state, therefore, does not negate the nonstate orientation of the strike movement as a whole. In the rhetoric and methods of the movement, it is clear that those mobilized by the strike viewed themselves as the producers of value that is captured and directed by the state. The demand that these values be returned to those who produced them, and that they have more directive control over their productive and associative relationships, thus signals an attempt to take as much power and resources from the state as possible, through struggle, and to put it in the hands of those who create and sustain life.

Chamoiseau's emphasis on "the horizontal plenitude of the living" and his images of auto-mimesis make sense only in this political context. In his narratives and political writings, Chamoiseau echoes the sentiment that was heard again and again during the 2009 General Strike: the peoples of Martinique and Guadeloupe have the capacity to sustain and reproduce their own lives. The state, by contrast, has only diminished this capacity by undermining local production and promoting a neocolonial economy, in which foreign imports overwhelm the capacity of local producers. In this context, the general strike is a removal of the power that creates life, the power of social production and reproduction, and a display of auto-mimetic powers, creative capabilities outside of the capitalist circuit. Like the moth that moves in spaces "que les clartés et les commerces oublient (forgotten by light and commerce)" and seeks to display his wings, "captent la moindre clarté qui suinte de la nuit (capturing the least light that seeps out of the night" (*PL* 21), the general strike embodies a beauty that is meant to inspire imitation – a process of global transformation that Chamoiseau and Glissant imagine as being possible when "le monde fait Tout-Monde et qu'il amplifie jusqu'à l'imprévisible le mouvement d'aile du papillon (the world becomes *Tout-Monde* and expands unto incalculability the movement of a butterfly's wing)."[38]

## L'État français comme un corps étranger

The extraordinary creativity displayed in the 2009 French Antillean General Strike, in its tactics, its literature, and its political self-reflection, may seem to suggest that there is something fundamentally new about its political vision. It's tempting to regard its models of nonstate space, horizontality, and collective auto-mimesis as staging a break with twentieth-century social movements and heralding novel, twenty-first-century forms of struggle. Is there not something decidedly "postmodern" about a political metastasis that occurs outside central parties and state-centric structures, spreading transnationally like a contagion, and bringing a carnivalesque assemblage of groups into relation under the heading of *liyannaj*: a creole term that, as many have noted, stresses processuality more than self-identity?

And yet, the historical imagination expressed in the many communiqués and interviews devoted to the 2009 General Strike emphasizes, time and again, the continuity between current struggles and those of previous centuries. "La France donne de l'argent aux Antilles pour que les Antillais achètent des produits français (France gives money to the Caribbean for the Caribbeans to buy French products)," writes Édouard Glissant, "C'est un circuit colonial (It is a colonial circuit)" controlled by "les Békés … les descendants des grands propriétaires fonciers (the *békés* … the descendants of the large landowners)" and "les maîtres des rouages de l'import–export (the masters of the machinery of the import and export trade.)"[39]

The continued relevance of earlier struggles against *békés* and the colonial power is therefore continually highlighted: one LKP communiqué provides a brief history of the 1910 Guadeloupe General Strike and the 1925 strike of small planters in Petit-Canal.[40] Another outlines the 1952 Guadeloupe General Strike, stressing the aid provided by workers to "nombreux jeunes se mobilisent dans les principales artères de la ville (many youth mobilizing in the main arteries of the city)"[41] and drawing parallels between the current actions of "l'État colonial (the colonial state)" and the massacre perpetrated by France in Le Moule.[42]

Apropos of its organizational methods, LKP members stress old-fashioned footwork more than novel technologies of struggle: "Des réunions, le soir, auprès de trois, quatre, cinq adhérents – pour les aider à bâtir une section (Meetings in the evening with three, four, five members – to help build a section)," says LKP organizer Eddy Damas of their organizing methods: "Des tractages, chaque semaine, sur les marchés, même à la sortie des cimetières – pour convaincre, et prendre la température … juste les vieilles ficelles du militantisme (Handing out flyers, every week, in the markets, even at the exit of cemeteries – to win people over and gauge their sentiment … just the old tricks of activism."[43] Asked about email, he replies as follows: "Quand tu distribues un papier, ça n'est même pas l'information qui compte. C'est grâce à la poignée de main, grâce à l'échange autour, que l'on persuade lentement. Que nos idées se distillent dans le corps social (When you hand out flyers, it's not the information itself that matters. It's the handshake, the circulating around, that slowly wins people over. That allows our ideas to be distilled in the social body)."[44]

Similarly, Élie Domota explains that "Le LKP n'est pas un mouvement spontané. C'est une accumulation, une addition de luttes, de victoires, de défaites, d'expériences qui remontent à des dizaines d'années (The LKP is not a spontaneous movement. It is an accumulation, an aggregate of struggles, victories, defeats, experiences that date back dozens of years)."[45]

This sense that the 2009 General Strike was a resumption of a much older history of struggle is essential, because it draws attention to forms of exploitation, racial oppression, and social upheaval that link twenty-first-century upheavals to earlier ones, despite the significant social and economic changes that the French overseas departments and regions have undergone.[46] This sense of the radical transmissibility of the general strike over space and time was also evident in the discourse that linked struggles in Guadeloupe and Martinique to those of neocolonial spaces with economies and working populations quite different from theirs – Réunion, whose export market is still dominated by sugar, and Guinea, where industrial production and agriculture make up over 63 percent of the GDP.

In a global archipelago like this, where thousands of workers labor in bauxite mines using technologies dating back to the industrial revolution, while others sell cosmetics in shopping centers to European tourists, it makes little sense to generalize about "twentieth-century" and "twenty-first-century" forms of social struggle. By constellating workers belonging to so many sectors of this unevenly developed socio-economic landscape – fishermen, agricultural workers, fuel transporters, construction workers, health and hospitality workers – the 2009 General Strike challenged any notion that "twentieth-century" forms of struggle, such as the mass strike, are obsolescent or belong only to the "developing world," while others are appropriate only to post-industrial economies. The multiple temporalities that such a strike embraces and sets in relation invite us to rethink the way we periodize social, economic, and cultural developments on a world scale.

Rather than viewing the horizontal, nonstate, alliance-based methods of the 2009 General Strike as a "postmodern" form of struggle, remote from the historic workers' movement and its forms, we should be encouraged to view it as the resumption of a history of nonstate movements that have traversed the twentieth and twenty-first centuries, often occurring beneath official history, and obeying autonomous social patterns and organizational modes. The same is true of literary productions such as Chamoiseau's, which could be said to belong less to a theoretical narrative about postmodern literature, stemming from post-Fordism and the death of the historical worker's movement, than they do to an entirely different, subterranean nexus of works, spawned by eidetic rupture and nonstate space – an instauration of forms that is catalyzed at precise times, within and despite the larger narratives we tell, which link up to one another erratically, across cultures, according to local climatic conditions and geographies of struggle: a literature of nodes and islands, as opposed to a literature of clear lineages and traditions.

A reading practice attuned to such global nodes of literary production, which often crop up despite the official tradition, and do not necessarily bequeath a lineage of imitators, would not find its motivation in a hermetic tradition of stylistic techniques. Instead, it would seek to register those moments when existing traditions, styles of conduct and expression are suddenly inadequate, are voided, requiring a transformation of consciousness remote from centralized instruments of power. It would seek to locate within texts not so much their position within punctual political assemblages and concentrations of capital, but rather their dislocation, their being thrown back on more fundamental antagonisms, their lack of assimilation to the current "line," moments in which basic energies and balances of power intrude upon more polite discourses of "negotiation."

It would be a document of people in the process of transforming themselves – not, strictly speaking, a reappropriation of the master text, but a strange and untimely process of recomposition, removed from hierarchical structures of rule. Such breaks with tradition, and such a drive to innovate, have long been associated with global modernisms, as schemata of practices involving fragmentation, abstraction, and the mythic method. As we will see, the works of Asturias certainly embody recognizably modernist techniques, but do those of Sembene and Chamoiseau? The evidence suggests that eidetic rupture and nonstate narrative possess their own literary-historical geography, which exists beyond clear-cut distinctions between modernist, postmodernist, and realist forms of literature.

Turning to Ousmane Sembene's *Les bouts de bois de Dieu* makes this obvious. It is a text that documents, with more intensity and depth than almost any other text I can think of, the process of collective recomposition that nonstate narratives bring to life. And yet, it is a narrative that belongs to a very different time and place than Chamoiseau's *Les neuf consciences du Malfini* and *Le papillon et la lumière*. Set in French West Africa in 1947 and 1948, it deals with railwaymen who live under French colonial rule, in an economy that is overwhelmingly fueled by agricultural production.[47] But the mass strike carried out by these railwaymen evolved communication networks, organizational forms, and models of self-government that belong to the long, discontinuous history of nonstate space that was resumed in the French Antilles in 2009. In chronicling this event, Sembene's narrative represents moments of eidetic rupture, nonstate space, and organization that inform this present history, that elaborate its potentialities, and that exhibit what is in many ways an even more radical process of self-transformation.

Involving 19,000 workers along the 1,287 kilometers of rail line that stretches from Dakar, Senegal to Koulikoro in present-day Mali, the Dakar–Niger Railway Strike presented even more acute organizational dilemmas than the 2009 General Strike, which unfolded serially, under the auspices of the LKP in Guadeloupe, the Collectif du 5 février in Martinique, and a coalition of strikers in Réunion. Sembene's narrative reflects the complexity of carrying out a simultaneous transnational strike of this scope, skipping from organizational efforts in Bamako to those in Thiès and Dakar, and chronicling the nonstate practices of characters with marginal positions inside the railway union, or altogether outside of it. Especially difficult in this context were the tasks of combating the starvation tactics, police violence, and counterintelligence of the French state and maintaining solidarity along a front that stretched from the port city of Dakar to the capital of French Sudan.

In Sembene's account, the strike becomes a life or death struggle almost immediately, with the railway company colluding with state authorities and businesspeople to cut off water and electricity to workers' neighborhoods and to prevent strikers from being able to buy grain from local merchants. The first clash represented in the novel is between the police and the market women of Thiès, who fight with clubs, iron bars, and bottles, and, reinforced by the strikers, eventually succeed in driving the cops from the marketplace. As the strike continues, however, those who are carrying it out realize that alongside physical confrontations such as these, apparatuses of nonstate decision-making are necessary, to coordinate action and evolve strategic policy.

The first major test of this nonstate organizational machinery comes when the strikers must decide how to handle the case of one Diara, a ticket-taker who, guarded at all times by five policemen, is serving as a replacement laborer and informant for the railway company. In this moment of extreme exigency, and faced with a problem that is unprecedented in their experience, the workers construct a nonstate organ of self-regulation: an alternative adjudicative assembly, complete with jurors, witnesses, and a collective deliberative process, all designed to evolve binding, community-based solutions to problems like those posed by Diara – all outside of the legal apparatuses of the state. Up until this point in the narrative, the record-keeper of the local strike committee in Bamako, a worker named Tiémoko, had led a commando group that simply battered strike-breakers. But, in a conversation with another commando, Tiémoko suddenly feels this is inadequate; he asks "est-ce un résultat d'avenir (is that enough, for the future?)"[48] Though Tiémoko never specifies what he means by "un résultat d'avenir," it's clear that he is imagining a future in which the railway workers have replaced ad hoc forms of coercion with much more durable institutions of nonstate self-regulation. The nonstate trial of Diara provides an excellent example of this.

Sembene describes the crowd that throngs to the union building to witness the nonstate jury trial of Diara – a crowd not just of workers, but of their families, neighbors, and spiritual leaders: "pour tous ceux qui étaient présents, dans la salle ou sur l'estrade, c'était la première fois qu'ils participaient à un jugement (this was the first time that anyone there – in the hall or up on the stage – had taken part in a trial)" (BBD 132/ GBW 78–9). In fact, la loi, as a concept, evokes for this crowd not the indigénat or the Code Civil, but rather "les vagues souvenirs (vague memories)" (BBD 132/GBW 79 translation modified) of Bambara law, which had long ceased to exist in urban centers of French Sudan: "Inconsciemment (Subconsciously)," then, the crowd "éprouvaient une curieuse sensation de dépaysement (experienced a strange sensation of disorientation)," torn between this memory of tribal law and "des sentiments fraternels qu'ils éprouvaient les uns pour les autres, le ‹coupable› compris (the feeling of brotherhood that they had for each other, including the 'accused')" (*BBD* 132/ *GBW* 79 translation altered). Despite this feeling of deracination, however, the novelty of having to make such a weighty decision themselves "aiguisait leur curiosité (sharpened their curiosity)" – for many, it was "la première possibilité de jouer un rôle ‹d'homme›, leur rôle d'homme (the first opportunity to play the role of a man – of their own man)" (*BBD* 132/ *GBW* 79 translation altered).

What Sembene is describing here is the realization, on the part of the crowd, of nonstate capacities that they did not suspect they possessed. It is a moment that is impossible to explain according to racist–imperialist theories of "the organic incapacity for self-government" or more recent theories of the voiceless subaltern. This is because Sembene's crowd is creating, out of themselves, capacities that even they consider to be *beyond themselves*, beyond their customary practices, beyond their "comfort zone," beyond their understanding. This process of creation is therefore, according to a logic that only a subtly dialectical method can grasp, a process of *discovery* as well. In creating new capacities for self-government in response to unprecedented circumstances, they discover they had been invested with these capacities all along. They had simply never been called upon to exercise them.

The temporality of this process of simultaneous creation and discovery is complex, but understanding it will help us understand how populations, in moments of rupture and decision, are able to *create themselves* beyond themselves. In Sembene's narrative, this can be seen in the way the crowd's creation of an utterly unprecedented, "modern" process of self-government throws them back upon much older, customary forms of self-government which none of them has actually experienced before. The trial of the railway worker is, in some ways, projected back upon this ancestral past; the name given to his crime makes this clear – *dynfa* – a Bambara word that had almost completely fallen out of customary use, which means "treason."

But while the crowd projects itself back upon a remote ancestral past, it simultaneously projects itself forward onto a remote future which is even more foreign, yet which they are in the process of creating. Sembene notes that the meeting hall where Diara is being detained "avait perdu son apparence coutumière (had lost its customary aspect)" – not only is the hall overflowing with people, all of whom are invited to give testimony for or against Diara, but "on remarquait des présences féminines, ce qui était une nouveauté (the presence of women was noticeable, which was something new)" (*BBD* 131/ *GBW* 78).

Four women come forward; one recounts Diara's collaboration with a French soldier who forced her and her companions off the train and seized their return tickets without remuneration; another recounts Diara's stopping the train and making them get off: "huit femmes au plein milieu de la savane ... il faut le crucifier sur la place du marché! (eight women in the middle of the bush ... he should be crucified in the marketplace!)" (*BBD* 151/*GBW* 92 translation altered). It is an unsettling moment: "chacun était troublé en lui-même de cette nouveauté: des femmes qui venaient de prendre la parole au milieu des hommes (everyone was inwardly disturbed by this novelty: women who showed up to speak among men)" (*BBD* 151/ *GBW* 92 translation altered). However, the strike and the forces of repression, as well as of mutual aid, that it sets in motion reveal in an unmistakable way the roles women play that are essential to the survival of the community – roles that in this scene become part of a public conversation about strategy, tactics, and ethics for the first time.

The essential point here is that Sembene's crowd is evolving forms of discourse, affect, and practice that are, strictly speaking, unimaginable, even from the participants' own point of view. The crowd depicted is composed of largely illiterate smiths, lathe operators, fitters, stokers, engine drivers, and the sectors of the Bamako population with whom they have contact. For more than a century they have been told by the colonial government that they have an organic incapacity for self-government, that they are, in short "not real people, capable of directing themselves" but are instead "victims of geography or history who found themselves left behind by the modern world."[49] Their own political parties were oriented more toward political jockeying in the French parliament than toward workers in their own countries. Lamine Guèye, for example, eager to avoid alienating his "metropolitan allies," avoided making any public comment on the strike;[50] similarly, Houphuët-Boigny and Senghor "did not make the strike their own."[51]

With a history of such neglect and oppression, what do these workers have to draw on as a source of confidence and self-direction? What, in their lived experience, has prepared them for the effort at self-government Sembene represents?

In Sembene's novel, the answer lies both in nonstate rituals and customs that belong to the collective past and in nonstate capacities that are mobilized by the strike itself. Indeed, Sembene suggests that something about the negative space created by the strike allows the recovery of neglected rituals and customs at the same time as it allows the "remembrance" of future forms of life that are in the process of being created.

This exceedingly complex temporality is evoked in a passage that begins with an image of the sky itself seemingly emptied of all conventional associations by the withdrawal of labor: "au-dessus des toits, des arbres, des montagnes, il n'y avait plus qu'un immense vide bleu (above the roofs, the trees, the mountains, there was just an immense blue void)" (*BBD* 126/*GBW* 75 translation altered). Because of this suspension of the everyday, "on avait ressuscité des fastes des jours anciens, oubliés depuis des temps immémoriaux (the pageantry of an older time, forgotten since time immemorial, was revived)" (*BBD* 126/*GBW* 75 translation altered). Both military ceremonies and ceremonies of elegant display are "remembered" because of the strike: "des hommes armés de bâtons mimaient des combats au sabre dont les règles remontaient au temps du règne de El Mami Samori Touré (men armed with staffs performed the saber duels whose ritual dated from the reign of El Mami Samori Touré" (*BBD* 126/*GBW* 75), and at the same time, the young girls wore "les coiffures les plus compliquées, faites de tresses enchevêtrées ou curieusement séparées. Elles déambulaient dans les rues, s'abandonnant gracieusement au rythme des baras que l'on entendait à chaque carrefour (incredibly complicated hairdos of braided or curiously separated tresses. They strolled down the streets, gracefully abandoning themselves to the rhythms of the Bambara dances that could be heard on every corner)" (*BBD* 126/*GBW* 75–6 translation altered).

This language of ritual, display, and seduction is then carried over into the community's transformed perception of the railway itself. The passage is extraordinary:

> Tels des amoureux éconduits, ils revenaient sans cesse aux alentours des gares. Ils restaient là, les yeux fixés sur l'horizon, immobiles, échangeant à peine quelques phrases banales. Parfois, un îlot de cinq ou six hommes se détachait du groupe compact et partait à la dérive en direction de la voie. Pendant quelques instants, ils longeaient les rails puis soudain, comme pris de panique, ils se hâtaient de revenir s'agglomérer à la masse. Alors ils restaient là, accroupis ou debout au pied d'une dune, les yeux fixés sur les deux parallèles qui s'allongeaient sans fin pour aller se fondre au loin dans la brousse. Quelque chose de nouveau germait en eux, comme si le passé et l'avenir étaient en train de s'étreindre pour féconder un nouveau type d'homme, et il leur semblait que le vent leur chuchotait une phrase de Bakayoko souvent entendue: «L'homme que nous étions est mort et notre seul salut pour une nouvelle vie est dans la machine, la machine qui, elle, n'a ni langage, ni race.»
>
> (Like spurned lovers, they kept coming back to the areas surrounding the stations. They would stand there, motionless, eyes fixed on the horizon,

hardly exchanging even a few banal phrases. Sometimes, a little bloc of five or six men would detach itself from the larger mass and drift off in the direction of the tracks. For a few minutes, they would wander along the rails and then, suddenly, as though seized with panic, they would hasten back to the safety of the group they had left. Then again they would just stand there, or squat down in the shade of a dune, their eyes fixed on the two endless parallels, following them out until they joined and lost themselves in the bush. Something new germinated in them, as if the past and the future were coupling to breed a new kind of man, and it seemed to them that the wind was whispering a phrase they had often heard from Bakayoko: "The kind of man we were is dead and our only hope for a new life lies in the machine, the machine which, of itself, has neither a language nor a race.")

(*BBD* 127/*GBW* 76 translation altered)

How is this passage a document of emerging nonstate capacities? In what ways does it invite us to rethink the forms of self-transformation and agency available to nonstate actors in the colonial and neocolonial world?

One clue lies in the language of eroticism and ritual that surrounds the railway in this passage. Unlike the traditional community rituals that are revived during the strike, the nervous rituals surrounding the railway have no customary content – they are "incomplete" rituals, in the sense that they do not belong to the shared habitus of the community. And yet, the anxious, tentative dance of seduction the men perform seems aimed at integrating new forms of technology, know-how, and power into community patterns of practice, as if the competencies involved in taking the operations of the railway under their own direction could be "written into" the everyday forms of life that sustain their community.

This is not as far-fetched as it may sound – in fact, the military rituals Sembene mentions above date back not to the ancient Bamana Empire but to the anti-colonial army of resistance Samori Touré began developing in the 1880s. Though the saber duels Sembene mentions certainly were part of the ceremonial culture of Touré's army, what it was known for more than anything was its implementation of modern weapons and tactics, such as the breech-loading rifle, modern forms of military discipline, and platoons and companies organized according to European methods. What Sembene imagines in the railway passage is a similar attempt to integrate modern forms of social and economic know-how into the customary practices of his West African characters – not in the service of a hegemonic colonial agenda, but in the interest of developing their community autonomy and self-government.[52]

Notice also how the delicate process of reconciling community autonomy and technological know-how is performed directly by anonymous, rank-and-file strikers, not party delegates or state representatives. The strikers' ritualized and strangely erotic attitude toward the railway in fact seems to be an experiment in how far a community can go in the direction of economic development and technological modernization while still retaining a nonstate coordinative capacity over the social life of their community.[53]

Of course, such nonstate forms of community autonomy were consistently regarded as deviations from Soviet policy under Stalin and Khrushchev. It might be surprising, therefore, that Sembene, who cofounded the Communist-affiliated Parti africain de l'indépendance (PAI), would chronicle so meticulously the autonomous organizational networks of workers and their families, outside of party bureaucracies and other state structures. This interest in nonstate networks makes more sense, however, in the context of Sembene's increasing impatience with the Communist Party, which he abandoned in 1960 – the year of Senegal's independence from France and the year *Les bouts de bois de Dieu* was published.

Sembene's unflattering representation of the Communist-controlled Confédération générale du travail (CGT) in his novel is one symptom of this impatience with Communist officialdom. When a deputy of the CGT appears in the novel, it is only to castigate a railway worker for pursuing what he pejoratively refers to as a "grève politique (political strike)" (*BBD* 333/ *GBW* 217 translation altered). He sneers: "Vous ne voulez pas recevoir de directives? Eh bien, nous, nous ne marchons pas avec les diviseurs (You don't want to go by the union's general policies? Fine, we won't have anything to do with separatists)" (*BBD* 319/ *GBW* 206 translation altered). Instead of calling out CGT-affiliated locals to stand in solidarity with the strike, the CGT deputy convenes a meeting headed by himself, the governor-general, the local imam, and the mayor-deputy which is clearly designed to pressure the railway workers into ending the strike. To the imam's warnings about the evils of the strike and the politicians' advice that the strikers simply trust the government, the CGT deputy adds his voice: his union would adopt "une attitude d'attente à l'égard de la grève (a 'wait and see' attitude toward the strike)" since "il fallait éviter tout essai de ‹séparationisme› au sein de la classe ouvrière (it is necessary to avoid any attempts at 'separationism' within the working class)" (*BBD* 333/ *GBW* 217 translation altered).

Why such bureaucratic double-speak from a deputy of an organization that once represented the most radical aspirations of the French working class? The answer has everything to do with the takeover of the CGT by the Stalinist Parti communiste français (PCF). In the 1950s, the PCF saw African independence as a goal that should be contemplated only after Communist control had been secured in France. Their argument was that "colonialism was the source of African misery, that the trusts caused colonialism, that the trusts were powerful because of their position in France, that consequently the only sensible course for Africans was to ally with the French Communists, who attacked the trusts in France"; moreover, "if France were to leave immediately, economically backward Africa would but fall victim to British or American imperialism."[54] Thus, while the CGT did organize workers in African countries, they expected them to be subordinate to a centralized leadership in Paris.

One Communist-published paper even argued that because the French Constitution "contains undeniable progressive elements ... Communists of Africa favor the maintenance and implementation of the French Union within the framework of the Constitution."[55] In other words, Africans should fight imperialism not through a struggle for independence, but by "fighting for the preservation and the application of the principles of the Constitution" itself.[56]

The nauseating paternalism of French Communist officialdom toward workers and activists in French West Africa helps explain why Sembene – in the words of his biographer, Samba Gadjigo –"began to have strong misgivings about the leadership role of the Communist Party" by the time he published *Les bouts de bois de Dieu*.[57] Though he had organized dockers in Marseilles as part of the CGT, Sembene looks to the Dakar–Niger railway strike as the basis of a process that could allow Africans to govern themselves outside of party and state structures.

This nonstate orientation is remarkable, evolving as it did out of the largely state-based nationalist fervor of African independence movements in the 1950s and 1960s. Though the process of decolonization these movements effected was one of the most courageous, sweeping, and successful acts of political will in the history of the world, it also evolved vertical concentrations of power and repressive state structures that, in Senegal as in so many other spaces, were to ossify into highly centralized, comprador neocolonial state apparatuses. In the very midst of this process, Sembene had the intellectual audacity to conceive a barely imaginable alternative: nonstate actors taking directive control of their workplaces, evolving decision-making apparatuses to coordinate productive work and interpersonal conflict-resolution on a mass scale. This is the vision expressed by the delicate, tentative confrontation between "the machine" and the railway workers in the passage above.

In revisiting the material space of the railway, now transformed into a nonstate space by the mass strike, the workers in the passage are nervously testing out the idea that they require neither employers nor white colonists and their native political allies to order social life on their behalf: "Leur communion avec la machine était profonde et forte, plus forte que les barrières qui les séparaient de leurs employeurs, plus forte que cet obstacle jusqu'alors infranchissable: la couleur de leur peau (Their fellowship with the machine was deep and strong; stronger than the barriers which separated them from their employers, stronger even than the obstacle which until now had been insurmountable – the color of their skin)" (*BBD* 128/*GBW* 77). Passages like these stage a fundamental break not merely with racist colonial theses about Africans' "organic incapacity for self-government," but also with party- and state-centered forms of anti-colonial initiative.

What is occurring is not merely a shift in belief and opinion, but a rupture in these nonstate actors' basic lived perception of how social life is reproduced, and their shaping relationship to this process. In other words, an eidetic rupture has occurred, which involves not so much an "Aha-Ereignis" of synthesis and fulfillment as a terrifying sense of collective capacities that have been suspended over a social void and mobilized in a search for new methods of recombination. "Un îlot de cinq ou six hommes se détachait du groupe compact" – it is almost as if these shifting aggregations of men are the untested synaptic relays of a social mind that is accustoming itself to new tasks. As they return to the larger mass, "comme pris de panique," they seem to ask "How can we subdivide ourselves, allocate tasks, install executive functions, without severing these functions from the group as a whole? How can we imagine ourselves as equipped to govern – not merely our work processes, but our neighborhoods, our social relations, the processes whereby machines and materials are set in motion and put to use?"

These are exactly the kinds of questions that arose in the 2009 General Strike in the French Antilles and in the 1944 Guatemalan General Strike. In each of these cases, a mass strike which at first could have been dismissed as having "narrowly" economic objectives gave rise to questions involving a restructuring of the social world as a whole, and the confidence of ordinary people to be nodes of that restructuring. In French West Africa and the contemporary French Antilles, it bears repeating, this eidetic rupture is inextricably bound up with the racial dynamics in these French regions. "Quand j'étais petit (When I was little)," Élie Domota explained, "je lisais *BLEK, YATACA, ZAMBLA* et *AKIM*! Comme tous les jeunes de mon âge! (I was reading *BLEK, YATACA, ZAMBLA,* and *AKIM*! Like all kids my age!)" – comic book narratives in which "le héros, tout seul le plus fort dans la forêt, commande tous les nègres, tous les serpents, tous les gorilles, toutes les bêtes, le seul blanc commande tout le monde! (the hero, the strongest in the forest, gives orders to all the Negroes, all the snakes, all the gorillas, all the animals – the sole white orders everyone else around!).[58] Similarly, "dans les activités professionnelles, celui qui symbolise la réussite ne nous ressemble pas! (in professional activities, those who symbolize success do not look like us!)" – "Nos enfants dans leur développement, lorsqu'ils regardent la télévision ne voient personne qui leur ressemble! (Our children, as they grow up, don't see anyone who looks like them on TV!)"[59]

Referring to the pre-war sentiments of his onetime schoolmates, Sembene's cousin and friend Doudou Guèye expressed a similar view: "At school, in all our songs, we celebrated the glory of France, her strength and her beauty; they also told us that we were all, whites and Blacks, her children."[60]

Rupturing this eidetic regime comes as a profound shock, as seen in the words of one commentator during the 2009 General Strike:

> On a vu [sur la chaîne privée Canal 10] le préfet entouré de ses collaborateurs, tous blancs, lire comme au théâtre un texte du ministre, se lever et s'en aller (…). Quasiment au même moment, les syndicats patronaux presque tous blancs eux-aussi, quittent aussi la pièce. Dans la grande salle, il ne reste que des Noirs. C'était très fort. Et ceux qui restent – la délégation LKP et les élus politiques – se mettent tous à parler en créole. L'État français comme un corps étranger.

> (We saw [on the independent channel, Channel 10] the prefect surrounded by his colleagues, all white, read theatrically a text of the Minister, get up and leave … Almost simultaneously, the employers' organizations, almost all white as well, left the room. In that large room, only blacks remained. It was an incredible feeling. And those who were still there – the LKP delegation and the local elected representatives – all started speaking Creole. The French state as a foreign body.)[61]

This moment of rupture, in which the body of empire is suddenly and shockingly perceived as a foreign body, a body lodged in oneself, is not exclusive to the history of mass strikes. Frantz Fanon memorably describes the anguish of a similar moment of demystification that occurred to him when a French brat pointed at him and said "Mama, see the Negro! I'm frightened!"[62] It is a rupture that has all of the complexity of a colonized people's internal diversity, and sometimes happens according to the slow-motion temporality Chamoiseau chronicles in *Les neuf consciences du Malfini* and sometimes in a lightening-quick shock like the one described above. But, as Chamoiseau notes, during mass strikes, "des rigidités se précisent et tremblotent, tandis que des virtualités étonnantes se révèlent

(Rigidities become conspicuous and begin to break up, while amazing potentialities are revealed)" ("J"). The complete withdrawal of labor power not only tends to terrify the colonial and neocolonial power into committing tactical errors – for example, the imperial contempt displayed by the French Secretary of State who left Guadeloupe prematurely, on what must have seemed to be more important matters – but also mobilizes populations outside of prevailing structures of racial patronage and assimilation. In the French Antilles, this makes active and plain to see the fact that the regions' black populations have the social skills to render the entire edifice of empire, with its dependencies, patronages, and forms of racism, obsolete – to reveal them as "archaisms," in Chamoiseau's language.

It is this profound non-necessity of empire that Sembene underlines in his mass-strike chronicle as well. The fellowship between the black railway workers and "the machine" is stronger than the obstacle of skin color not because of some universal law of work, but because it is through their ability to imagine themselves as a directive force installed comprehensively within their own material life processes that these nonstate actors are able to grasp, for the first time, the obscene imposition of empire, its status as an extrusion, a foreign body, irrelevant to the reproduction of life. As in Chamoiseau's narratives, this comprehensive sense of their ability to substitute themselves for empire is built up neither through party propaganda nor via an intellectual grasp of the fallacies of racist logic. It seizes nonstate actors unexpectedly when the mass strike reveals them to be the material, intellectual and affective force that reproduces life in the colony, and it does so only on condition that they void and negate colonial systems of dependency themselves.

This process does not resemble the strategies of reappropriation intricately theorized by so many postcolonial theorists, in that it does not take place in the phenomenological nexus where colonial and neocolonial subjects absorb, internalize, and then redeploy the sign-systems of empire, according to a logic of semiotic slippage, excess, and recoding. But, as I've stressed, this is not because mass strikes and eidetic ruptures are somehow more deliberate or straightforward than these forms of resignification – just the opposite. What the subject of eidetic rupture *intends* is never to dismantle his or her own basic apperceptive framework. If such a dismantling occurs, it is because the material, intellectual, and interpersonal resources that must be marshaled to maintain the strike are so immense, and involve so many forms of social intransigency, that to secure even the most modest of its goals will demand a struggle requiring the evolution of an entirely new body of capabilities – a body which one does not yet inhabit. It is a body that exists only as a function of the spatial practices whereby a community elaborates its occupation and recombination of the material of life.

Of the three authors examined here, Miguel Ángel Asturias provides the most detailed internal cartography of this collective process. Like Chamoiseau and Sembene, he represents moments of eidetic rupture that occur when nonstate actors perceive their own activity to be the constitutive ground of social being. But Asturias' focus is on the complex network of faculties and sensitivities that nonstate actors must develop to navigate the complex web of class forces and tactical alignments involved in the process of revolutionary transition.

## Un fenómeno atmosférico

The 1944 General Strike in Guatemala was, in many ways, just as surprising as the 1947–1948 Dakar–Niger railway strike. In 1944 Guatemala was ruled by a dictator, trade unions were illegal, and its economy was dominated by United Fruit, which administered the country's only important Atlantic harbor, owned every mile of railroad track within its borders, and possessed a telephone and electricity monopoly. The country was occupied by thousands of US soldiers, to protect the Panama Canal during World War II, but also to keep Guatemala within the orbit of the United States' political and economic interests.[63] With this double investiture of force – Guatemala's own military and the massively powerful imperial presence to which it was subordinate – it is difficult to imagine a situation less conducive to the emergence and metastasis of nonstate space.

And yet, in June of 1944, a week-long general strike conducted by plantation workers, sectors of the urban proletariat, students, and professionals succeeded in bringing the almost 14-year-long dictatorship of General Jorge Ubico to an end. Then, after four months of political maneuvering on the part of the dictator's allies to help him stay in power through electoral manipulation, armed workers and students joined with insurgent elements of the military to overthrow Federico Ponce, who was poised to continue the policies of Ubico. This popular mobilization made possible democratic congressional and presidential elections by December 1944.

How was all of this possible? With a highly centralized state willing to unleash military repression on any form of workers' organization, and with all political parties other than Ubico's Liberal Party having been declared illegal, what political resources did the dissident sectors of Guatemala's population have to draw upon?

Miguel Ángel Asturias' novel *Los ojos de los enterrados* offers some intriguing answers to this question. The novel chronicles the organizational efforts of its protagonist, Octavio Sansur, and the workers, students, and professionals with whom he comes into contact. Orphaned as a child and raised by a fortune teller in the slums of Guatemala City, Sansur becomes involved in a conspiracy to assassinate the president. But when the plot is discovered and Sansur goes into hiding working as a fruit hauler, he realizes that an assassination plot, like street fighting or a coup d'état, "cae en cierta forma dentro de lo militar y lo policial," (falls in a certain way within the sphere of the military and the police," even if it is directed "contra la dictadura (against the dictatorship)."[64] A revolutionary strike, on the other hand, "no forma parte de la máquina estatal y rompe con el orden establecido (is not a part of the state machinery and breaks with the established order)" (*OE* 219/*EI* 310). Such a strike "participa de lo político y lo social y tiene las características de un fenómeno atmosférico (is involved in social and political matters and has the characteristics of an atmospheric phenomenon)" (*OE* 219/*EI* 310).

In line with this new strategic orientation, Sansur takes up work with indigenous Guatemalans as an ash collector. This occupation allows him to enter the houses of former conspiratorial contacts without attracting the attention of the secret police, under the pretext of gathering their oven ashes, which he then sells to soap factories. After solidifying connections with his professional and military contacts and with Malena Tabay, a crucial ally in the teachers' union, Sansur travels to Tiquisate to help coordinate the general strike among the plantation workers. Within days, a party that had exclusive control over the government for seventy-three years implodes.

In broad strokes, that is the plot of the novel. What do its twists and turns teach us about the organizational models and epistemologies of the Guatemalan Revolution? What do the subtly literary characterizations, interpersonal dynamics, and social symbolism that Asturias mobilizes reveal about the potency of the general strike and the forms of knowledge it makes possible?

Near the end of *Los ojos de los enterrados*, Sansur is hiding in a dark railroad boxcar, waiting to be transported by militant railroad workers to Tiquisate to help prepare for the imminent general strike. A member of the underground network of radicalized workers leads Sansur, "temeroso de todos y de todo (afraid of everyone and everything)" (*OE* 391/*EI* 559) "por andenes, rieles, durmientes, cruzadillas (across platforms, rails, ties, switches)" (*OE* 391/*EI* 558), and deposits him in a dark, unused boxcar with a sandwich and a bottle of water. At this juncture, Sansur experiences what I've been calling an eidetic rupture. The material processes of the world around him suddenly appear as if suspended in space; in his mind's eye, they are abstracted from their everydayness and appear to be floating – one might say, "up for grabs":

> Sacó un pañuelo para secarse el sudor de las manos, de la cara, el sudor que le humedecía el pelo. Ruido de máquinas, y más lejos, el despertar de la ciudad. De pronto se oía cerca el tantaneo llamando a misa, tan distinto del sonido de las campanas de las locomotoras que llegaban o salían raudas. Una sirena ronca perforó el cielo. La de "El Zapote." Las siete de la mañana. Adentro los trabajadores de la cervecería. Y las sirenas agudas de los aserraderos. Las siete. Adentro los trabajadores a mover las trozas de madera hacia los dientes de las sierras. Bocinas. Congestión de tráfico. En esa esquina de la estación, siempre. Siempre. Timbres, pitazos y cascos de caballos, ecos en forma de cáscara de naranja sacada intacta, al resbalar y reafirmarse en las piedras de los patios de la estación, tirando de carromatos que van a cargar o descargar en las plataformas de los almacenes que entregan y reciben mercaderías y bultos.
>
> (He took out a handkerchief to dry the sweat on his hands, his face, the sweat which dampened his hair. A sound of machinery, and farther off the awakening of the city. Suddenly, close by, he heard the bells calling people to mass, so different from the locomotive bells of the engines that were coming and going rapidly. A hoarse whistle perforated the sky. That of El Zapote. Seven in the morning. The brewery workers inside. And the sharp whistles of the sawmills. Seven o'clock. Inside the workers were moving slabs of wood toward the teeth of the saws. Horns. Traffic congestion. Always at the corner by the station. Always. Buzzers, whistles, and horses' hooves, echoes in the shape of an orange skin that had been removed intact, slipping and straightening up on the stones of the station courtyard, pulling handcarts coming to be loaded or unloaded on the platforms of the warehouses that deliver and receive merchandise and packages.)
>
> (*OE* 391/*EI* 559)

This eidetic rupture shares many of the characteristics that we have seen in the eidetic ruptures that appear in the work of Chamoiseau and Sembene. Note how social space here suddenly seems lifted from its moorings – the material practices that animate it still available to sensible intuition, but severed from the false naturalness that made them appear part of an integral social whole. The literary device at work here, which we see in Chamoiseau and Sembene as well, involves what I'd call an eidetic inventory: an anatomization of the capabilities and relationships that make social reproduction possible, but one that is abstracted, at the level of literary technique, from the conventional associations and regulatory mechanisms that have, up until now, populated social space. For each of these authors, this literary technique encodes the state of socio-spatial suspense created by the general strike. Stylistically, this involves creating narrative oases in which diegetic sequencing is abandoned in favor of a literary tabulation of the networked practices and energies that the general strike interrupts. Notice, for example, how in this passage the congestion of motorcars is juxtaposed with horses carrying loads, barely able to stand on the unnaturally smooth tarmac – a stark image of the uneven development of Guatemala City, where the internal combustion engine shares the same social space as the pack animals of the peasantry. A similarly stark unevenness is visible in Sansur's mental comparison of the churchbells and the factory's steam whistles – a highly intimate, ritualized, and centuries-old invitation to fellowship coexisting with the impersonal, mechanical regimentation of the shop floor. This highly layered and disjunctive social space, with all of the work-processes that sustain it, seems strangely arrested in this passage – almost as if narrative continuity has broken down completely. But, crucially, the narrative mode in which these abstracted social processes are presented is not one of proairetic inertia or "empty time." Instead, it involves a saturation of the narrative field with a sense of the recombinative potential possessed by the disconnected elements of the diegetically interrupted scene.

Asturias creates this effect by focalizing the disconnected material practices of the city through the consciousness of a character who can hear but cannot see them. What takes center stage in this narration is therefore Sansur's ability to recombine, intuitively, the complex and uneven exchange relationships that permeate the city, almost from scratch, as if this apperceptive mode somehow "belonged" to a city on the verge of transforming its own distributions of work and political agency on the most fundamental level. The image Asturias uses to capture this sense of transformative potential is that of an orange peel lifted intact from the orange, as if the processes of the world around him were a living, floating membrane, carefully severed from its current environment and in search of a new social body.

This vision is made possible because of Sansur's careful preparatory work for the general strike: plantation workers, railway workers, teachers, professionals, and students have all been carefully "severed" from their fidelity to the ruling social order and are preparing to hold themselves, their labor, and their everyday fidelities in suspense, in what seems to many like an unnatural state.[65] This network of workers in the countryside, urban proletarians, and bourgeois elements in the city is evoked by the image of Sansur hiding on the railway – a railway which, itself, makes many of these spatially remote connections possible. His extreme anxiety is also a reflection of the anxious coalition of the bourgeoisie, the petit-bourgeoisie, landless peasants, and agricultural and industrial workers that carries out the general strike – an uneasy mélange of social forces both within and without the orbit of state space who, under slightly changed circumstances, could just as easily be fighting each other.

This anxiety produces another kind of eidetic rupture as Sansur bunks in the hut of the workers who receive him after his train ride – this time, a rupture that concerns his bourgeois girlfriend, Malena Tabay. Throughout the novel, Malena – like the bourgeoisie itself – has been something of a wild card with respect to the workers' movement and its main diegetic representative, Sansur. A young love of the impoverished Sansur, she nevertheless had a romantic fling with a young officer, Cárcamo, when Sansur went into hiding. Having reestablished contact with her, Sansur is tortured with anxiety about her relationship with the man who now serves as a commander in the dictator's army. He's particularly fixated on references to Cárcamo in Malena's journal, which concludes with the incomplete sentence "todo concluyó en que él era más joven que yo, y … (it ended with the fact that he was younger than I, and …)" (*OE* 141/*EI* 195). This "and" takes on an almost supernatural horror for Sansur, embodying as it does both the threat of her infidelity toward him and, much more significantly, the threat of the bourgeoisie's infidelity toward the workers planning the general strike. The idea that teachers, like Malena, and other professionals might easily "break" in favor of reactionary elements in the dictator's military becomes an obsession for Sansur.

Having concluded his political conversation with the workers in the hut, Sansur is falling asleep, thinking of the ultimatum that dissident students have issued to the government: within 24 hours, Ubico must restore the university's legal autonomy from the state, or else a general strike will be declared. In his drowsy condition, the 24 hours of the ultimatum dilate into "ochenta y seis mil cuatrocientos segundos (eighty-six thousand four hundred seconds)" (*OE* 396/*EI* 565), which are counted by the frogs that are chirping in the Tiquisate night.

In this atmosphere of suspended time, which evokes the nonstate creative powers that are being born all around him, Sansur and Malena suddenly seem suspended themselves. Sansur's vision is of the two of them bathing in the decelerated time of the frogs: "Veinticuatro … veinticuatroooo oooooohoras … ooa … ooa … ae … ae … ae … ae … veinticuatroooo oooooohoras, fatales … Caricias, burbujas y … de pronto el agua que se solidifica y ellos que logran quedar con las cabezas fuera de aquella camisa de fuerza que atrapaba sus cuerpos convertida en un témpano de espejos (Twenty-four … twenety-foooouuu … uuua … uuua … ae … ae … ae … ae … twenty-foooouuuur fateful hoooouuuurs … Caresses, bubbles, and … suddenly the water solidifies and they manage to stay there with their heads out of the strait-jacket that was trapping their bodies, changed into an ice-cake of mirrors …)" (*OE* 396/*EI* 566). This unpleasant image is of the fluid, creative, nonstate temporality of the imminent strike being denatured, frozen into an ice-bath that traps Sansur and Malena in an isolated, bourgeois happiness, fit only for the "las pobres imágenes pornográficas, las que se compran en postales (sad pornographic pictures that can be bought on postcards)" (*OE* 397/*EI* 566).

Sansur asks how his fantasies of marriage and its private satisfactions could be reconciled with "el coro de las parejas que pedían el diluvio … ¡el diluvio! … ¡el diluvio! … como única solución (the chorus of couples asking for the deluge … the deluge! … the deluge! … the only solution)" (*OE* 397/*EI* 567). Another vision seems to provide the answer:

Sus cabezas … (al licuarse el espejo en el diluvio, se quedaron sin cuerpo), sólo sus cabezas, sus cabezas buscando otros cuerpos …

¡Este, ése y aquél … señalando un cuerpo de campesina para Rosa Gavidia!

¡Este, ése y aquél … señalando el cuerpo de un húsar mostachudo para el capitán de infantería León Cárcamo!

¿Y él? … (¡Este, ése y … él …).

Él, sin su cuerpo, sólo su cabeza, entre ellos dos, entre la campesina y el capitán, haciendo de referee, pero no era un cuerpo a cuerpo boxístico, si no un cuerpo a cuerpo amoroso y había que separarlos, ¡horror!, para que no siguiera la reproducción del mismo tiempo de hombres y mujeres nacidas para carne de bombardeo o carne de fábricas …

(Their heads … [as the mirror dissolved in the deluge they were left without bodies], only their heads, their heads looking for other bodies …

This one, that one, the other one … pointing to the body of a peasant girl for Rosa Gavidia! …

This one, that one, the other one … pointing to the body of a mustachioed hussar for León Cárcamo, Captain of Infantry!

And he? … [This one, that one, and … he …].

He, without his body, only his head, between the two of them, between the peasant girl and the Captain, acting as a referee, but it was not the clinch of a boxing match, it was the clinch of a love match, and he had to separate them, oh, horror!, so that there would be no continuation of the time of men and women born to be the flesh of bombardment or of factories …)

(*OE* 397/*EI* 567)

The eidetic rupture in this reverie is so thorough that it allows Sansur to imagine affects that had been frozen in a secluded, bourgeois ice-bath to be severed from the private sphere and drift at large. The image is of an affective transivitism that the deluge of the general strike makes possible, with impulses that once belonged to Rosa Gavidia (Malena's pseudonym) embodying themselves in a peasant girl, crossing lines of class and culture in a network of creative energies.

It is an extremely anxious vision, however, in which the fluidized affects of Malena, while seeming to effect a merger with the peasantry and proletarians such as Sansur, could just as easily conjoin with the forces of reaction. Moreover, this is precisely what happened in the aftermath of the Guatemalan Revolution, as Asturias knew all too well by the time he published the final version of his novel in 1960. Rallying behind a coup that was directed by CIA head Allen Dulles (who had served as legal advisor to United Fruit), the bourgeoisie sided overwhelmingly with Castillo Armas, who initiated a 30-year-long killing rampage against Guatemala's workers and peasants.

Of what value, then, are visions of possibility such as those above? Don't they document more than anything the attempt on the part of workers and peasants to rely on affective connections with the bourgeoisie that, time and again, are ruthlessly betrayed?

Not necessarily. It is true that large sectors of the bourgeoisie turned against the leaders of the Guatemalan Revolution just ten years after its inception. But Asturias' novel suggests that this shift toward reaction was already anticipated by the tactical orientations of worker and peasant organizers before the revolution had even begun. This is visible in Sansur's dream image of himself trying to delay what seems like an inevitable union between Malena Tabay and the "little officer" for as long as possible. He anticipates the almost magnetic pull of the bourgeoisie to the forces of repression, and this anxiety is built into his vision of suspended, fluidized, creative affects that – temporarily – allow new cross-class alliances to be formed.

The complex emotional attitude Sansur must maintain is echoed in the chirping of crickets he hears all around him, which signifies both a primordial, atmospheric procreative power and the danger that the military and professional classes could monopolize this conjunctive power to bolster the forces of repression: "y … y … y … aquella penúltima letra del alfabeto … con su forma misteriosa de germen, de atadura, de conjunción copulativa (and … and … and … that penultimate letter of the alphabet, with its mysterious form of a seed, a link, a copulative conjunction)" (*OE* 142/*EI*

196 translation altered) is what he hears "multiplicado por un grillo, por mil grillos, por millones de grillos … crii … y … y … criii … y … y … y … crii … y … y … y … (multiplied by a cricket, by a thousand crickets, by millions of crickets … chirraa … and … and … chirraa … and … and … and … chirraa … and … and … and …)" (*OE* 142/*EI* 196 translation altered).

The stridulation of crickets signifies both the capacity of the Guatemalan people to recombine their productive energies in new forms of social organization and the terrifyingly impersonal process of shifting class alliances that was occurring on the eve of the 1944 General Strike. So, while the crickets' seemingly endless chirping evokes "la mentalidad mítica (the mythic mentality)"[66] and "el tiempo primordial (the primordial time)" that Adalbert Dessau and Francisco Solares-Larrave both describe in their respective accounts of Asturias' work, it never broadens into the kind of mythic vision which contains "los elementos con los cuales una cultura determinada configura su visión de mundo (the elements with which a given culture shapes its worldview)."[67] On the contrary, the numinous quality this sound takes on is meant to evoke a society falling back on what Aída Toledo calls "la memoria original (originary memory)" – but one lacking in the kind of cultural nationalism belonging to "el período onírico asturiano (Asturias' oneiric period)."[68]

In practical terms, this means Sansur must continually be testing out new bonds of political affect and solidarity, even as he recognizes that these bonds are suspended over a social void, and could be easily broken in the most violent ways. This practico-affective attitude should be recognized as a highly sophisticated resource that Sansur and his contacts have had to develop and on which they must continually rely. It is an emotional and cognitive habit that corresponds to one of the greatest operational assets of insurrectionary organizations: their extraordinary level of tactical and strategic fluidity. While the command structure of hierarchical military organizations lends itself to contextual stupidity and inflexibility, the insurrectionary organization Sansur is involved with invests each militant with the strategic knowledge to make decisions based on contextual knowledge that is developing in real time. This can place enormous emotional and intellectual pressure on individual militants, since they must develop an impersonal, strategic attitude toward projects, interpersonal dynamics, and combat situations that are affectively charged in the extreme. But it also results in a complexified fighting force able to advance and retreat in highly fluid ways, not just on the battlefield, but in the domain of political alliances, affective solidarities, and forms of social organization.

Asturias illustrates this practico-affective attitude in many of the
micropolitical negotiations and tactical reversals staged by the revolutionaries
in *Los ojos de los enterrados*. Sansur and Florindo Key, for example, at first
planned to assassinate Cárcamo. Though he was a childhood friend of
Sansur's, they put sentiment aside and plot his death since "en nombre de
su ley, ellos ejecutan a los trabajadores que reclaman mejor sueldo, mejor
trato, menos horas de trabajo, en las plantaciones del Caribe (in the name
of his law they execute workers who demand better pay, better treatment,
fewer hours of work on the plantations on the Caribbean coast)" (*OE* 304/
*EI* 432). However, when they discover that Cárcamo neglects to hand over
documents that would have implicated Malena in revolutionary activity,
the conspirators decide to protect him with their lives – not because they
now trust him, but because of his immense tactical value.

Similarly, the two Samuels of the novel, the brothers known as Samuelon
and Samuelito, single out an officer and teach him to play the guitar, deliberately attempting to enlist him into a fragile solidarity with the workers'
movement, and constantly checking in with the movement about his
affective orientation. An organizer named Rámila explains that such a
careful disposition is necessary when dealing with "militares que a la hora
de la hora, por salvar el pellejo o sus bienes, se ponen a favor del pueblo,
para luego cambiar y volver a ser sus verdugos (military men, who, at the
right moment, in order to save their skins and what they have, will join the
side of the people, so they can change later on and go back to being their
executioners)" (*OE* 348/*EI* 496).

This ability to pursue an "experimental" tactical line while tolerating
the possibility of contradictions and reversals is audible in the political
debates of the militants as well. At one point, Samuelon is advocating
for a strategy of subversion, as opposed to outright armed confrontation: "Me gusta más el papel de taltuza … Y cavando el edificio se van
a quedar bajo sus escombros, con todo y sus policías, y sus bancos, y sus
jueces, y su presidente, y su comandantes, y sus generales (I'd rather play
the part of a gopher … And with the building undermined, they'll be left
under the ruins with their police and everything, their banks, their judges,
their president, their commandants, and their generals" (*OE* 325/*EI* 462–3)
translation altered slightly). The responses of his comrades are extremely
instructive. One mocks him: "Y en eso despertaste (And then you woke
up)" (*OE* 325/*EI* 463), but the debate continues – disagreement, negativity,
and the ability to tolerate contradiction are among the practical resources
of the group. Rámila, who disagrees with Samuelon, nevertheless shakes
his hand: "¡El compañero me hace la competencia … muy bien … qué

bien habla! (This comrade is competition ... very good ... You speak very well!)" (*OE* 325/*EI* 463). Samuelito responds "¿Y aquí, Rámila, cómo ve la cosa? (And how do things here look to you, Rámila?)" (*OE* 325/*EI* 463). His brother echoes his question, "¡Sí, sí, que nos diga cómo ve la cosa! (Yes, yes, tell us how you see things!)" (*OE* 325/*EI* 463).

The resource that is on display in this passage is not a resource in the sense that weapons, ammunition, and comestibles are. But in some ways it is even more important than these forms of material. The ability to advance an argument, a maneuver, an affective tie, energetically, while at the same time having the capacity to suspend it – in a sense, to be suspending it even as one advances it, anticipating other paths, the possibility of errors of procedure or intelligence – this is a resource that belongs to horizontally-organized political formations, and one that constitutes the very material of their being. And crucially, this is not simply an operational resource for the day-to-day prosecution of an insurrection, but a resource that allows militants to imagine future worlds, future social systems, future ways of organizing affect, solidarity, and forms of motivation.

Asturias emphasizes this futurally-oriented disposition in his characters' actions and fantasies. In one of Sansur's debates with politicized workers, he describes the nonstate space that the Guatemalan people are constructing as "el paréntesis de luz que se abría en el cotidiano vivir de gentes de pan y sueño ... y dando permanencia de futuro a la marcha de campesinos y obreros hacia el poder (the parenthesis of light that was opening up in the daily life of people of bread and dreams ... and giving the permanence of a future to the march toward power of workers and peasants)" (*OE* 393/*EI* 561). But this future is never depicted in the novel, which concludes with the idea that "los enterrados que esperaban el día de la justicia (those who were interred and waiting for the day of justice)" could not close their eyes yet, as the workers and peasants were only "en el umbral esperanzado de ese gran día (on the threshold of that great day)" (*OE* 482/*EI* 695).

This image is derived from the Mayan belief that the dead can only close their eyes and sleep when the injustices of their lifetime have been redeemed. It's telling, therefore, that the main indigenous character of the novel, Juambo, whose land was stolen by United Fruit without compensation, is still adrift at the end of the novel, wandering in the negative space opened up by the strike: "Sólo él en las calles ... Sólo él entre los bananales (he alone on the streets ... he alone in the banana groves)" (*OE* 480/*EI* 692) while the strike threatens "la rápida invasión de la maleza a los cultivos, la avalancha de los insectos que en horas se comían todo, lo devoraban, lo destruían, lo pudrían (the rapid invasion of underbrush onto the plantings, the avalanche of insects which in a matter of hours would eat everything up, devour it, destroy it, putrefy it)" (*OE* 480/*EI* 692–3 translation altered).

Though in 1952 the Árbenz administration would begin implementing one of the most far-reaching agricultural reform acts ever envisioned in Latin America, redistributing to peasants what would amount to 1.4 million acres of land that United Fruit had left uncultivated, it is significant that Asturias' novel makes no mention of the political leaders who would come to power in the wake of the revolution, nor the political jockeying in military and professional circles that would help cement their rule. Asturias describes Árbenz as "un visionario ... uno de los nuevos héroes de la América nuestra"[69] and, in *Week-end en Guatemala*, represents his overthrow by the United States as a grotesque atrocity (even the US Sergeant that the novella focuses on refers to it as a betrayal of "el espíritu de América (the spirit of America)."[70] But in *Los ojos de los enterrados*, it is clear that nonstate forces, with their capacity to bring the productive life of the state to a standstill, are the ones who force the state to act, grudgingly and with much temporizing, in their interests.

As Cindy Forster notes in her study of campesinos in the Guatemalan Revolution, plantation workers, both indigenous and Ladino, provided the coordination and physical force that in large part allowed the revolution to succeed, and their forms of organization were autonomous from both the state and the middle-class organizations with which they liaised.[71] Other historians of the revolution have noted that these nonstate forms of organization in no way found their consummation in the Arévalo regime that came to power after elections (with suffrage of the male population) in 1944. On the contrary, Arévalo's social program was weak and confused; the Labor Code he supported in 1947 established an eight-hour workday, but continued to define unions on farms employing fewer than 500 people as illegal. Arévalo encouraged agricultural cooperatives and implemented a national program of social security, but did not hesitate to use the army to suppress strikes in the countryside. Labor discontent under Arévalo's presidency thus led to frequent strike activity throughout his administration. A strike during the 1945/46 harvest in the department of San Marcos threatened massive crop losses; this was followed by another series of strikes during the 1946/47 harvest. The railway union, whose workers play crucial roles in Asturias' novel, struck in 1944, 1945, 1946, 1947, 1949, and 1950, adopting a strong developmentalist stance that outstripped anything Arévalo was willing to implement. In 1949, the union declared it would support "any national firm that competes with or establishes national services similar to those foreign companies have at the present time in a monopolistic form."[72]

This is why Forster sees the Árbenz administration, which did institute sweeping land reform and social policies, as the result of nonstate forces which continued mobilizing for six years after the initial ouster of Ubico had already been accomplished.[73] Nonstate forces, in other words, compelled state action, by maintaining their organizational bonds and tactics throughout the revolution, until the process was cut short by the overwhelming military power of the United States in 1954.

This agonistic relationship between state and nonstate actors is a recurring motif in the literary works I have examined in this chapter. In Chamoiseau's *Les neuf consciences du Malfini*, it is visible in the autonomous organizational activity that is evolved outside the inflexible, xenophobic state apparatus of Colibri, and in *Le papillon et la lumière* it is evoked by the luminous, self-creative powers that become available only when nonstate actors take direct action to assault and immobilize the French neocolonial regime. In Sembene's *Les bouts de bois de Dieu*, it can be seen in organizational networks the railway workers maintain outside of the politicking of their local elected officials and the PCF-aligned union representatives who try to break their strike. In all of these cases, nonstate forces create networks of communication, intelligence, and physical force that are in a position to outlast the moment of political crisis, and out of which nonstate forms of social organization can be built.

These nonstate resources are not of a kind that demands literacy or "breeding." Middle-class political organizations do not have a monopoly on their potency, nor are elite subjects called on to "speak for" subaltern nonstate networks, whose numbers, discipline, and forms of delegation allow them to speak clearly for themselves. Our difficulty in picturing how ordinary people – transport workers, shantytown dwellers, railway workers, fruit haulers – could discover and cultivate such resources therefore has far more to do with our own theoretical limitations than any ontological incapacity among nonstate actors themselves. Indeed, in the literature I have examined in this chapter, the nonstate networks of ordinary people offer by far the most ambitious, capable, and well-organized force for change, in the face of state forces that are immobilized or complicit with colonial and neocolonial agents.

Nevertheless, bringing these nonstate forces into view is only the first step in our theoretical itinerary. The question of how the organizational forms and systems of self-government inaugurated by the general strike could possibly be prolonged, spatially and temporally, so as to secure lasting mechanisms of delegation, remains open at this point, and requires much more thorough investigation. It is to this question of the durability of nonstate self-government and its reach across national borders and populations that the next chapter turns.

### Notes

1  Françoise Thull and Pierre Mabut, "Guadeloupe and Martinique Workers Call General Strikes to Protest Economic Racism," *San Francisco Bay View: National Black Newspaper,* February 13, 2009. www.sfbayview.com/2009/02/guadeloupe-and-martinique-workers-call-general-strikes-to-protest-economic-racism/.

2  Even the USA, which had not seen a general strike since 1946, witnessed a general strike being called in Oakland, California in 2011, which shut down the Port of Oakland and was supported by locals of the International Longshore and Warehouse Union, the United Brotherhood of Carpenters, the Service Employees International Union, and the Oakland Education Association. See Michael A. McCarthy, "Occupying Higher Education: The Revival of the Student Movement," *New Labor Forum: A Journal of Ideas, Analysis, and Debate*, April 8, 2012. www.newlaborforum.cuny.edu/2012/04/08/occupying-higher-education-the-revival-of-the-student-movement/.

3  See Raúl Zibechi, *Territories in Resistance: A Cartography of Latin American Social Movements*, trans. Ramor Ryan (Oakland: AK Press, 2012).

4  Eugene W. Holland, *Nomad Citizenship: Free-Market Communism and the Slow-Motion General Strike* (Minneapolis: University of Minnesota Press, 2011), 150, 156.

5  www.cia.gov/library/publications/the-world-factbook/geos/xx.html.

6  www.oecd.org/tad/benefitlib/trade-costs.htm.

7  www.atag.org/facts-and-figures.html.

8  The exact figure is 21.6 percent of workers, worldwide. International Labour Organization, *World of Work Report*, 2014. www.ilo.org/global/research/global-reports/world-of-work/2014/lang--en/index.htm.

9  Edward Said, "Foreword," in *Selected Subaltern Studies,* ed. Ranajit Guha and Gayatri Chakravorty Spivak (Oxford: Oxford University Press, 1988), vi.

10  See especially Guha's excellent analysis of the "primordial networks and many different means of verbal and non-verbal communication" involved in this deliberative process (Ranajit Guha, *Aspects of Peasant Insurgency in Colonial India* [Durham: Duke University Press, 1999], 9).

11  As Masood Ashraf Raja correctly notes, Sembene's representation of the strike reflects these high political stakes: not just labor relations, but "all aspects of a colonized life become subject to the demands of a new socio-political order structured specifically by the strike itself" (Masood Ashraf Raja, "Ousmane

Sembène's *God's Bits of Wood*: The Anatomy of a Strike and the Ideologeme of Solidarity," in Gordon Collier, ed., *Spheres Public and Private: Western Genres in African Literature* [Amsterdam and New York: Editions Rodopi, 2011], 434).

12 Éloïse A. Brière argues, along these lines, that, with the onset of the strike, "l'édifice colonial commence à se fissurer (the colonial edifice begins to crack)" – accordingly, she correctly describes the strikers as participating not just in a narrowly economic struggle, but in "la construction d'espaces libérateurs – précurseurs de l'indépendance (the construction of liberated spaces – precursors of independence)" (Éloïse A. Brière, "Recycler l'histoire de la décolonisation: Fiction et lieux de mémoire," *French Colonial History*, 8 [2007], 142. Translation mine.)

13 Élie Domota and Guillaume Davranche, "Élie Domota (UGTG): 'Libérations nationale et sociale doivent aller de pair,'" *Alternative Libertaire*, April 6, 2013. www.alternativelibertaire.org/?Elie-Domota-UGTG-Liberations. Translation mine.

14 André Lucrèce, "Guadeloupe, Martinique, des sociétés marquées par le sceau du déclassement," *Gens de la Caraïbe*, February 28, 2009. www.vers-les-iles.fr/livres/2009/Lucrece_opinion_1.html. Translation mine.

15 See Robert J. Alexander and Eldon M. Parker, *A History of Organized Labor in Panama and Central America* (Westport: Praeger, 2008), 219.

16 See Deborah Levenson-Estrada, *Trade Unionists against Terror: Guatemala City, 1954–1985* (Chapel Hill: University of North Carolina Press, 1994), 16.

17 The awkwardness of centering the story around the civil engineer near the end of the novel is registered by two excellent studies: Ashley Dawson's, which suggests "perhaps this servant of the state glosses a little too quickly over the forms of biopower that the municipal government continues to wield within Texaco," and Michael D. Rubenstein's, which questions whether the electricity brought by the civil engineer "could make up for centuries of oppression and exploitation" (see Ashley Dawson, "Squatters, Space, and Belonging in the Underdeveloped City," *Social Text*, 22:4 [Winter 2004], 30; and Michael D. Rubenstein, "Light Reading: Public Utility, Urban Fiction, and Human Rights," *Social Text*, 26:4 [Winter 2008], 36). I'd suggest that Chamoiseau's shift onto the terrain of fable and abstract philosophical narration is a way to move away from the forms of state-sponsored resolution that the novel invokes – especially since the forms of mutual aid and resistance the squatter characters embody are far more important to the novel's internal momentum than the statist resolution *Texaco* halfheartedly proposes.

18 Ernest Breleur *et al.*, *Manifeste pour les "produits" de haute nécessité* (Paris: Éditions Galaade, 2009), 4–5. Translation mine.

19 *Ibid.*, 5.

20 *Ibid.*

21 The exact language of the demands is as follows: "Un salaire minimum guadeloupéen calculé sur le coût réel de la vie en Guadeloupe ... L'arrêt

des saisies immobilières des propriétés des guadeloupéens … Création
d'une structure assurant un véritable service public de la formation
professionnelle" (LKP, «LIYANNAJ KONT PWOFITASYON – Mi nou!
nou gwadloupéyen – KA NOU VLE …» [archive, no longer available
online], January 20, 2009).

22  *Manifeste pour les "produits" de haute nécessité,* 2.

23  *Ibid.,* 7.

24  *Ibid.,* 9.

25  The exact language of these demands is as follows: "Mise en place d'un
véritable service de transport des usagers … Droit à l'organisation de
formation syndicale ouverte à toutes les organisations syndicales de
Guadeloupe … La création d'une pépinière artisanale et agricole qui serait
la vitrine de nos produits du terroir … Redynamisation des bassins de vie
par le développement économique d'activités de terroir (exemples: agro-
transformation, pêche …) … Prise en compte dans la programmation des
médias de la langue et de la culture guadeloupéenne par la présence de
représentants des associations culturelles dans les conseils d'administration
… Contamination des terres par la chlordécone: Définition de mesures
sanitaires pour protéger les populations des zones contaminées («LIYANNAJ
KONT PWOFITASYON – Mi nou! nou gwadloupéyen – KA NOU
VLE …»).

26  Patrick Chamoiseau, "J'ai vu un peuple s'ébrouer … Nous n'avons jamais été
aussi vivants," *Le Monde,* March 13, 2009. www.lemonde.fr/idees/article/2009/
03/13/j-ai-vu-un-peuple-s-ebrouer-nous-n-avons-jamais-ete-aussi-vivants-
par-patrick-chamoiseau_1167622_3232.html. All translations mine. Hereafter
cited as "J".

27  Patrick Chamoiseau, *Les neuf consciences du Malfini* (Paris: Gallimard, 2009),
38. Hereafter cited as *M*. All translations mine.

28  Édouard Glissant, *Poetics of Relation,* trans. Betsy Wing (Ann Arbor: The
University of Michigan Press, 1997), 89.

29  Patrick Chamoiseau, *Texaco* (Paris: Gallimard, 1992) 282–3. English translation: Patrick Chamoiseau, *Texaco,* trans. Rose-Myriam Réjouis and Val
Vinokurov (New York: Vintage, 1998), 257.

30  Richard Watts, "Poisoned Animal, Polluted Form: Chamoiseau's Birds at the
Limits of Allegory," *Pacific Coast Philology,* 46:2 (2011), 185.

31  Wendy Knepper, "Colonization, Creolization, and Globalization: The Art and
Ruses of *Bricolage,*" *Small Axe,* 21 (October 2006), 84–5.

32  Stella Vincenot, "Patrick Chamoiseau and the Limits of the Aesthetics of
Resistance," *Small Axe,* 30 (November 2009), 69.

33  Patrick Chamoiseau, *Le papillon et la lumière* (Paris: Éditions Philippe Rey,
2011), 15, 14–15. Hereafter cited as *PL*. All translations mine.

34  Yarimar Bonilla, "Guadeloupe Is Ours: The Prefigurative Politics of the Mass
Strike in the French Antilles," *Interventions: International Journal of Postcolonial
Studies,* 12:1 (2010), 126.

35 Élie Domota and Guillaume Davranche, "Élie Domota (UGTG): 'Libérations nationale et sociale doivent aller de pair,'" *Alternative Libertaire*, April 6, 2013. www.alternativelibertaire.org/?Elie-Domota-UGTG-Liberations. Translation mine.

36 LKP, «LIYANNAJ KONT PWOFITASYON – Mi nou! nou gwadloupéyen – KA NOU VLE …»

37 Serge Apatout and *Alternative Libertaire*, "Guadeloupe, pour l'appropriation de la mémoire et du travail," May 1, 2002. http://ugtg.org/spip.php?page=imprimer&id_article=636.

38 Édouard Glissant and Patrick Chamoiseau, *Quand les murs tombent: l'identité nationale hors-la-loi?* (Paris: Éditions Galaade, 2007), 11. My translation.

39 Édouard Glissant, "Dans la Caraïbe, le monde entier est venu," interview by Arnaud Robert, *Le Temps*, March 20, 2009. www.vers-les-iles.fr/livres/2009/Glissant_2009_1.html. Translation mine.

40 UGTG, "De la grève de 1910 au LKP: Un siècle de luttes en Guadeloupe," August 31, 2009. http://ugtg.org/article_1066.html.

41 LKP, "Meeting de solidarité du LKP: 14 Février 1952 La grève des ouvriers au Moule noyée dans le sang!," February 12, 2012. http://ugtg.org/article_1713.html. Translation mine.

42 *Ibid.*

43 Josef Kohlhaas, "La gwève généwale pour les nuls," *Fakir,* October 15, 2009. www.fakirpresse.info/La-gweve-genewale-pour-les-nuls. Translation mine.

44 *Ibid.*

45 Rosa Moussaoui and Élie Domota, "Élie Domota: Le capitalisme conduit inexorablement à la barbarie," *L'Humanité,* September 18, 2009. www.humanite.fr/node/423888. Translation mine.

46 In 1910, for example, the economy of Guadeloupe was dominated by agricultural production, and the General Strike that occurred that year was carried out by agricultural workers working on the estates of former slaveholders. Today, industries like food processing, textile manufacture, tourism, and retail trade are the backbone of the region's economy. But the continuities between twentieth- and twenty-first-century struggles that were highlighted by participants in the 2009 General Strike cut against the widely held belief that contemporary social struggles are the product of fundamental shifts in the nature of global capitalism, the organs of struggle that confront it, or the political subjectivities evolved within this context. Wholly absent in the discourse surrounding the 2009 General Strike was the idea that financialization or "immaterial production" had fundamentally altered the relations of exploitation in capitalist society, diminished the effectiveness of the general strike as a political tool, or voided the political will of working people in the French Antilles.

47 For an excellent analysis of Senegal's colonial economy, see Catherine Boone, *Merchant Capital and the Roots of State Power in Senegal: 1930–1985* (Cambridge: Cambridge University Press, 1992), esp. 31–77.

48  Ousmane Sembene, *Les bouts de bois de Dieu* (Paris: Le Livre Contemporain, 1960), 141. Hereafter cited as *BBD*. English translation: Sembene Ousmane, *God's Bits of Wood*, trans. Francis Price (Oxford: Heinemann, 1962), 85. Hereafter cited as *GBW*. Unless otherwise noted, English translation is that of Price.

49  James A. Jones, "Fact and Fiction in *God's Bits of Wood*," *Research in African Literatures*, 31:2 (2000), 117–31.

50  James A. Jones, *Industrial Labor in the Colonial World: Workers of the Chemin de Fer Dakar–Niger 1881–1963* (Portsmouth: Heinemann, 2002), 26.

51  Frederick Cooper, " 'Our Strike': Equality, Anticolonial Politics, and the 1947–48 Railway Strike in French West Africa," *The Journal of African History*, 37 (1996), 82.

52  Marian Aguiar makes a similar point when she argues *vis-à-vis* Sembene's representation of the railway's modernity that "the meaning of technology … change[s] as it travels and becomes situated in a new terrain of cultural practices" – a process she refers to suggestively as a "rupturing of the technology" (Marian Aguiar, "Smoke of the Savannah: Traveling Modernity in Sembene Ousmane's *God's Bits of Wood*," *Modern Fiction Studies*, 49:2 [2003], 296).

53  Kwaku Addae Gyasi notes that such moments make of the strike "an opportunity for self-affirmation," and F. Case also makes reference to the "collective participation in decision-making processes" on display in *Les bouts de bois de Dieu* (see Kwaku Addae Gyasi, "From *God's Bits of Wood* to *Smouldering Charcoal*: Decolonization, Class Struggle, and the Role of Women's Consciousness in Postcolonial West Africa," *French Colonial History*, 5 [2004], 179; and F. Case, "Workers Movements: Revolution and Women's Consciousness in *God's Bits of Wood*," *Revue Canadienne des Études Africaines/Canadian Journal of African Studies*, 15:2 [1981], 278). What I add to this conversation is an analysis of the importance of the nonstate, nonparty, nonbureaucratic community networks that link the labor actions of the railway workers to the total life process of the community they inhabit – the links that transform labor action into coordinated nonstate space.

54  Ruth Schachter Morgenthau, *Political Parties in French-Speaking West Africa* (Oxford: Clarendon, 1964), 25.

55  *Ibid.*, 27.

56  *Ibid.*

57  Samba Gadjigo, *Ousmane Sembène: The Making of a Militant Artist*, trans. Moustapha Diop (Bloomington: Indiana University Press, 2007), 124.

58  Élie Domota, "Rapports de race et de classe dans la société guadeloupéenne." http://ugtg.org/article_731.html. One minor correction: *Zembla* is the title of the comic book that the website renders as "*ZAMBLA*." Translation mine.

59  *Ibid.*

60  *Ousmane Sembène: The Making of a Militant Artist*, 59.

61  Éric Favereau and Antoine Guiral, "Le surprenant succès du LKP, objet politique non identifié," *Libération.fr*, March 4, 2009. www.liberation.fr/france/2009/03/04/le-surprenant-succes-du-lkp-objet-politique-non-identifie_463225.

Cited in Christine Chivallon, "Guadeloupe et Martinique en lutte contre la «profitation»: du caractère nouveau d'une histoire ancienne," *Justice Spatiale/ Spatial Justice*, 1 (2009). www.jssj.org/wp-content/uploads/2012/12/JSS1-7fr1. pdf.

62 Frantz Fanon, *Black Skin, White Masks*, trans. Richard Philcox (New York: Grove, 2008), 112.

63 See Susanne Jonas, *The Battle for Guatemala: Rebels, Death Squads, and U.S. Power* (Boulder: Westview Press, 1991), esp. 22.

64 Miguel Ángel Asturias, *Los ojos de los enterrados* (Buenos Aires: Editorial Losada S.A., 1960), 219. Hereafter cited as *OE*. English translation: Miguel Ángel Asturias, *The Eyes of the Interred*, trans. Gregory Rabassa (New York: Delacorte Press, 1973), 310. Hereafter cited as *EI*. Except where noted, this excellent translation is the one used.

65 This image is a far cry from what Arturo Arias describes, in reference to Asturias' early work, as "un espacio simbólico metaideológico que crea símbolos nacionales para uso cotidiano (a meta-ideological symbolic space that creates national symbols for everyday use)" (Arturo Arias, "Transgresión erótica y recodificación de símbolos en *Mulata de Tal*," in *Cien años de magia: Ensayos críticos sobre la obra de Miguel Ángel Asturias*, ed. Oralia Preble-Niemi [Guatemala City: F&G Editores, 2006], 22, online at www.literaturaguatemalteca.org/arias28.html; translation mine). According to Arias' argument, early works such as *Hombres de maíz* (1949) embodied the intention "por forjar una cultura nacional popular que fuera empleada por el estado democrática ladino para su consolidación nacional (to forge a popular national culture that was used by the *ladino* demo-cratic state for its national consolidation (*Ibid.*, 22), whereas a later work such as *Mulata de Tal* abandons this unifying cultural agenda and, in fact, "no cree en la posibilidad de un estado (does not believe in the possibility of a state)" (*Ibid.*, 23). Within the chronology Arias establishes, then, *Los ojos de los enterrados* is closer to the nonstate imagination of a work like *Mulata de Tal*, but it mobilizes this nonstate imagination in moments of eidetic rupture that are national in scope, which suggests the novel is not just one of transgression but an attempt to imagine a nonstate political reconfiguration.

66 Adalbert Dessau, "Mito y realidad en *Los ojos de los enterrados*, de Miguel Ángel Asturias," in *Homenaje a Miguel Ángel Asturias: Variaciones interpretativas en torno a su obra,* ed. Helmy F. Giacoman (New York: Las Americas Publishing Company, 1971), 211. Translation mine.

67 Francisco Solares-Larrave, "El mito crítico: una construcción contestataria en *El espejo de Lida Sal*," in *Cien años de magia: Ensayos críticos sobre la obra de Miguel Ángel Asturias*, ed. Oralia Preble-Niemi (Guatemala City: F&G Editores, 2006), 181, 184. Translation mine.

68 Aída Toledo, "Tras la pista de *El alhajadito*," in *Cien años de magia*, 145. Translation mine.

69 Miguel Ángel Asturias, "Jacobo Árbenz," *Alero*, 4 (April–June 1971), 18, 19.

70  Miguel Ángel Asturias, *Week-end en Guatemala* (Buenos Aires: Editorial Goyanarte, 1956), 41. Translation mine.

71  See Cindy Forster, *The Time of Freedom: Campesino Workers in Guatemala's October Revolution* (Pittsburgh: University of Pittsburgh Press, 2001).

72  See Jim Handy, *Revolution in the Countryside: Rural Conflict and Agrarian Reform in Guatemala, 1944–1954* (Chapel Hill: University of North Carolina Press, 1994), 28.

73  See Cindy Forster, *The Time of Freedom.*

# CHAPTER 2

# Nonstate Internationalism: From Claude McKay to Arundhati Roy

In the previous chapter, we examined the mass strike as a socio-political act of resistance that opens up nonstate capabilities, processes, and spaces in the colonial and neocolonial world. In the 2009 General Strike in the French Antilles, the Dakar–Niger Railway Strike of 1947–1948 and the Guatemalan General Strike of 1944, as in so many of the mass strikes that have occurred in the twentieth and twenty-first centuries, the extra-legal organizational structures made necessary by the strike allow for a vision of democratic decision-making on a large scale that serves as an imaginary alternative to the postcolonial state's vertical concentrations of power. In the literature and theory devoted to them, strikes such as these are repeatedly pictured as mass pedagogical organs, awakening unprece-dented styles of communication, technical competencies, and habits of critique amidst the general population, making possible large-scale forms of self-government outside the aegis of the state.

The aftermath of these strikes, however, must prompt us to ask whether such forms of broad, horizontal, nonstate self-government can be anything but evanescent phenomena – nonstate spaces contracting as quickly as they dilated, suffocated by neocolonial political regimes and imperialist war. Guatemala is by far the most tragic case. In the wake of the 1944 General Strike, the revolutionary government of Jacobo Árbenz was overthrown in an undeclared war, funded by the United Fruit Company and directed by the CIA, which led to one of the longest and most sickeningly brutal counterinsurgency campaigns in modern history.

In the case of French West Africa, the Dakar–Niger Railway Strike brought about significant gains for Senegalese workers, and demonstrated to the French the potential cost of opening up another theater of counter-insurgency operations. But the Union Progressiste Sénégalaise's consolidation of maraboutic authority and Wolof aristocratic rule in the countryside and its eventual banning of opposition parties, political student organizations, and all national-level confederations of trade unions other than its own Union national des travailleurs sénégalais and Confédération nationale des travailleurs sénégalais created major obstacles to the forms of democratic expression and nonstate initiative represented in Sembene's account of the 1947–1948 strike.

The fallout of the 2009 General Strike of the French Antilles is less easy to assess, in part because it is still occurring. In principle, the LKP had all of its main demands met, including a housing rent freeze, a ban on evictions, the setting aside of 64,000 hectares of farmland for future use, and a €200 monthly increase for Guadeloupe's lowest-paid workers.[1] But infringements of the Jacques Bino accord of February 26, 2009 caused the LKP to call for new mobilizations just one year and nine months after the 2009 General Strike.[2] Certainly, some of the more ambitious visions awakened by the general strike – Chamoiseau's vision of regional interdependencies and food sufficiency, for example – have not yet come to pass.

All of this invites us to ask how it could ever be possible to *institutionalize* the horizontal decision-making practices that evolve in nonstate space. This question is even more pressing given the transnational character of both the Dakar–Niger Railway Strike and the General Strike in the French Antilles. What nonstate logistical and executive apparatuses could ever have the kind of scope to solidify democratic processes and political life on such a scale? What could take the place of the state in coordinating such efforts on a national and international level?

These days, such questions often arise in the context of debates about cosmopolitanism. Nongovernmental organizations often take pride of place in debates such as these, in part because of the positive change many such organizations have been able to effect by means of their transnational organizational efforts. But, for quite some time, theorists have been sounding notes of skepticism about cosmopolitanism as a *political* project. Take Craig Calhoun's contribution to *Debating Cosmopolitics*. When "a large proportion of global civil society – from the World Bank to non-governmental organizations setting accountancy standards – exists to support capitalism and not pursue democracy," what credible *institutions* of global self-government can we point to?[3] Ultimately, Calhoun argues, if cosmopolitan democracy is to be "more than a good ethical orientation for those privileged to inhabit the frequent traveler lounges, it must put down roots in the solidarities that organize most people's sense of identity and location in the world"; in other words, it must be built from the ground up, from "networks of directly interpersonal social relations, such as those basic to local community."[4]

This ideal of local autonomy within transnational self-government is frequently invoked in contemporary theories of global democracy.[5] But its practical corollary – what this ideal would look like in terms of institutions, practices, and regulative mechanisms – is often difficult to visualize. For example, in *A Critique of Postcolonial Reason*, Gayatri Spivak notes that invocations of local, concrete experience all too often construct the fantasy image of a general will based on "the credit-baited rural woman" who can be " 'formatted' … through UN Plans of Action" in the service of an unquestioning "financialization of the globe."[6] Similarly, in *Spectral Nationality*, Pheng Cheah questions the capacity of local social negotiations to develop a contemporary political life beyond the nation state: "in the current conjuncture, nationalism cannot be transcended by cosmopolitan forms of solidarity," since transnational assemblages lack the organizational coherence and numerical density necessary to make them effective political agents.[7] Moreover, "*the unevenness of political and economic globalization* makes the nation-state necessary as a political agent for defending the peoples of the South from the shortfalls of neocolonial capitalist global restructuring."[8]

In terms of its institutional imagination, then, cosmopolitan theory faces something of an impasse. According to Cheah, celebrations of "endless hybrid self-creation and autonomy from the given" too often ignore globalization's other face – forced migrancy, underdevelopment, and neocolonial domination – and tend to articulate purely cultural models of transformative agency, which fail to consider "framework[s] for the distribution and regulation of economic resources and capabilities to satisfy human needs."[9] At the same time, Cheah admits that the real-world emancipatory resources of the postcolonial state are perpetually undermined by "comprador indigenous elite[s] in collaboration with multinational capital."[10] If it is difficult to imagine this transnational administrative elite transforming itself into a neutral arbiter of international justice, it is often just as difficult to imagine local communities evolving their own structures of international self-government without access to the formidable resources of state and interstate institutions.

Faced with this politico-institutional impasse, cosmopolitan theorists often speculate about the kinds of transnational organizational bodies that could bypass the state and represent the will of national populations directly. David Held's idea of United Nations-backed "People's Assemblies" belongs to this discursive regime; so did the 1990s-era enthusiasm that surrounded the creation of the International Criminal Court, which pretends to act outside specific national interests, but which is too often an obvious instrument of them.[11] Cosmopolitan fictions like these, with their ideology of universalism and their practical alignment with Western imperialism, invite critiques like those of Timothy Brennan, who argues that cosmopolitanism is "a discourse of the universal that is inherently local … a Pax Americana dressed up as 'international law.' "[12] "Internationalism," according to Brennan, is a more useful term, as it is "an ideology of the domestically restricted, the recently relocated, the provisionally exiled," that is, an ideology "addressed to those who have an interest in transnational forms of solidarity, but whose capacities for [accomplishing them] have not yet arrived."[13]

But while it may offer a more flexible, and less Eurocentric, conceptual rubric than cosmopolitanism, "internationalism" has a fraught history of its own. As Perry Anderson notes, the dominant form of internationalism in the twentieth century was international communism, which by the time of Stalin's ascendancy within the Communist Party of the Soviet Union in 1922 had become synonymous with autocratic government and a "perverted" internationalism, in which "the activities of the Third International were utterly subordinated to the interests of the Soviet state, as Stalin interpreted them."[14] In more recent history, as Anderson also notes, "internationalism" has deteriorated to the point where it operates as a "codeword for forward policies to be pursued by the American state at large" denoting, first and foremost, "the right of the international community to blockade, to bomb, to invade peoples or states that displease it."[15]

In this chapter, I ask whether it is possible to imagine an internationalism that is external both to the "international community" of capitalist states and to the comparably sordid history of authoritarian communism. What precedents are there for imagining such a nonstate internationalism? Can such a thing be adumbrated at all without steering into cosmopolitan culs-de-sac involving "neutral" governing bodies inspired by supposedly universal ethical precepts?

I've chosen to examine the work of Claude McKay and Arundhati Roy precisely because they reject both the "internationalism" of capital and that of authoritarian communism, while at the same time articulating forms of political internationalism with axes of power outside the nation-state. In Roy's case, this vision of nonstate internationalism is articulated in the context of the anti-globalization movement, and in her writings on the Naxalite insurgency and Narmada Bachao Andolan in India. In McKay's case, it is articulated in the context of black internationalism and early twentieth-century forms of anti-Soviet proletarian internationalism.

I bring together these spatially and temporally remote forms of internationalism in this chapter to demonstrate that questions about nonstate space, subnational groups, territorial occupation, and international democratic institutions unite the twentieth and twenty-first centuries in the most urgent ways, despite the historiographic categories we commonly use to divide them. The populations Roy and McKay focus on – economic migrants, national minorities, peasants, factory workers, and the "developmental bourgeoisie" – participate in processes and dreams that were never "put to rest" with the twentieth century. They have been recurring in nonlinear, spatially transitive ways up to the present day.

The project of nonstate internationalism is an especially illuminating example of these continuities, because of its relevance to populations who have been marginalized by the political structures of institutional communism, but who nevertheless remain committed to an anti-capitalist social imagination. Claude McKay was one such thinker. When visiting the Soviet Union in 1922, he went as a delegate not of the American Communist Party but of the African Blood Brotherhood, a self-organized network for racial solidarity and self-defense. Because of his externality to the American Communist Party and his association with British "Left Wing" Communists, who critiqued Lenin for emphasizing centralized party politicking over mass initiative, McKay was received with hostility in Moscow, and ultimately was thrown out of the Lux Hotel and placed in a dilapidated room furnished with nothing but an army cot. Identifying himself as an "unorthodox comrade sympathizer" and a "radical dissident," he even feared being denounced as a spy.[16]

This points to the fact that McKay's internationalism in the 1920s was not identical to that of the Communist International. The term McKay applies to himself – "radical dissident" – referred, at the time, to radicals who dissented from Soviet orthodoxy itself: anarchists, anarcho-communists, syndicalists, and Left Wing Communists with "anarchist" tendencies like Sylvia Pankhurst and Rosa Luxemburg. Therefore, when McKay blasts the Comintern in 1937, for "believ[ing] only in the principle of dictatorship," he does so not from the perspective of status quo anticommunism, but in the name of *social revolution and the triumph of workers' democracy.*[17] Indeed, McKay's most energetic indictment of the Comintern is that they "have nothing but contempt (which is sometimes concealed) for genuine workers' democracy."[18]

The political vision McKay opposes to this is one of nonstate internationalism: an internationalism in which race-based organizations, workers' councils, and municipal labor organizations would interlink on a transnational level, forming the basis of a non-hierarchical, decentralized form of self-government. It is a vision that is based, in part, on the model of the anarcho-syndicalist Industrial Workers of the World (IWW), which McKay joined in the 1920s, and which argued that an international network of workers' councils, with delegates elected from local rank-and-files, could take over the functions that states, parties, and professional politicians currently fulfill. But it is a political vision that also owes much to black internationalism – especially its insistence that black populations develop their own political leaders, economic infrastructure, and mutual aid networks. McKay provides only a skeletal image of what such a nonstate, black internationalism like this would look like in his nonfiction works. But if we look carefully at fictional works like *Banjo* we can see McKay evolving a flexible, speculative structure that allows him to articulate a powerful vision of nonstate internationalism. In these cases, literature takes over where political analysis hardly dares to tread, and allows McKay to conceive a barely imaginable alternative to capitalist and Communist states, rooted in the networked democracies of nonstate populations of economic migrants and African-descended groups.

Amazing as it may seem, given her social and cultural distance from McKay, Arundhati Roy finds herself in a position similar to his, both in her attempts to stake out an anti-capitalist politics outside the aegis of institutional Communism, and in terms of the way her fiction maps out socio-political possibilities that are barely articulable in the language of political polemic. Her complex position is in part a reflection of the complex politics of the anti-globalization movement. While confronting neoliberal capitalist globalization with the powerful concept that "another world is possible," the movement has achieved no consensus about what this alternative might look like, producing instead an impressive variety of theories and narratives, ranging from Zibechi's analysis of peasant cooperatives in the Andes to Naomi Klein's documentation of worker-run *fábricas ocupadas* in Argentina. What many of these efforts have in common, however, is an attempt to imagine nonstate political alternatives, and this often takes shape as an attempt to recuperate the anarchist, syndicalist, and Left Communist intellectual tradition that McKay was drawing on in the early twentieth century.

For example, one of the first texts to be associated with the anti-globalization movement was John Holloway's *How to Change the World without Taking Power*, which critiqued the state-focused praxis of international communism, and proposed various forms of nonstate politics in its place. Oral histories of the *fábricas ocupadas* movement have a similarly dissident quality. They center on the idea of autogestion, which dates back to the anarchist movements in Argentina, Algeria, and France. In recent years, a *Left Communist Reader* has even appeared, along with works like *Left of Karl Marx: The Political Life of Black Communist Claudia Jones*, *In the Cause of Freedom: Radical Black Internationalism from Harlem to London, 1917–1939*, and *Cartography of Revolutionary Anarchism*, which are in the process of reconstructing the dissident internationalist world in which Claude McKay moved.

Arundhati Roy's theoretical and literary work is very much a part of this ongoing conversation about nonstate alternatives. In her 2011 *Walking with the Comrades*, she describes the necessity of developing "an imagination that is outside of capitalism as well as Communism,"[19] and in a speech to the People's University of the Occupy Wall Street movement, Roy said "we are not fighting to tinker with reforming a system that needs to be replaced."[20] But replaced with what? It is a question about nonstate political forms that haunts not just Roy, but the anti-globalization and Occupy movements as well.

In what follows, I'll argue that Roy's narratives *The God of Small Things* and *Walking with the Comrades* provide a vision of nonstate internationalism that is as powerful and complex as any theoretical document produced by the anti-globalization movement. Like McKay's narratives, Roy's proceed from a profound impatience with the landscape of existing institutional political actors – in her case, the Indian state, including the institutional Indian Communist Party (Marxist) (CPI[M]), as well as many of the NGOs that have allied with Western capital to coopt resistance movements of the Global South. And like McKay, she turns to populations of economic migrants, peasants, and workers to imagine a nonstate internationalism that could rival that of capitalist state and interstate institutions.

But how could displaced peasants, poorly armed insurgents in the countryside, or Untouchable factory workers, isolated even from most of their coworkers, ever evolve nonstate networks and capacities of international scope? It's a question similar to what McKay had to ask in the 1920s, when he tried to imagine a nonstate internationalism forged out of economic migrants, West Indian peasants, and African American workers.

These populations all confront a cosmopolitan impasse, in the sense that their spatial displacements, economic transactions, and communication networks are all constrained in ways that bar access to the cosmopolitan ideal that has been articulated in recent philosophy and political theory. But, in many ways, it is precisely this cosmopolitan impasse that is the doorway to forms of nonstate internationalism that are impossible to imagine from the perspective of disembedded, "universal" actors of the kind so often associated with the cosmopolitan ideal. One could even say that Roy's novel *The God of Small Things* is structured around precisely such a detour around the politics of cosmopolitanism. In this sense, it's a good place to start opening up questions about nonstate internationalism that link twentieth-century literature to contemporary literatures of neo-liberalism, radical critique, and nonstate imaginaries.

## The Cosmopolitan Impasse

What does it mean to say that *The God of Small Things* is structured around a cosmopolitan impasse?

Let's look at Roy's narrative. On a diegetic level, this impasse is literal: twin siblings Estha and Rahel, along with their mother, uncle, and great-aunt, are traveling by car to Cochin, where they plan to see *The Sound of Music* at a local cinema and pick up their half-British cousin Sophie at the airport. En route, their sky-blue Plymouth is delayed at a railroad crossing and swarmed by a demonstration organized by the Travancore-Cochin Marxist Labour Union. Trapped in the car, their great-aunt is compelled by some of the demonstrators to wave a red flag and chant "Inquilab Zindabad." Though their great-aunt is outraged, the incident is untraumatic for the twins – Rahel's main preoccupation is her excitement over seeing her friend Velutha, a factory employee of Untouchable caste, among the demonstrators.

Benign as this impasse may appear, it anticipates a series of traumatic incidents about to occur in quick succession in the novel: Estha's molestation by a soft-drink vendor in the theater, their cousin's drowning in the Meenachil river, their uncle's closing of his pickle factory amidst communist agitation, and Velutha's murder at the hands of the police for his cross-caste affair with Estha and Rahel's mother.

Somehow the brief pause at the railway crossing emblematizes all of these traumas, but how and why? The key to this question lies in the social symbolism that Roy layers with incredible rigor around this scene.

From the very outset, the family's car ride is set in a transnational context. The rice fields and rubber trees they pass, as well as the Communists in the Kerala countryside, are likened to the rice fields, rubber trees, and Communists of Vietnam, which, in the winter of 1969, were under bombardment by US forces: "further east," Roy writes, "in a small country with similar landscape (jungles, rivers, rice fields, Communists), enough bombs were being dropped to cover all of it in six inches of steel."[21] The import of this connection isn't entirely clear, until the railway crossing gate descends and the twins are greeted by the sight of the "level-crossing lunatic," Murlidharan, who lost both arms fighting for the British in Singapore in 1942, and was rewarded with nothing more than a railway pass. Having lost his mind, and also the railway pass, he sits naked on the milestone by the railroad crossing, near a sign that reads "BE INDIAN, BUY INDIAN."

Contributing to this symbolic nexus of imperialism and underdevelopment is the fact that the sky-blue Plymouth carries a rickety sign advertising uncle Chacko's pickling factory, which boasts an illustration of a kathakali dancer which Chacko hopes will give his products a "Regional Flavor and would stand them in good stead when they entered the Overseas Market" (*GOST* 46).

The family outing is therefore part of a complex cosmopolitan itinerary, in which the twins look forward to confirming their deep identification with Anglophone culture through cinema, and in which Chacko looks forward to receiving his half-British daughter – the product of a cosmopolitan romance he enjoyed during his time at Oxford – all under the banner of Paradise Pickles and Preserves, a small-scale industry which Chacko naively hopes will one day enter into global circuits of commodity exchange.[22] Surrounding this emotionally charged cosmopolitan journey are reminders of imperialist violence and economic maldevelopment the family would prefer to ignore: Murlidharan's mutilated body, sacrificed to the interests of the British Empire; the billboard exhorting Indians to buy native products, an imperative that registers India's underdeveloped industrial infrastructure; and the railway itself, built by the British to speed the extraction of raw materials from India's "spice coast."

But the most overt obstacle to the family's cosmopolitan fantasies is the demonstration that engulfs them – a demonstration of CPI(M) organizers, students, and paddy workers, who are demanding an hour-long lunch break, a modest raise, and that Untouchables no longer be addressed by their caste names. Though the Naxalite movement that was active in Kerala in 1969 was separate from the CPI(M), and in fact had concentrated its forces in a separate party (called the Communist Party of India [Marxist-Leninist]), Roy writes that "there was an edge" to the anger of this protest "that was Naxalite, and new" (*GOST* 67). What does this mean? And why does Roy stage this encounter between "Naxalite anger" and the cosmopolitan journey of her protagonists?

In her 2011 narrative *Walking with the Comrades*, Roy explains that one of the principal reasons for the current phase of Naxalite struggle is the failure of institutional Communism to serve as a progressive alternative to mainstream electoral politics in India. "The major Communist parties," she writes, "have managed to survive in the mainstream only by compromising their ideologies so drastically that it is impossible to tell the difference between them and other bourgeois political parties any more" (*WC* 197). "Few," she adds, "would associate the word 'revolutionary' with the CPI or the CPM any more" (*WC* 197). Worse yet, Communist governments have recently unleashed police violence in Nandigram, Singur, and Jangalmahal, all in the name of neoliberal development projects – a move that has further alienated them from their constituency. The Naxalites, by contrast, have remained consistent in their strategy: "the redistribution of land, by violent means if necessary, was always the centrepiece of their political activity" (*WC* 198). Thus, the Naxalite movement, for all its faults, "shone a light on the deeply embedded structural injustice of Indian society," and, despite having little organizational purchase outside forested areas, has "a presence in the popular imagination, an increasingly sympathetic one, as a party that stands up for the poor against the intimidation and bullying of the State" (*WC* 199).[23]

In 1969, the Naxalites served a similar social-symbolic role: in a decade that saw economic stagnation, acquiescence to predatory US neoliberal policies, and a famine that killed thousands of people while state forces aided in the burning of grain, Naxalism was viewed by its supporters as an attempt to end neo-feudal forms of exploitation among India's largely rural population and set it on the path to agricultural modernization and autocentered economic development. In his 1974 study, Biplab Dasgupta stressed this socio-economic basis of the Naxalite movement's popularity: Naxalism expressed, within its fairly narrow scope of activity, a much larger dissatisfaction that a country of "vast scope for establishing large … industrial undertakings" had been relegated to such extreme economic dependency and political stasis.[24]

No doubt, this popular dissatisfaction was expressed in the electoral arena in 1967, when the Congress Party lost its majorities in half of Indian states and Communist-led united-front governments took power in West Bengal and Kerala. But, even at this early stage, the two principal Marxist parties maintained a "subservience to the control of the rural elite," "abandoning the lower classes in practical terms" while enjoying lower-class votes thanks to clientele networks controlled by the dominant peasantry.[25] To the adivasis, students, and urban, petit-bourgeois elements who constituted its leadership, Naxalism represented the possibility of seizing and cultivating land that electoral parties would never redistribute, despite hollow talk about land reform. It also represented the networking of nonstate "liberated zones" such as those established in the original Naxalbari uprising in 1967, which saw the establishment of village committees to take over schools and the organization of nonstate judicial organs. The goal of this agrarian revolution was to jump-start the Indian economy by means of a socio-political process similar to that of neighboring China, which evolved from an impoverished colonial dependency to an emerging world power within only a few decades.

The Naxalite movement therefore embodied a model of *modernization* that promised an alternative both to Western capitalism and to the Soviet state. By the 1960s, both the United States and the USSR were heavily invested in the Indian economy, with the United States swaying India into ceasing all trade with Vietnam and Cuba, liberalizing its imports, accepting foreign ownership of Indian industries, and devaluing the rupee, and the Soviet Union using India as a major export market for its capital goods and armaments industries. At this time, the Naxalites were the only political organization in India to describe their country as "a neo-colony of U.S. imperialism and Soviet socio-imperialism,"[26] and to propose a model of economic modernization external to this combined regime of capitalist and state-communist underdevelopment.

As Samir Amin notes in a recent collection devoted to the Naxalite movement, this model of modernization diverged both from free-market ideologies of development and from the Marxism of the Second International, which postulated that "all societies had to first pass through a stage of capitalist development ... before being able to aspire to socialism."[27] By imitating the Chinese model, the Naxalites hoped, simultaneously, to break with neo-feudal property relations in the countryside and implement a project of autocentered industrialization under the rubric of collective ownership. Domestically, their party program called for "abolish[ing] the caste system, remov[ing] all social inequalities and all discrimination on religious grounds and guarantee[ing] equality status for women."[28] And globally, they saw themselves as part of a new kind of internationalism, remote from US-controlled institutions and Soviet social imperialism – based instead on "the national liberation struggle of the colonial people surg[ing] forward like a torrent throughout Asia, Africa and Latin America."[29]

All the same, as Roy herself notes, it is difficult to imagine that the Naxalites, if ever they acceded to power, could avoid the statist pitfalls of

Stalinist Russia and Maoist China, with their history of purges and mass executions. In fact, she suggests that it is only as a nonstate force that the Naxalites can be imagined as part of a democratic project. In *Walking with the Comrades*, she notes that "when the Party is a suitor wooing the people, attentive to their every need, then it genuinely is a People's Party. But after the Revolution how easily this love affair can turn into a bitter marriage. How easily the People's Army can turn upon the people" (*WC* 122). In Roy's literary imagination, then, the Naxalites represent not so much an empirical guerilla organization in a specific phase of struggle as a socio-political impulse toward forms of nonstate modernization and internationalism that are still almost impossible to conceive in contemporary neoliberal India.

This is how the "Naxalite anger" that surrounds Rahel and Estha in *The God of Small Things* should be interpreted. It isn't that of actual insurgents – it couldn't be, since during this phase of their activity the Naxalites limited their efforts to armed campaigns in the countryside and had no program of economic struggle such as that conducted by the paddy workers in Roy's novel. Instead, the Naxalite edge to the demonstration expresses a more general anger over social inequality and economic violence that cannot be expressed in electoral terms, and which is shared by urban workers, landless peasants, students, and petit-bourgeois sympathizers alike. As Roy also stresses, this anger is shared by touchable and Untouchable demonstrators who are marching together – a flouting of caste divisions that has a "Naxalite" quality as well. Whereas institutional Communism in Kerala "never overtly questioned the traditional values of a caste-ridden, extremely traditional community" (*GOST* 64), Naxalism in its various manifestations had always stood for militant cross-caste organizing in the service of India's most marginalized populations. In this context, then, "Naxalite," though it literally refers to Maoist-inspired revolutionaries and their state-syntonic worldview, evokes more generalized forms of social anger that have no place in the language of electoral parties, and which, of necessity, activate nonstate imaginations of political activity.

Interrupting the cosmopolitan fantasies of Rahel and Estha's family with this Naxalite anger is Roy's way of demonstrating the social and economic impasses that ordinary Indians confront in the state-sponsored itinerary that is supposed to usher in India as an equal player in globalized regimes of accumulation. Ever since the 1950s, Indian development economists have stressed that land reform is the most urgent precondition of their country's economic modernization. In the words of D. Narayana and Raman Mahadevan, "it is no coincidence that the greater part of southern and western India that came under the raiyatwari tenure system during the colonial period," which recognized the legal proprietorship of all registered holders of land, comprises "precisely the regions that have experienced relatively better growth in the post-independence period" – the more democratic nature of land ownership making possible a "trajectory of capital accumulation" that was "more broad-based and heterogeneous."[30]

On points such as these, Naxalite theorists are in perfect accord with mainstream Indian development theory. But while Congress and CPI party leaders, with their deep ties to jotdar constituencies, indefinitely postponed meaningful land reform, Naxalites proposed to effect it forcibly through nonstate means.

It's at this complicated nexus of Indian developmental politics and nonstate insurgency that Chacko's somewhat depressing, billboard-porting car stands. The pickle factory whose products it advertises is exactly the kind of small-scale, labor-intensive industry that could most benefit from agricultural modernization and transform itself into an engine of "bottom-up" growth. As the authors of the South Commission's Draft Report argue, "small-scale industries … are by definition more employment generating (or labor intensive) than very large scale industries because their technologies are linear" – therefore, they "do more to widen the base of the technological arts than the giant large scale industries."[31] This, in turn, generates a local consumption base that allows industry to develop, since "as income grows," it allows "the production structure [to change] due to changes in income elasticities of demand in favour of manufactured goods."[32] Moreover, this is precisely the regime of production for domestic consumption that the Left Democratic Front proposed in Kerala, beginning in the late 1960s – the exact time and place of the cosmopolitan impasse Roy stages in *The God of Small Things*.

And yet, Chacko's advertisement-carrying car is left to idle tragically in front of a "BE INDIAN, BUY INDIAN" sign, during the exact period in which the state-sponsored, people-centered planning agenda in Kerala is imploding. Before long, his half-British daughter, the emblem of his own cosmopolitan aspirations, will die; his sister will die in exile, ostracized because of an affair she has with Velutha (one of Chacko's factory employees); and his factory will be abandoned, destined to house only some dilapidated machinery and a barn owl.

Chacko's ruin, the ruin of his sister, the ruin of Rahel and Estha, and the much more violent ruin of Velutha all presage the ruin of a modernization project that implicates not only India's nascent developmental bourgeoisie but also the country's most radical attempt at land reform, nonstate political organization, and the removal of caste distinctions and women's oppression – an attempt expressed through the "Naxalite anger" in Roy's narrative. *The God of Small Things* is, in this sense, a traumatized, desperate insistence on the viability of this modernization project, against all odds, and in the context of a neoliberal political climate that, since 1991, seems bent on replaying the 1960s-era economic programs that Roy represents in her novel – only on a far more expansive scale.

So how does Roy imagine this modernization project, outside of the institutional Communists who evade it and the bourgeois who fail it?

The migration of a "Naxalite" nonstate political imagination into urban areas – among factory workers, Untouchables, and even sectors of the petit-bourgeoisie, is what Roy stages in the social-symbolic layering of her novel. This is most obvious in the role that Velutha, as a Naxalite activist and an Untouchable factory worker, comes to assume in her narrative. Velutha, who has a brilliant engineer's mind, who "mended radios, clocks, water pumps" and "knew more about the machines in the factory than anyone else" (*GOST* 72) represents exactly the kind of local initiative and technical competence that development theorists had hoped to harness as part of a social program of "bottom-up" development. Moreover, he works at exactly the kind of infant, high-employment-generating industry that is so often the victim of monopoly-focused, neoliberal development models. Velutha's affair with the factory owner's sister, which, tellingly, begins with a series of engineering acts – he devises intricate toy windmills and boats for her pleasure – is thus not Roy's way of coating over rigid caste distinctions with a sentimental gloss. It is her way of evoking locally-based forms of self-development that could constitute an alternative to India's current path of state-based, neoliberal economic restructuring – an alternative that Roy can imagine taking shape only in a nonstate atmosphere of cross-caste alliances and extra-legal formations.[33]

If this sounds far-fetched, look at how Roy describes Velutha and Ammu's first sexual encounter: "As he rose from the dark river and walked up the stone steps, she saw that the world they stood in was his. That he belonged to it. That it belonged to him. The water. The mud. The trees. The fish. The stars. He moved so easily through it. As she watched him she understood the quality of his beauty. How his labor had shaped him. How the wood he fashioned had fashioned him. Each plank he planed, each nail he drove, each thing he made had molded him" (*GOST* 316). In this peculiarly Marxist variety of eroticism, Velutha is simultaneously a locally-embedded force of the rural environment and a self-developing power in the urban world of the factory – a capacity for self-shaping reflected back on itself and developing itself through its activity. Because of this capacity for all-sided development, Velutha attains an almost godlike stature in the novel, serving both as a neo-modernist agricultural deity whose birthmark, like a lucky leaf, "made the Monsoons come on time" (*GOST* 70) and as a representative of the human potential activated by industrialization.[34]

However, this capacity to bridge rural and urban self-development, this ability to absorb and develop local forms of know-how, is stifled in the novel – held back by caste divisions, class oppression, and neoliberal socio-economic paradigms. Velutha's dangerous and socially placeless affair with Ammu is thus a way of imagining the liquidation of these blockages by fiat, ahead of the socio-political development arc modern India has set for itself and outside any "reasonable" rubric of caste desegregation and social policy. There is something "Naxalite" about it, in its insistence on cross-caste relationships and models of self-development that have no place in state institutions or their policies. This is strangely in keeping with the ways in which Naxalism itself is often described as a "love affair" between the urban petit-bourgeoisie, who make up much of its cadre, and rural populations of adivasis and peasants. Public intellectuals have exhausted themselves trying to account for the strange attraction that has caused "bright" medical students and intellectuals to head to the countryside and attempt to bring about land reform by force of arms. The attraction has been described as a "tryst" and a "seduction" of late, and has even spawned a novel entitled *Romance of a Naxalite*.[35]

What Arundhati Roy suggests is that this "foolish romance" is the product of impatience with a history of underdevelopment in India that dates back to the British Raj, and which persists in the contemporary Indian state's refusal to implement meaningful, broad-based moderni-zation initiatives in the countryside, except in isolated examples such as Operation Barga and some land reforms carried out in Andra Pradesh, both political responses to Naxalite operations (*WC* 199). The "romance" of Naxalism is a product of this political crisis – of the sense that the human potential of India's population can be developed only in nonstate space, through nonstate political instruments and nonstate strategies.

The image of Velutha as a socio-political bridge, conveying nonstate geographies of struggle from the countryside to the heart of Kerala's struggling infant industries is, no doubt, "unrealistic." How could nonstate forms of rural self-government ever be politically reconciled with a mass-based urban development regime in the current political cli-mate? How could a militia movement like the Naxalites ever be imagined as part of a broad-based movement for sustainable change? The African

National Congress (ANC), which did effect exactly this kind of transition, is an inappropriate model, according to one recent theorist, as the Naxalites lack the "moral, political and popular mandate" possessed by the ANC in South Africa.[36] Even Roy balks at the image of the Naxalites assuming a broader leadership role in India, citing their "doctrinal inflexibility, their reputed inability to countenance dissent, or work with other political formations" (*WC* 208).

*The God of Small Things*, then, does not offer a program of mass-based change encompassing rural and urban India, nor does it "recommend" Naxalism as a solution to India's endemic poverty and neoliberal agenda. Instead, it registers a profound dissatisfaction with institutional Communism and with certain forms of cosmopolitan discourse, and then institutes a highly flexible process of phenomenological layering in an attempt to imagine a nonstate internationalism that could counteract India's current path of neoliberal social engineering. The focal point of this nonstate imagination is not really Velutha and Ammu's romance, but the vast panoply of social forces that are brought together in this conjuncture, in all of their conflictuality and dissonance.

Contemplate, for example, the fact that Ammu and Velutha's desire for each other is awakened in the midst of a "Blue army" of discontented workers who are staging a work stoppage that has emptied Chacko's factory. As the Untouchable man and the landlady admire each other's qualities, Estha ruminates in the empty factory, idly stirring its vats, which have been transformed into appropriate raw material by the workers' collective exit. Opining that he and Rahel "just might" have to become Communists, Estha carries the Marxist flag that was foisted upon their great aunt during the demonstration and runs away from home, establishing a "Mobile Republic" on the bank of the Meenachil river, in the exact location Ammu and Velutha use for their first tryst.

This innocent reinvention of communism by Estha and Rahel, in a nonstate space of their own design, quite literally prepares a place for Velutha and Ammu: they first bed down in the clearing that the children opened up earlier that day when they moved an aging boat to establish their communist "Mobile Republic." An affair so shot through with images of striking workers, abandoned machinery, nonstate space, and remobilized communisms obviously has nothing to do with narrative sentimentality or the "easy personal solutions [that] are offered for intractable social conflicts," as Aijaz Ahmad has described it.[37] Instead, the erotic encounter is a speculative instrument that Roy uses to imagine all the untapped capacities of India's underclass coming alive and developing themselves within the orbit of properties, affects, and infrastructures that are imagined to be the sole possession of its industrial bourgeoisie.

Recall that Velutha is the only character who really knows how to run and repair the industrial infrastructure that belongs to Chacko; Velutha "knew more about the machines in the factory than anyone else" (72). Likewise, Velutha is able to enter into and respond creatively to the vernacular, Malayalam-centered world of Rahel and Estha far more effectively than Chacko, their Oxford-educated, Anglophile guardian. In other words, Velutha possesses all the dynamism, potential, and scope that is supposed to be the property of the developmental bourgeoisie – he "belongs to" its infrastructures, its technics, and even its local expressive cultures far more than Chacko does. All that Velutha lacks is access to the clientele networks and systems of favoritism from which Chacko benefits due to his proximity to the personnel of the Communist-run state. This proves decisive in the end, as Velutha is turned away by the self-seeking Communist leader, Comrade Pillai, when he seeks help after his affair with Ammu is revealed – a betrayal that leads directly to his death at the hands of the police.

This complex plotting positions the Untouchable, Naxalite Velutha as a force of ingenuity and indigenous self-development far more dynamic than the postcolonial bourgeoisie – but one that is stifled by the patronage networks that bind the Communist state to the Indian business class. Rahel and Estha's adoption of Velutha's Naxalite brand of communism, however, sets up an intriguing counterfactual situation: what if the indigenous modernization project Velutha embodies were developed outside of the clientelistic inertia of the Indian state? Is it possible to imagine a new generation of Indians developing nonstate spaces of self-development, based not on neoliberal doctrines or party chauvinism, but on local networks of power and decision-making?[38]

It is through such a process, almost unimaginable in the current neoliberal conjuncture in India, that Roy imagines the erasure of caste blockages and class divisions that have prevailed in India for so long. Such a nonstate internationalism, she suggests, may come not from NGO projects or Western-backed liberalization programs, but from fiercely local battles waged against local power brokers who administer the social logic in which caste oppression, clientelism, and economic stagnation are perpetuated.

This perspective radically challenges the cosmopolitan project in the ways it has been conceived in the past. It is an internationalist vision that cannot be administratively implemented, one that cannot be brought into being through "universal" instruments, human rights bodies, capitalist development initiatives, or global forums. It is territorially based, in the sense that it is articulated first through national and subnational struggles, and transnational only by virtue of a long detour through which local, mass-based struggles lead to new modernization paradigms and new forms of nonstate internationalism. Roy gestures toward this new kind of internationalism when she describes the necessity of rediscovering a politics external to both capitalism and Communism – an imagination that, at the same time, resides in "people who go to battle every day to protect their forests, their mountains and their rivers" (*WC* 213–14).

Such a project belongs to a futural political imagination, in the sense that neither the Naxalite insurgents, nor the global justice movement, nor the multiple nonstate agents of the developing world possess insurrectionary capabilities or mass-based international political organs capable of realizing it.

But this futural imagination has a long history. Nonstate internationalism is not an innovation of the last decade or so. It was the most powerful political idea of the twentieth century – though its history was quickly muffled beneath the statist communisms that came to act in its name. The global justice movement, with its sensitivity to local power networks, minority subjects, and immigrant populations, is beginning to recover questions about locality and internationalism that belong to a largely forgotten history of early-twentieth-century political inquiry.

Claude McKay is one of the most powerful literary voices of this forgotten history, both in the rigor with which he thinks through the position of minority subjects and immigrant populations within the politics of internationalism and in his articulation of local power networks of workers and the unemployed. Works like *Banjo*, *The Negroes in America*, *Harlem: Negro Metropolis*, and *Amiable with Big Teeth*, in this sense, belong to the same speculative universe as *The God of Small Things*, in that they are attempting to imagine a nonstate internationalism that is almost unimaginable in their contemporary political conjuncture.

But how does McKay imagine such a nonstate internationalism? How does his work offer alternatives to current debates about cosmopolitanism and transnational governance?

### Black Self-Organization

Let's begin by reflecting on the remarkable contemporaneity of Claude McKay's political position. Long before the Khrushchev report, long before the Soviet imperialist crises in Hungary and Czechoslovakia, long before the collapse of the Soviet Union itself, McKay had been developing a critique of Soviet-style authoritarian communism, and searching for black proletarian political alternatives to it. Like many in the anti-globalization and Occupy movements of the twenty-first century, McKay was attracted to anarchist and syndicalist forms of thought, seeing in them an emphasis on local democratic networks and political autonomy lacking in state-communist political models. And like many contemporary theorists, McKay turns to the transnational as a response to the realities of populations at the margins of national political representation: peasants, metropolitan workers, the colonized, and people of African descent. He is thus intimately concerned with the problem of international and community self-government, but his intellectual commitments and figural devices are very different from much of what is to be found in current debates about cosmopolitanism and transnational governance.

To begin with, McKay holds out little hope that any "ethical" cosmopolitanism, disconnected from mass bases of power and self-government, could end the forms of hierarchy and domination he witnessed in Jamaica, the United States, and France. Instead, McKay develops a political vision in which race-based organizations, workers' councils, and municipal labor organizations would constitute a transnational network of nonstate self-government.

This project for international self-government places McKay within the orbit of what Cheah calls "socialist cosmopolitanism," and such scholars as Greta Le Seur, William J. Maxwell, Mark I. Solomon, Gary Edward Holcomb, and Winston James firmly establish McKay's intimate relationship with socialist and communist forms of thought.[39] Nevertheless, McKay always maintained a critical distance from institutional Communism, expressing reservations about political centralization and the dangers of authoritarian rule. McKay never joined the Communist Party, and instead joined the anarcho-syndicalist IWW, which insisted that immediately recallable worker-delegates could occupy executive functions within an international system of self-government, without introducing the class hierarchies that stubbornly persisted in authoritarian communist regimes.

All of this points to the fact that McKay's internationalism in the 1920s was not identical to that of the Communist International, but was instead a complex amalgamation of anarchism, syndicalism, and black nationalism. Little has been written about this dimension of McKay's thought. Kathryne V. Lindberg notes that McKay was "influenced by the rhetoric and direct action of Syndicalism"[40] and Gary Edward Holcolm refers to McKay's *Banjo* as a "queer black anarchist manifesto."[41]

In what follows, I would like to add to these eloquent critical voices by opening up an inquiry into McKay's nonstate internationalism. Like other nonstate internationalists of the early twentieth century, McKay registers his distance from institutional Communism in various ways, but remains committed to a non-hierarchical model of international self-government, viewing democracy not as a disembedded process, administered by a permanent caste of professional politicians, but rather as a process of shaping participation in workplaces, communities, and social production as a whole. Realizing that such forms of self-government could never sustain themselves in isolation from transnational currents of migration and wealth, McKay tries to imagine a framework for the democratic integration of transnational constituencies, while at the same time rejecting the idea that parties, politburos, and unrecallable central committees could serve this integrative function without relapsing into authoritarian forms of governance. What makes McKay a nonstate internationalist is precisely this suspicion of unregulated central direction and his attempts to imagine forms of delegation, referral, and self-regulation that allow directive control to be rooted permanently and inalienably in local democratic communities.

In what follows, I analyze McKay's 1929 novel *Banjo* in the context of his participation in debates over local autonomy and self-government that are rooted in the political nexus of nonstate internationalism. My argument is three-fold. First, I argue that McKay's representations of transnational patterns of interaction do not celebrate any administratively implementable cosmopolitan ethic of humanitarianism, tolerance, or hybridity. Instead, they are partial examples of an as yet unrealized political project, in which specifically African-descended subjects establish self-organized, racial structures of proletarian democracy within a larger multi-ethnic international.

Second, I argue that this vision of black self-organization, while related in some ways to black nationalism, points much more emphatically to forms of black autonomy within a larger, decentralized framework of global self-government, whose closest analogues are the kinds of collectivist anarchism and syndicalism articulated by nonstate internationalists. Finally, I argue that the group dynamics in *Banjo* evoke the rudimentary structures of local negotiation that would constitute the building blocks of any decentralized, global democracy along nonstate internationalist lines. McKay explicitly juxtaposes the circulation of ideas and know-how among the vagabonds of Marseilles with the circulation of commodities on the longshore in order to evoke powers of judgment, creation, and self-organization that are currently trapped within the commodity-form, expressing themselves only virtually in the fluidity and multiversality of global flows of wealth. Staging scenarios in which diasporic Africans reappropriate these powers of judgment, creation, and self-organization in concrete, local negotiations, but with a plasticity and scope that rivals that of global capital itself, is McKay's way of imagining a futural, postcapitalist political form, in which local racial affiliations and labor networks become sites of transnational democratic agency, while at the same time remaining embedded within community networks and ethnic solidarities.

To understand how McKay imagines such a mutual imbrication of the global and the local, and how this image of locally-embedded transnational self-government differs from some of our contemporary fantasies about transnational governance and cosmopolitan subjectivity, we should first examine the models of political internationalism and local autonomy McKay mobilizes in his work.

### Anarchism and the Negro Bund

About halfway through *Banjo*, we are introduced to the character who most richly embodies McKay's dissident internationalism, a Haitian intellectual named Ray who fraternizes with the group of proletarian beachcombers whose collective life *Banjo* chronicles. Ray reads the socialist paper *Humanité* and describes himself as a revolutionary with proletarian politics. But the more Ray mixes in the "rude anarchy of the lives of the black boys – loafing, singing, bumming, playing, dancing, loving, working," the more they seem to embody "the irrepressible exuberance and legendary vitality of the black race," which Ray worries might suffer "under the ever tightening mechanical organization of modern life."[42] In other words, despite his socialist internationalism, Ray is concerned about the mechanism and centralism of currently existing forms of socialism. His travels, and especially his travels to Africa, which allow him to "observ[e] and appreciat[e] the differences of human groups" alert him to the fact that "just as what was helpful for one man might be injurious to another, so it might be with whole communities of peoples" (*B* 325).

This concern for black autonomy causes Ray to reject the socialism of what he calls the "Nordic philosophers": "He did not think the blacks would come very happily under the super-mechanical Anglo-Saxon-controlled world society of Mr. H. G. Wells. They might shuffle along, but without much happiness, in the world of Bernard Shaw" (*B* 325). He then concludes his meditation by suggesting that black people would perhaps "have their best chance in a world influenced by the thought of a Bertrand

Russell, where brakes were clamped on the machine with a few screws loose and some nuts fallen off" (*B* 325). This is an important addition, since it signals Ray's alignment with a tradition of dissident internationalism, in which local, semi-autonomous networks form the basis of a global system of self-government.

McKay's attraction to Russell's model of self-government lies in its fusion of anarchism, with its emphasis on local autonomy, and socialism, with its vision of international solidarity and economic coordination. As Russell points out in *Proposed Roads to Freedom*, "modern Anarchism … is associated with belief in the communal ownership of land and capital," and thus in terms of "the *economic* organization of society … does not differ from that which is sought by Socialists."[43] Where anarchism and socialism differ is primarily in their sense of the democratic model that could secure this condition of communal economic control and prevent it from giving rise to new forms of hierarchy and domination. On this score, Russell prefers the democratic model of syndicalist anarchism, with its vision of locally self-governing industries, linked by regional decision-making bodies staffed by elected and recallable rank-and-file delegates from the locals. In Russell's opinion, this model of self-government is superior to statist socialism, which threatens to reinstate "the remoteness of the seat of government from many of the constituencies" – a condition in which "legislators live in comfort, protected by thick walls and innumerable policemen from the voice of the mob," and in which these legislators come to feel it "an essential part of statesmanship to consider what are called the interests of the community as a whole, rather than those of some discontented group," with "interests of the community as a whole" being defined vaguely enough "to be easily seen to coincide with self-interest."[44] Russell's solution to this problem is to "[allow] self-government" not just to industrial councils, but "to every important group within a nation in all matters that affect that group much more than they affect the rest of the community."[45] He concludes that "the government of a group, chosen by the group, will be far more in touch with its constituents, far more conscious of their interests, than a remote Parliament nominally representing the whole country."[46]

It is easy to see why McKay was attracted to this model of anarchist self-government. It explicitly refers to "subordinate nations or groups"[47] as constituencies entitled to self-government, and thus roots itself in the kinds of African diasporic networks that McKay would like to see included in an international framework of self-government. It is a political vision that McKay often articulates in relation to the idea of a "Negro *Bund* "[48] – his vision of a radical, self-organized workers' organization modeled on the Jewish Bund, which would form an autonomous element within an international network of workers' organizations.

In a conversation with Karl Radek and in an informational pamphlet written for the Third International, McKay describes the Jewish Bund, in its relationship with the Communist International, as a model for black diasporans to follow. In *The Negroes in America*, McKay suggests that a movement "similar to the Jewish Bund in Russia," but organized by Negroes, is already evidenced by "the rise of such organizations as the Friends of Negro Freedom ... and the African Blood Brotherhood (among whose members are some communists)."[49] And in an article for the *Jewish Frontier*, McKay goes further, arguing that "wherever a distinct group of people is living together, such a people should utilize their collective brains and energy for the intensive cultivation and development of themselves, culturally, politically and economically."[50] In this connection, McKay mentions Jewish Youth organizations, the Jewish Historical Society, the Jewish Publications Society, Jewish Physical Culture, the Jewish Legion, Jewish War Veterans, the Jewish Occupation Committee, as well as "Jewish hotels, theaters, clubs, stores, printing establishments, colleges and hospitals" as examples that should be followed by diasporic Africans.[51]

As I will explain momentarily, McKay's emphasis on cultural and economic development certainly owes something to the black nationalism of Marcus Garvey. But McKay's image of a self-organized black cultural and political bloc is a vision of political agency that extends well beyond the entrenched hierarchies and business ethic of Garveyite nationalism. McKay's references to the Jewish Bund are especially instructive in this respect, since the Bund exhibited a mode of racial organization fundamentally different from that of Garvey's Universal Negro Improvement Association (UNIA). The General Jewish Labor Bund was a socialist labor organization and an international organ of racial self-defense and cultural development. But in 1905 and 1917 it was also an actively revolutionary force, mobilizing tens of thousands of workers to occupy factories and reorganize them along collectivist lines. As a consequence, the Bund came to assume the status of a political personage, with functions and rights within the Third International similar to those of the workers' councils.

While McKay was working for Sylvia Pankhurst's radical periodical *The Workers' Dreadnought*, she published an article in the paper that clearly showed the unique status of the Bund in the Soviet International. Reproducing a document originally published in *Pravda*, Pankhurst's article outlined the regulations governing the election of rank-and-file delegates to citywide workers' councils in the Soviet International. For example, local workplaces employing up to 500 workers were entitled to send one rank-and-file delegate to the citywide council, and "those employing over 500 [to] send one representative for every 500 men."[52] But it was not just local factory councils that were represented in the citywide council. Trade unions were also entitled to send a number of deputies that was proportional to their membership, and non-Russian political organizations were also allotted seats at the citywide council. The Jewish Bund is listed as one of the non-factory-based political organizations entitled to representation in the International, along with the Polish Socialist Party (Left), the Polish and Lithuanian Social Democratic Party, the Lettish Social Democratic Party, and the Jewish Social Democratic Party.[53]

In other words, in 1918, the power base of revolutionary democracy was a patchwork phenomenon, with race-based organizations such as the Bund being accorded political representation along the same lines as the revolutionary factory councils and the trade unions. This was a source of discontent for Lenin, Trotsky, and the young Stalin, all of whom sought to centralize decision-making power in the hands of the Bolsheviks, fearing that provisions for the "national-cultural autonomy" of Jews would promote distrust and conflict among the working class as a whole. In a 1903 essay entitled "The Position of the Bund in the Party," Lenin makes this clear, arguing that the Jewish organizational autonomy endorsed by the Bund "runs counter to the interest of the Jewish proletariat, for it fosters among them, directly or indirectly, a spirit hostile to assimilation, the spirit of the 'ghetto.'"[54] Similar language appears in Stalin's 1913 *Marxism and the National and Colonial Question*, written under the guidance of Lenin: "It is to be expected that the Bund will take another 'forward step' and demand the right to observe all the ancient Hebrew holidays ... The maintenance of everything Jewish, the preservation of *all* national peculiarities of the Jews, even those that are patently noxious to the proletariat, the isolation of the Jews from everything non-Jewish, even the establishment of special hospitals – that is the level to which the Bund has sunk."[55]

In his *History of the Russian Revolution*, Trotsky explains how this position does not contradict Lenin's support for the right of nations to self-determination: the right to self-determination consists only in the right to *secession*, the right to resist "the forcible retention of this or that nationality within the boundaries of the general state."[56] Nevertheless, "within the framework of the party" itself, "Bolshevism insisted upon a rigid centralism, implacably warring against every taint of nationalism which might set the workers one against the other or disunite them."[57]

McKay clearly objects to this "rigid centralism," favoring instead organizational models featuring the kind of counterbalanced political forces
that existed in the Third International in 1918, before the majority Bundists
were organizationally absorbed into the Communist Party. The political
structure outlined in Pankhurst's article, in which autonomous racial
groups and local labor organizations would be integrated into the structure
of political self-government, as coherent voting blocs able to oppose legislation not in their collective interests, corresponded much more closely to
McKay's political ideal. Such a political model allowed McKay to imagine
that organizations for racial self-defense and labor action such as the
Friends of Negro Freedom and the African Blood Brotherhood could be
part of a "Negro Bund," functioning as autonomous racial blocs within a
larger international framework of self-government.

This political perspective owes something to black nationalism and
something to socialism, but its suspicion of centralization and authoritarian leadership reflects, more than anything, the strong anarchist strain
within the tradition of dissident internationalism.

Indeed, it was precisely their critiques of authoritarian communist
leadership and their emphasis on mass self-organization that caused the
internationalists of the *Workers' Dreadnought* to be associated with anarchism by Lenin. While McKay was working for the *Workers' Dreadnought*
in 1920, Lenin critiqued the paper's contributors in his pamphlet *Left-
Wing Communism: An Infantile Disorder* for their tendency to support
mass self-government much more strongly than the kind of parliamentary
compromises and shifting allegiances performed by the Bolshevik party.
*The Workers' Dreadnought* published Lenin's pamphlet in its entirety, as well
as a lengthy serial rebuttal by Herman Gorter. Gorter's "semi-anarchist"
insistence that "an ever greater mass [take] things in hand – a mass that is
conscious of its responsibilities, that searches, propagates, fights, strives,
reflects, considers, dares, and carries out" clearly found a strong complementary vibration within McKay's own mass-based literary imagination.[58]
In fact, when McKay uses the term "anarchy," it is synonymous not with
"chaos" or mass confusion, but precisely with the forms of collective self-
organization that Gorter and Pankhurst stress, and which McKay experienced first-hand in the African Blood Brotherhood.[59]

For example, in the passage from *Banjo* above about the "rude anarchy"
of the beach boys, "anarchy" is a predicate of "loafing, singing, bumming,
playing, dancing, loving, working" – in other words, "anarchy" corresponds
to life processes that achieve order through spontaneous contact and vital
negotiation, rather than through a superimposed form of order. This is

why the term appears again in *Harlem: Negro Metropolis* when McKay is describing the complexly self-adapting dance steps executed by a Harlem sect known as the Divinites. Describing the creation of a vital and self-mediating whole out of a diverse mixture of dance traditions, McKay notes:

> There is anarchy in the movement. In that fervid atmosphere the religious words of the sing-dance fit perfectly the music-hall ditty to which they are adapted. Rampant individual steps punctuate the rhythm. Fragments of every conceivable dance measure whirl about: a rare huddly of Guinea fetishers, an ecstatic Senegalese plunging to the call of the tom-tom, a patter of Moroccan flamenco, an Irish jig, a briefly oblique schottishe, the one-step, the rhumba; altogether they make one glorious variation of all the dances of creation.[60]

One might expect "anarchic" dancing to be vital but inharmonious and filled with collisions. But "anarchy" for McKay means exactly the opposite of this. Adaptation, individual punctuation, the development of a planless whole out of different traditions, the creation of a kinetic international: these are the predicates of "anarchy" for McKay.

However, the kind of anarchism that McKay develops is not just one of spontaneity and planless action. It is one that evolves in a complicated dialectic between local, self-organized initiative and large-scale planning. This is one of the principal positive characteristics of nonstate thinking that nonstate internationalists like McKay and Roy share: the need to imagine a carefully orchestrated political and economic modernization project that could unfold outside the aegis of state bureaucracies, including those of the postcolony. Roy imagines such a project in terms of local, self-governing, Naxalite-esque groups launching the kind of development initiatives that the Indian bourgeoisie is unable to direct because of its refusal to implement land reform and the modernization project it entails.

In McKay's text, it is a question that the political conversations of his characters constantly revolve around – especially *vis-à-vis* the modernization project embodied in Garveyite black nationalism. As Bugsy says of a black saloon keeper who espouses Garveyite ideas, "That saloon-keeper is race talking all the time, and he is robbing his countrymen them, too, giving them more rotten stuff to drink than the white man" (*B* 92). Banjo agrees: "He grabbed his, all right, and growed thin like a mosquito doing it. Look how his cheeks am sunkin'" (*B* 77). Much more than simple *ad hominem* attacks, these comments take aim at the self-serving acquisitiveness that McKay associates with Garveyism and the black business class whose aspirations it voices. In Banjo's philosophical dialect, it represents a political sterility that is akin to sexual sterility: a willed removal of one's sensual and creative energies from the forms of mutual aid his everyday interactions embody.

Ultimately, though, McKay's most successful attempts to imagine a modernization project outside of Garveyite party politics unfold not in conversations between his characters, but through the structural relationship between Ray, who is positioned as an advocate of the large-scale, planned mobilization of social surplus, and Banjo, who embodies much more local initiatives of self-government.

## Diaspora and Self-Government

In the first few pages of *Banjo*, we are introduced to Lincoln Agrippa Daily, nicknamed Banjo, "heaving along from side to side, like a sailor on the unsteady deck of a ship … patroll[ing] the magnificent length of the great breakwater of Marseilles, a banjo in his hand" (*B* 3). Several years earlier, Banjo had renounced his US citizenship and left the southern United States as a sailor on a transatlantic commercial liner. After a circuitous journey that brought him to the ports of London, Alexandria, Istanbul, and Bologna, Banjo arrived in Marseilles, unattached, without a country, and determined to live in the moment. His unsteady stride belongs to this transitory existence, as if the rhythm of his life on the beaches and byways of Marseilles had something of the unsteadiness of transatlantic sea travel. Even his casual search of the breakwater for errant food containers is described in nautical terms, as a deck patrol aimed at identifying and remedying threats to the security and seaworthiness of the ship.

This first glimpse of Banjo is of a man immersed in the vagaries of his hand-to-mouth existence, but who nevertheless possesses a practical competence that allows him to navigate his transitory existence with skill. Banjo's first experience on the beach reflects his attunement to the engineering of material processes and human relationships. From his vantage point on the breakwater, Banjo suddenly sees "black bodies dropping" out of "the bottom of one of the many freight cars along the quay" (*B* 3). He is immediately intrigued by the practical implications of the scene. Had the rail jumpers made holes in the bottom of the car, reengineering it so as to make their escape with ease? Or had they simply seized upon and repurposed an existing design element of the train? He approaches the strangers and asks them about what he has just seen, adding that he had never come across a boxcar with a hole in the bottom in all of his hoboing in the United States. The leader of the gang replies "P'raps not. They's things ovah here diffarant from things ovah theah and they's things ovah theah diffarant from things ovah heah. Now the way things am setting with me, this heah hole-in-the-bottom box car is just *the* thing for us" (*B* 4). Impressed with the man's rhetorical inventiveness, Banjo replies "You done deliver you'self of a mouthful that sure sounds perfect" (*B* 4). The rail jumper responds "I always does. Got to use mah judgment all the time with these fellahs heah" (*B* 4).

Compare this scene to the first glimpse we have of Ray – a Haitian intellectual living among the transnational proletarian groups whose collective life McKay's novel chronicles. McKay's most autobiographical character, Ray mixes with the itinerant groups of African-descended characters he meets in the port city of Marseilles. However, Ray is separate from the proletarians' "loose, instinctive way of living" (*B* 319) and has an approach to life that is more intellectualistic and detached than theirs. Whereas we see Banjo and his gang developing everyday technologies to reappropriate goods on the waterfront, Ray is often to be found rhapsodizing in a much more abstract way about the global commercial flows that pass through Marseilles on a daily basis:

> He loved the docks ... There any day he might meet with picturesque proletarians from far waters whose names were warm with romance: the Caribbean, the Gulf of Guinea, the Persian Gulf, the Bay of Bengal, the China Seas, the Indian Archipelago. And, oh, the earthy mingled smells of the docks! Grain from Canada, rice from India, rubber from Congo, tea from China, brown sugar from Cuba, bananas from Guinea, lumber from the Soudan, coffee from Brazil, skins from the Argentine, palm-oil from Nigeria, pimento from Jamaica, wool from Australia, oranges from Spain and oranges from Jerusalem. In piled-up boxes, bags, and barrels, some broken, dropping their stuff on the docks, reposing in the warm odor of their rich perfumes – the fine harvest of all the lands of the earth. (*B* 67)

How can we explain the ecstatic tone of this passage, which seems to position Ray as an uncritical celebrant of the pleasures of global trade? Strangest of all is the aestheticizing attitude Ray adopts when he eventually does begin to imagine the working conditions of laborers in the African diaspora: "Eternal creatures of the warm soil, digging, plucking for the Occident world its exotic nourishment of life, under the whip, under the terror. Barrels ... bags ... boxes ... Full of the wonderful things of life" (*B* 67). For a contemporary reader, it is extremely difficult to imagine how Ray's attitude toward the "wonderful things of life" here can be reconciled with his knowledge of the whipped bodies of the colonized laborers who are producing them. Such an attitude is even more difficult to explain on the part of a character who, like McKay, aligns himself explicitly with revolutionary proletarian politics. How are we to make sense of this?

The first thing to note is that Ray's reverie takes place in a world in which the production of goods has been completely subsumed and conditioned by the production of surplus value. In Marx's terms, "the value-creating possibility, the realization [*Verwertung*] which lies as a possibility within [the worker], now likewise exists as surplus value, surplus product, in a word as capital, as master over living labor capacity, as value endowed with its own might and will," confronting him in his abstract, object-less, purely subjective poverty."[61] This comprehensive abstraction of the workers' creative energy is visible in the disarticulated signifiers of locales and commodities McKay lists in the passage above. But what of the "possibility" alluded to in Marx's passage? What of his alternative vision of wealth, imaginatively stripped of "the limited bourgeois form" and visible as "the universality of individual needs, capacities, pleasures, productive forces, etc., created through universal exchange … the absolute working-out of [humanity's] creative potentialities"?[62]

In *Banjo,* this possibility is visible at first only as an elision: "Barrels … bags … boxes …" McKay's ellipses suggest some excess existing beyond the tightly contained goods on the breakwater and the policed bodies that produced them. This excess is visible in the breaches of the containers "dropping their stuff on the docks," displaying a mass of goods ready to be appropriated by beachcombers like Banjo and Malty.[63] This sensually appropriable "stuff," which disseminates itself in excess of private property regulations, is a clear cognate of Banjo's "joy stuff" – a term he uses to encompass his musical and intellectual virtuosity, his powers of consumption, his sexual vitality, his ability to disseminate aesthetic pleasure, and his ability to respond productively to the creative energies of his audience. The dock scene therefore envisages the productive powers and creative virtuosity of a global network of producers escaping from the commodified roles to which they are annexed and combining with one another in an international locale – an imaginary space where social surplus becomes denuded of its "private life" as individually accumulated surplus value.[64]

So does this image celebrate an actually existing political subjectivity – a "spirit of the cosmopolitical community," perhaps, in the process of breaking with the "retrograde ideology" of nationalism and other "territorialized imaginations of identity"?[65]

Not exactly. First, note the image of the creatures of the soil, "digging, plucking for the Occident world." These policed bodies are always visible behind the migrant populations McKay evokes; indeed, they cannot be clearly distinguished from the migrants depicted in this passage, and this is part of McKay's point. As Dipesh Chakrabarty reminds us, "pre- or noncapitalist" regions should not be regarded as completely exterior to capitalism itself; instead, "Marx allows us to read the expression 'not yet' deconstructively as referring to a process of deferral internal to the very being (that is, logic) of capital."[66] This is because, as David Harvey makes clear, forms of naked domination and direct coercion are not exterior to capitalism's "purely economic" forms of surplus value extraction – they are, in fact, part of a process of accumulation by dispossession, in which influxes of "cheaper labour power, raw materials, low-cost land, and the like"[67] are forcibly created, allowing continued accumulation even in the face of stagnant effective demand in core, industrialized regions. In addition to this violent abstraction of local labor power into globalized circuits of capital, there is another kind of "difference-with capital" to which Chakrabarty points, and which constitutes "the ground of constant resistance to capital."[68] He locates this resistance in Marx's conception of living labor as "the excess that capital, for all its disciplinary procedures, always needs but can never quite control or domesticate," and which is embodied in "the person-cum-laborer's bodily habits, in unself-conscious collective practices, in his or her reflexes about what it means to relate – as a human being and together with other human beings in the given envir-onment – to objects in the world."[69]

For Chakrabarty, the upshot of this confrontation between living labor and "the process of abstraction that is constitutive of the category of labor" is a constant "translation" that "constitutes the condition of possibility for the globalization of capital across diverse, porous, and conflicting his-tories of human belonging" – not a "beyond of capital," but a constant negotiation between the universalism of capital and the particularity of locally-embedded, living contexts of experience.[70] McKay illustrates a sim-ilar tension between local contexts of experience and global capital flows, which Chakrabarty's insights about abstract labor are extremely helpful in elucidating. But McKay's speculative horizon is, undoubtedly, a *beyond of capital*. What he envisions is not so much a negotiation between global capital and local contexts of experience – his images of the whip, the terror, invoke a space in which *non-negotiables* predominate – as a perspective from which the circulating values of global capital could be viewed as the abstract body of a political subject currently prevented from emerging through sheer applications of force. The ecstasy of Ray's reverie is easier to understand from this perspective; he is not imagining a guilty, negotiated settlement between the "wonderful things of life" and the whipped bodies of colonized laborers. He is imagining another global horizon, in which human populations have the same kind of mobility and multiversality that commodities have – where surplus value, which can move freely about the globe in large part because those who produce it are forcibly prevented from doing so, can be glimpsed as an appropriate social surplus, available to new combinations and new dispersions.[71]

Obviously, this post-statal world did not exist in McKay's time, just as it does not exist in ours. McKay's Marseilles, like Ray's reverie about social surplus, is therefore not an image of actually existing cosmopolitan subjects nor of punctually realizable migratory politics. It is an image of workers who still bear the traces of agricultural life, traditional cultures, and the terror of the plantation, developing robust but politically incomplete models of self-organization in a political space where capital has eroded many of the traditional rituals and communal ties of agricultural life. In representing this transitional space, McKay is profoundly interested in what Chakrabarty calls the "unself-conscious collective practices" that belong to the life-processes of workers. But McKay does not stage a *negotiation* between his migrants' unconscious social reflexes and the Enlightenment universals that constitute the "categorical structure"[72] of global capital. Instead, he projects a political horizon in which social reflexes, forms of association – the entire terrain of collective habits and practices Chakrabarty refers to – condense in self-organizational structures and contend for the kind of comprehensiveness and directive force that currently belong to capital alone.

Banjo, in this sense, embodies the self-organizational practices that could transform the raw social surplus of Ray's rhapsody into a transnationally mediated structure of political and economic self-administration. Consider, for example, that when Banjo patrols the breakwater, he is searching for errant commodities, bags, or boxes of comestibles that have been diverted from their intended destination – foodstuffs that have, in a sense, "escaped" from the circuit of capitalist production and consumption, and in which he can share. But, strangely, he performs this act of reconnaissance as if he were on deck patrol on a commercial liner, where one of his duties would be to check on the integrity of whatever deck cargo his ship might be carrying. Banjo stands at the intersection of these two models of the commodity: as well-guarded private property, on one hand, and as a mass of appropriable use-values on the other. And it seems somehow appropriate that the next image in the passage is that of human bodies "escaping" from shipping containers and conversing with Banjo, as if to evoke the human capacities for creation, judgment, and organization concealed within the commodity form. This clearly evokes what Brent Edwards refers to as *Banjo*'s "attempts to locate what eludes or exceeds the logic of capitalist civilization."[73] But what is the exact relationship between commodities, human productive powers, and modes of political organization in this passage?

In his autobiography, *A Long Way from Home*, McKay indicates that he trained himself in Marx's ideas in order to keep up with the "Socialists, Communists, anarchists, syndicalists, one-big-unionists and trade unionists, soap-boxers, poetasters, scribblers, [and] editors of little radical sheets" whom he met at the International Club in London from 1919 to 1921.[74] But the first Marxist McKay came to know was a Harlem intellectual named Hubert Harrison, whose combination of black nationalism, socialism, and anarchism is closely related to McKay's own. Harrison advocated a program of Negro self-determination, with an emphasis on disciplined intellectual training, personal development, and mutual aid. But, like McKay, he emphasized the need for local efforts at community development to link up with international socialist movements. His range of intellectual reference reflects this eclecticism. In opposing a Negro delegation to the Paris Peace Congress, he mentions the stern treatment Marx, Lenin, and two anarchists – Peter Kropotkin and Errico Malatesta – suffered at the hands of the French authorities, and in a column he edited for *New Negro*, entitled "Our Little Library," he recommends Kropotkin's anarchist tract *Mutual Aid*, alongside books like Edward Wilmot Blyden's *African Life and Customs* and Sir Sidney Olivier's *White Capital and Coloured Labor*.[75] McKay's political attitude would be similarly eclectic, borrowing from black nationalism as well as anarchism, syndicalism, and socialism.

No doubt the forms of locally-rooted racial self-organization and mutual aid on display in *Banjo*'s encounter with the rail jumpers owe something to black nationalist forms of self-improvement and community development. They reflect the idea that blacks should "not go begging to the white race either for help, leadership or a program" – the core principle of Garvey's UNIA, which Harrison celebrated in a 1923 article for the *Associated Negro Press*.[76] Similarly, McKay notes with praise "the amazing energy and will to uplift awakened in the Negroes by Garvey."[77] But even while he served as the principal editor of Garvey's *Negro World*, Harrison would denounce the staunch hierarchies and authority worship of Garvey's organization, and McKay would similarly criticize Garvey for his opposition to labor politics of all kinds.[78] By the early 1920s both Harrison and McKay would become members of the anarcho-syndicalist IWW, whose emphasis on workers' self-management and federated locals of black and white workers appealed to their belief in the need for a flexible, international structure in which radical blacks could operate. Ultimately, McKay's political vision in the 1920s and 1930s was of all-black political organs like the Harlem Union and the African Blood Brotherhood relating on an international level to other self-governing locals.

The forms of racial self-organization evoked in *Banjo* are thus the product of an eclectic mix of political tendencies that Harlem intellectuals like McKay and Harrison drew upon in the 1910s and 1920s. Harrison's exhortation "let us go to Africa … study engineering and physics, chemistry and commerce, agriculture and industry … learn more of nitrates, of copper, rubber and electricity; so we will know why Belgium, France, England and Germany want to be in Africa" has the ring of Garvey's back-to-Africa worldview.[79] But note how Harrison appeals directly to a broad base of African Americans ("let *us* go") to develop themselves intellectually and combine their knowledge, in the absence of any top-down organizational structure. This model of self-education draws on the writings of anarchist theorists Francisco Ferrer y Guardia and Peter Kropotkin, who, as Jeffrey B. Perry notes, were important influences on Harrison.[80] Understanding the ways in which such anarchist forms of thought circulated within McKay's immediate intellectual milieu will shed a great deal of light on the decentralized networks and forms of self-organization that McKay represents in *Banjo*.

## Rituals of Association

In 1914 and 1915 Hubert Harrison taught at the Ferrer Center, an educational center organized according to the anarchist principles of Ferrer and Kropotkin. The most important principle of this anarchist pedagogy is what Kropotkin called "integral education," an approach that combines scientific instruction with concrete, hands-on training in invention and manufacture. It is an approach geared toward eliminating the social division of labor between intellectual work and manual work. Under the right political conditions, Kropotkin hoped it could help create a new kind of productive unit: the self-governing factory council, simultaneously responsible for scientific innovations, engineering projects, and the day-to-day manual work of social production. Linking these local, non-hierarchical units on a global level would, Kropotkin hoped, allow former colonies to participate in a decentralized international, in which the global division of labor would be replaced by a regional "variety of pursuits – intellectual, industrial, and agricultural – corresponding to the different capacities of the individual, as well as to the variety of capacities within every human aggregate."[81]

Harrison's model of African American self-education draws on these anarchist themes of self-organization and orientation toward social action. In an essay entitled "Education and the Race," Harrison compares African Americans to Russian workers "in the dark days of ... Czarist despotism," when "loyalty to interests that were opposed to theirs was the prevailing public sentiment of the masses."[82] Through "secret classes of instruction ... knowledge spread, enthusiasm was backed by brains" and "the workingmen of the cities studied the thing they were 'up against,' gauged their own weakness and strength as well as their opponents'," and ultimately swept away the czar's regime in the Russian Revolution.[83] Similarly, African Americans should make use of the "free schools and colleges" that are permitted to exist openly in America, and "become a race of knowledge-getters," mastering "the knowledge that can build ships, bridges, railroads and factories" and "the knowledge which harnesses the invisible forces of the earth and air and water."[84] Harrison's image, in other words, is of African Americans becoming engineers, scientists, and intellectuals not so they might fit in with capitalist America, but so that they might develop what Kropotkin imagines in *Fields, Farms and Factories*: a decision-making power capable of integrating local, industrial self-organization with political self-government on a global scale. At this level of generality, people of African descent would link up internationally with self-governing bodies composed of all the races of the world. Until this becomes possible, however, Harrison believed that self-organization must proceed along racial lines, to maintain "defensive structures of racial self-protection."[85]

This anarchist emphasis on self-organization and self-government is something we repeatedly encounter in McKay's work as well. Banjo's interest in the physical architecture of the breakwater and in the engineering specifications of the railroad cars reflects this black proletarian character's orientation toward the kinds of practical, scientific, and engineering competency for which Harrison advocates. Moreover, it is this spontaneous knowledge-seeking attitude that first causes Banjo and the rail jumpers to galvanize as a group. In a loose and self-organizing educational structure, the rail jumpers teach Banjo how to make the technology of the railway his own, with special attention to the differences between European and American trains. And, as their conversation makes clear, it is questions such as these, involving the technologies of everyday life, that lead to the complexified competencies and decision-making processes of these characters. It is the practical requirements of daily life that promote Malty's organizational competence, in what Kropotkin would see as a mutual interaction between practical exigency and intellectual self-development.

Of course, in this scene, Banjo and the rail jumpers are not literally taking command of the railways or the breakwater; instead, they are developing habits of mind and association that, under changed circumstances, could gear them affectively and practically toward organizational activity of this kind. In essence, they are practicing at the level of affect and micropolitical negotiation modes of activity that have no concrete corollary yet at the level of large-scale praxis. In this way, McKay singles out currents within everyday life where the logic of imaginable regimes of self-government is visible, though in an incomplete way. It is a narrative method that is especially useful to anarchist authors who are faced with the difficulty of providing examples of present human behavior patterns that could plausibly be extended into large-scale forms of self-government. In this respect, McKay, like Harrison, is in dialogue with Peter Kropotkin, much of whose polemical mode is geared toward such forms of partial exemplarity.

Take, for example, the models of self-organization Kropotkin furnishes in *The Conquest of Bread*. The first concerns the regulation of boat traffic in Holland; Kropotkin imagines a "state-loving socialist" asking the following question: without government, "who ... will undertake the regulation of canal traffic in the future society? Should it enter the mind of one of your anarchist 'comrades' to put his barge across a canal and obstruct thousands of boats, who will force him to yield to reason?"[86] In response, Kropotkin points to actually existing nongovernmental syndicates of boatmen, "free associations sprung from the very needs of navigation," which adjust "the right of way for the boats ... by the order of inscription in a navigation register" and which no one is permitted to contravene "under pain of being excluded from the guild."[87] In an ironical vein, Kropotkin notes that these syndicates have spread internationally without having to "wait for a great Bismarck to annex Holland to Germany, and to appoint an Ober Councillor of the General States Canal Navigation ... with a number of gold stripes on his sleeves, corresponding to the length of the title."[88] Instead, "associations have sprung up freely," come to an "international understanding," and recruited "volunteer adherents [which] have nought in common with governments."[89] Similarly, Kropotkin points to the English Lifeboat Association, a "spontaneous movement" composed of "hundreds of local groups ... along the coasts," who, outside of all governmental mechanisms, organized themselves to save the crews of foundering vessels, remunerated only by the "spontaneous subscriptions" of ratepayers.[90]

Like *Banjo*'s opening image of self-organization, these examples are incomplete. They represent only enclaves of free association within a larger capitalist system that conditions their organizational forms. But Kropotkin's method is to point out patterns of mutual aid that currently exist, in whatever form, in order to demonstrate modes of affect, practical competence, and organizational embeddedness that are already part of humanity's ensemble of relational attitudes, and which could be developed much more extensively in a society not organized around hierarchy and private accumulations of wealth.

This approach to political ontology seems to have made a significant impact on McKay. During his visit to the Soviet Union in 1922 and 1923, McKay went so far as to visit the dungeon in which Peter Kropotkin was confined in 1873 until his escape and journey to England in 1876. This homage to Kropotkin – a figure who to Lenin embodied the theoretical incorrectness of all anarchists – is a noteworthy addition to the long retinue of official visits to factories and military bases prepared for McKay by the Soviet government. Indeed, Kropotkin's critique of the Russian Revolution as a triumph of authoritarianism and his concern for Lenin's suppression of the workers' councils are part of a dissident internationalist tradition reflected in McKay's own critiques of authoritarian communism.

In articles he wrote for *Socialist Call* and *New Leader* in 1937 and 1938, McKay condemns the Soviet Union's "government by dictatorship," its support for the "indefensible imperialistic interests of European nations," its role "along with the Nazis and Fascists, in helping to destroy Democracy in Spain," its opportunistic relationship to African American workers, and its "criminal slandering and persecution" of those "who have remained faithful to the true traditions of radicalism and liberalism."[91] This list of criticisms is revealing, in that it stems not from an allegiance to status quo American anticommunism, but rather from a tradition of critique defined by dissident Marxism, anarchism, syndicalism, and Left Communism – in short, a tradition of dissident internationalism. Note McKay's reference to Spain, which points to Stalin's liquidation of the self-governing anarchist collectives and independent Marxist and anarchist militias: self-organizing groups to which McKay ascribes the possibility for genuine "Democracy." Note also McKay's reference to the impending Second World War as an expression of Europe's imperialist ambitions – not a popular view among liberals, conservatives, or orthodox Communists during this period. Finally, note that McKay's critique of Communism is based on its opportunism toward African Americans – the fact that, to avoid precipitating a revolt of white workers, the Communists avoided demanding that they "make places for colored workers," limiting themselves to "an abstract crusade against Segregation and Race Prejudice, with fraternal contact as a proof of their sincerity."[92] But this does not turn McKay against radical labor agitation. Even as late as his 1940 *Harlem: Negro Metropolis*, McKay advocates for local, self-organized black unions such as the Negro Industrial Alliance, the Afro-American Federation of Labor, the Harlem Labor Union, the Harlem Artists' Guild, and the Metropolitan Guild as instruments of "self-development and community autonomy" for African Americans.[93]

All of this confirms the fact that McKay is criticizing Soviet Russia from a radical standpoint – from the position of workers' networks, minority organizations, and self-governing collectives that McKay believes are capable of administering democracy without aid from centralized organs such as the Comintern. Indeed, the title of McKay's article for *Socialist Call* is "I Believe in the Social Revolution and the Triumph of Workers' Democracy." In 1937 the idea that a movement for workers' democracy must be resumed outside of the aegis of the Communist Party – that organs of democratic self-government should be organized and directed by workers themselves – was common only in the world of dissident internationalism. McKay moved in this world, with its many overlapping circles, rubbing shoulders with figures like Daniel De Leon, Sylvia Pankhurst, Herman Gorter, and Bill Haywood. But he never aligned himself with any of the anarchist, syndicalist, or Left Communist movements in a permanent way. Instead, he appropriated and rewrote elements of this theoretical tradition to develop an autonomous vision of black proletarian self-organization.

## Figures of Self-Development

Turning back to *Banjo* with these models of self-organization in mind, it is easier to see why Banjo's and Ray's encounters are so often staged against the backdrop of global commerce. Ray's Marxist intellectualism is able to project the cosmopolitanism of global trade as an abstract terrain of social surplus – during their first walk together, Ray guides Banjo to a prospect from which cargo ships can be viewed, abstractly, as "little splashes of many colors bunched together" (*B* 70), just as their last stroll together is among "the boxes and barrels and the loading and unloading of ships", about which Ray exclaims to himself "Commerce! Of all the words the most magical" (*B* 307). But it is Banjo who embodies the structures of mutual aid which alone allow Ray to imagine this immense social surplus within the context of a political project of self-government. Ultimately, Ray is too far removed from these forms of group-formation to serve as a fitting emblem of proletarian self-organization. Accordingly, his relationship with Banjo should be characterized not so much as a process of complementary political education as a gradual permeation of Ray's abstract theories with the concrete structures of mutual aid which Banjo embodies. Banjo and the other proletarians on the dock "possessed more potential power for racial salvation" (B 322), from Ray's perspective, than did black intellectuals and Garveyites, precisely because their everyday praxis is organized not around state-syntonic economic accumulation and business acumen, but around forms of group association that, to Ray, possess a proto-political structure: "In no other port had he ever seen congregated such a picturesque variety of Negroes … *It was as if every country of the world where Negroes lived had sent representatives drifting in to Marseilles.* A great vagabond host of jungle-like Negroes trying to scrape a temporary existence from the macadamized surface of this great Provençal port" (B 68, emphasis mine).

McKay's evocation here of "jungle-like" Negroes arriving at the center of capitalist commerce is essential, because it skips, in a very pointed way, the intermediate phase so often associated with cosmopolitan models of subjectivity – namely, the development of a native bourgeoisie and the forms of statecraft that are its corollary. One of the best ways to account for the positive dimensions of both McKay's and Roy's politics, in fact, is to register the depth of their critique of comprador bourgeoisies, and the creativity with which they imagine mass-based political alternatives to them. Long before Frantz Fanon's critique of the comprador bourgeoisie, which focuses on its tendency simply to take over the "business offices and commercial houses formerly occupied by the settlers … identif[ying] itself with the Western bourgeoisie" (B 152–3), McKay noted the "enthusiasm of the bourgeoisie of decolonizing nations for exploiting their own people."[94] And long after the golden age of decolonization, Roy reminds us of the Indian bourgeoisie's role in handing over "the land of millions of people … to private corporations … for Special Economic Zones (SEZs), infrastructure projects, dams, highways, car manufacture, chemical hubs, and Formula One racing."[95]

Reading back and forth between these two imaginative moments allows us to reconstruct a literary problematic that centers not so much on practices associated with the postcolonial state as on a longer, even more thorny, historico-literary complex, in which nonstate alternatives to elite governance in the colonial and postcolonial world take center stage. For both McKay and Roy, this means imagining a political subject that can insert itself directly into modernization projects and apparatuses of self-government, without the mediation of national bourgeoisies or the communist parties that so often act as agents of state accumulation in their own right. This is why both *Banjo* and *The God of Small Things*, so far removed in space and time, center on figures of self-development, remote from state-centric processes of governance, yet possessed of many-sided capacities for social mediation that seem to rival those of capital itself: Banjo, who boasts that his "self-makings" (*B* 303) exceed those of the black nationalist character Goosey, and Velutha, whose engineer's mind has all the vitality and capacity for creative evolution that the middle-class industrialist Chacko lacks.

Of course, McKay's and Roy's narratives belong to very different political environments and geospatial intersections, and the nonstate imaginings they offer differ in many respects. The casual and semi-anonymous technologies of encounter and cooperation employed by Banjo and the rail jumpers are an "example" of an internationalism in which decision-making power would be continually referred back to the organizational know-how of local, nonstate agents rather than being focalized through fetishized leadership figures – they therefore stage a scenario in which structures of political belonging are the product of portable technologies of cooperation and self-defense, rather than the result of party edicts or a territorial national mythos, and are in this sense much closer to the porous, semi-anonymous, administrative locals of anarchist and syndicalist internationalism than to nationalist models of sovereignty. Roy's literary geography, by contrast, is organized around the territorially-based insurgencies of Naxalite militants, and the possibility that such a nonstate political protagonist could jump-start a project of development and self-government left deliquescent by the national bourgeoisie and its Communist allies. Note, however, how failures of state-centric governance lead both McKay and Roy not to pre-capitalist fantasies of rural community life, but to affirmative politics based on the modernization projects and broadened forms of political organization their nonstate politics make imaginable.

This is a good way to account for the positive nonstate political imagination that evolves out of the century-long cosmopolitan impasse addressed by both McKay and Roy. It is an imagination that is nonstate not because of any simple investment in pre-state organic communities, but because of its vision of development projects and mechanisms of self-government directed by forces outside of the failed postcolonial bourgeoisie – the class that, as

McKay put it in 1921, "chafe[s] under the foreign bit because it prevents them from using to the full their native talent for exploiting their own people."[96]

If we can imagine the "world" in world literature not in terms of actually existing ethical communities, but in terms of precisely these kinds of speculation about new modes of democratic practice, then it becomes easier to see how McKay and Roy both contribute to a world literature problematic that affiliates very different historical moments and geographical locations. This affiliation is based not on genealogies of literary-historical prestige but rather on a shared attempt to project, in discontinuous and geographically specific ways, a new kind of political "self" as the substrate of self-government in the Global South. That this "self" belongs neither to the state apparatuses of the postcolonial bourgeoisie nor to the corporate persons of multinational NGOs and donor agencies renders it illegible within many of our current discourses on transnationality, oscillating as they so often do between nationalist state-building and the "universal" values that supposedly animate institutions of cosmopolitan humanitarianism.

World literature, as I hope I've shown, can disrupt rigid theoretical frames such as these by revealing potentialities for self-government that exist within the actual social worlds of the Global South, but which achieve self-definition only in the inexistent, futurally-oriented worlds that literary works are able to construct. In this chapter, I have brought such potentialities to light by focusing on the systems of self-rule evolved by economic migrants, workers, and indigenous insurgents, and conceiving of these as part of a nonstate modernization project that links the Asian subcontinent to the black Atlantic by way of an intricate world-literary itinerary. In the next chapter, we will pursue yet another world literature problematic that radicalizes the future-oriented capacities of world literature, locating nonstate space within the potentialities for self-government that evolve over the *longue durée* of world-systemic change and capitalist crisis.

### Notes

1  Richard Fidler, "Guadeloupe: General Strike Scores Victory, Spreads to Other Colonies," *Green Left Weekly*, March 13, 2009. www.greenleft.org.au/content/guadeloupe-general-strike-scores-victory-spreads-other-colonies.

2  Rosa Moussaoui, "Le LKP lance une nouvelle grève," *L'Humanité*, December 15, 2010. www.humanite.fr/16_12_2010-le-lkp-lance-une-nouvelle-grève-460268.

3  Craig Calhoun, "The Class Consciousness of Frequent Travelers: Towards a Critique of Actually Existing Cosmopolitanism," in Daniele Archibugi, ed., *Debating Cosmopolitics* (London: Verso, 2003), 92.

4  *Ibid.*, 112, 98.

5  Calhoun, for example, mentions David Held, who looks to a futural form of cosmopolitanism in which people "would be citizens of their immediate political communities, and of the wider regional and global networks which impacted upon their lives" (David Held, *Democracy and the Global Order* [Cambridge: Cambridge University Press, 1995], 233. Cited in Calhoun, "The Class Consciousness"). See also Selya Benhabib, *Another Cosmopolitanism* (Oxford: Oxford University Press, 2006); Partha Chatterjee, *The Politics of the Governed: Reflections on Popular Politics in Most of the World* (New York: Columbia University Press, 2004); Amitai Etzioni, *From Empire to Community: A New Approach to International Relations* (New York: Palgrave, 2004); and Pierre Hamel, Henri Lustiger-Thaler, Jan Nederveen Pieterse, and Sasha Roseneil, eds., *Globalization and Social Movements* (New York: Palgrave, 2001).

6  Gayatri Spivak, *A Critique of Postcolonial Reason: Toward a History of the Vanishing Present* (Cambridge: Harvard University Press, 2003), 259.

7  Pheng Cheah, *Spectral Nationality: Passages of Freedom from Kant to Postcolonial Literatures of Liberation* (New York: Columbia University Press, 2004), 312.

8  *Ibid.*, 300.

9  *Ibid.*, 301, 299.

10  *Ibid.*, 351.

11  Chandler levels a strong criticism of the models of international justice and "humanitarian intervention" often invoked in cosmopolitan theory. Especially forceful is his critique of the pseudo-impartiality of the Hague War Crimes Tribunal, which indicted Croatian-Serb leader Milan Martić for the use of rockets bearing cluster munitions against Zagreb, the Croatian capital, but which ignored NATO's "making military targets of city bridges, factories, marketplaces, residential neighborhoods and TV studios, with slight or no military value," as well as NATO's own use of cluster bombs in their attack on Niš in May 1999 (David Chandler, "International Justice," in Daniele Archibugi, ed., *Debating Cosmopolitics* [London: Verso, 2003], 35). Nevertheless, Chandler holds to a model of international law based on interstate regulations, whereas dissident internationalism looks beyond the state form for its models of political regulation.

12  Timothy Brennan, "Cosmopolitanism and Internationalism," *New Left Review,* 7 (January–February 2001), 81.

13  *Ibid.*, 77.

14  Perry Anderson, "Internationalism: A Breviary," *New Left Review,* 14 (March–April 2002), 11.

15  *Ibid.*, 24, 23.

16  Claude McKay, *A Long Way from Home* (New York: Harcourt, Brace & World, 1970), 162, 164. Fittingly, what turned the tide of party opinion in favor of McKay was a mass-based phenomenon – a "spontaneous upsurging of folk feeling" for him – which the party leadership decided to exploit for its propaganda value (*Ibid.*, 167).

17  Claude McKay, *The Passion of Claude McKay: Selected Poetry and Prose, 1912–1948,* ed. Wayne F. Cooper (New York: Schocken, 1973), 227.

18  *Ibid.*

19  Arundhati Roy, *Walking with the Comrades* (New York: Penguin, 2011), 214. Hereafter cited as *WC.*

20  Arundhati Roy, *Capitalism: A Ghost Story* (Chicago: Haymarket Books, 2014), 96.

21  Arundhati Roy, *The God of Small Things* (New York: Harper, 1997), 35. Hereafter cited as *GOST.*

22  Alex Tickell's observation in this context that "the family group confined in the foreign, socially contained space of the sky-blue Plymouth could be seen as a fitting analogy for the creative situation of the postcolonial author," is therefore astute (see Alex Tickell, "*The God of Small Things*: Arundhati Roy's Postcolonial Cosmopolitanism," *The Journal of Commonwealth Literature,* 38:1 [2003], 74). What I add to his analysis is the sense that this scene, in addition to emblematizing Roy's own anxieties about her positioning *vis-à-vis* the English-speaking world, stages the more generalized difficulties confronting postcolonial India in its attempts to realize the dreams of economic development and transnational cooperation that are part of the cosmopolitan ideal.

23  As Pranav Jani accurately notes, the criticism of institutional communism in *The God of Small Things* is "*not* the same as the anticommunism prevalent among post-Cold War elites," but is in fact "a marker of its leftist politics" (Pranav Jani, "Beyond 'Anticommunism': The Progressive Politics of *The God of Small Things*," in Ranjan Ghosh and Antonia Navarro-Tejero, eds., *Globalizing Dissent: Essays on Arundhati Roy* [New York: Routledge, 2009], 59, 49). Critics such as Nagesh Rao, Priyamvada Gopal, and Akin Adesokan have all helped to correct this misperception, seeing in Roy's work, alternately, a "'radical cosmopolitanism' ... closer to, although not identical with, a form of Marxist internationalism" (Nagesh Rao, "The Politics of Genre and the Rhetoric of Radical Cosmopolitanism; or, Who's Afraid of Arundhati Roy?," *Prose Studies,* 30:2 [2008], 169), a critique of a "postcolonial national democracy that ... act[s] like a colonizing power toward large sections of its citizenry" (Priyamvada Gopal, "Concerning Maoism: Fanon, Revolutionary Violence, and Postcolonial India," *South Atlantic Quarterly,* 112:1 [2013], 117), and a rejection of once-radical figures of anti-imperialist struggle who, once in power, foster unresponsive "governmental bureaucracies" (Akin Adesokan, *Postcolonial Artists and Global Aesthetics* [Bloomington: Indiana University Press, 2011], 172).

24  Biplab Dasgupta, *The Naxalite Movement* (Bombay: Allied Publishers, 1974), 211.

25  Ross Mallick, *Indian Communism: Opposition, Collaboration and Institutionalization* (Delhi: Oxford University Press, 1994), 14.

26  Dasgupta, *The Naxalite Movement,* 143.

27  Samir Amin, "What Maoism Has Contributed," in Santosh Paul, ed., *The Maoist Movement in India: Perspectives and Counterperspectives* (London: Routledge, 2013), 18.

28  Dasgupta, *The Naxalite Movement,* 146.

29  *Ibid.,* 142.

30 D. Narayan and Raman Mahadevan, "Introduction," in D. Narayan and Raman Mahadevan, eds., *Shaping India: Economic Change in Historical Perspective* (London: Routledge, 2011), 12–13.

31 See Vijay Prashad, *The Poorer Nations: A Possible History of the Global South* (London: Verso, 2012), 131.

32 P. M. Mathew, "The Industrial Stagnation of Kerala: Some Alternative Explanations," in B. A. Prakash, ed., *Kerala's Economic Development: Issues and Problems* (New Delhi: Sage Publications, 1999), 287.

33 This reading dovetails nicely with Yumna Siddiqi's interpretation of Velutha as "an antithesis to the vision of the state" (Yumna Siddiqi, *Anxieties of Empire and the Fiction of Intrigue* [New York: Columbia University Press, 2008], 174) and Anuradha Dingwaney Needham's highlighting of the "resistant properties" of this "oppressed subaltern subject" as "the motors of social, disciplinary, and epistemological transformation" (Anuradha Dingwaney Needham, "'The Small Voice of History' in Arundhati Roy's *The God of Small Things,*" *Interventions: International Journal of Postcolonial Studies,* 7:3 [2005], 370). What I would add to this is that Velutha's externality to statist optics and elite structures of power does not mean he is external to a vision of modernization and development, conceived according to Roy's nonstate imagination. So, while Velutha may embody "a certain nostalgia for the pre-colonial" according to Miriam Nandi's excellent analysis, Roy's uniting him with a representative of the failing developmental bourgeoisie represents not so much an attempted return to an impossible lost origin as socio-symbolic speculation about how socially generative potency such as Velutha's – Siddiqi calls it *metis*, referencing James C. Scott's idea of a "practical intuitiveness … outside the rationality of the state" (*Anxieties of Empire*, 174) – could participate in a form of nonstate modernization (see Miriam Nandi, "Longing for the Lost (M)other – Postcolonial Ambivalences in Arundhati Roy's *The God of Small Things,*" *Journal of Postcolonial Writing,* 46:2 [2010], 184).

34 In this sense, Devon Campbell-Hall is right to note that Velutha illustrates "the empowering possibilities of specialist manual skills in the battle to overcome social inequalities" (see Devon Campbell-Hall, "Dangerous Artisans: Anarchic Labour in Michael Ondaatje's *The English Patient* and *Anil's Ghost* and Arundhati Roy's *The God of Small Things,*" *World Literature Written in English,* 40:1 [2002–2003], 44). However, rather than seeing in this image of the skilled laborer a "rejection of international trends towards globalization" (42), I see it as an image of exactly the kind of bottom-up initiative that could fuel a project of alter-development and allow India to survive as an autocentered economy in a globalized world.

35 See C. V. Murali, *Dreams Die Young: A Student's Tryst with the Naxalite Movement* (Bombay: Frog Books, 2007) and Khademul Islam, who writes that "Bengal … was seduced by the siren song of the Maoists, a seduction that in practice meant CPI(M) for a time was simultaneously a party of elections and legislative compromise as well as attempting to contain radical/extremist factions that disdained those very elections and the corridors of state power"

(Khademul Islam, "Naxal Stories," *The Daily Star*, March 14, 2009. www. thedailystar.net/news-detail-79546).

36  Nirmalangshu Mukherji, *The Maoists in India: Tribals Under Siege* (London: Pluto Press, 2012), 110.

37  Aijaz Ahmad, ""Reading Arundhati Roy Politically," *Frontline*, August 8, 1997, 104–5 (republished in Alex Tickell, ed., *Arundhati Roy's* The God of Small Things [London: Routledge, 2007], 110–19).

38  I therefore agree with J. A. Kearney that the reader is meant to be "deeply moved by an intensified focus on the possible transcending of class and caste boundaries" that characterizes Roy's treatment of Velutha and Ammu's relationship (see J. A. Kearney, "Glimpses of Agency in Arundhati Roy's *The God of Small Things*," *Kunapipi*, 31:1 [2009], 129). What I would add to this is that this relationship is also meant to embody an unimaginable sociopolitical fusion between India's most exploited and marginalized populations and the machinery of development left under-used by the failing developmental bourgeoisie. This fusion is "disnarrated" in Laura Karttunen's sense of the term: it is "presented in the negative mode," in narrative space that the novel gestures toward without traversing, in order to draw attention to the social processes that render such a story impossible in the current context and invite speculation about what alternative possibilities such a story is capable of evoking (Laura Karttunen, "A Sociostylistic Perspective on Negatives and the Disnarrated: Lahiri, Roy, Rushdie," *Partial Answers: Journal of Literature and the History of Ideas*, 6:2 [2008], 435).

39  See Greta LeSeur, *Claude McKay's Marxism* (New York: Garland, 1989); William J. Maxwell, *New Negro, Old Left: African-American Writing and Communism Between the Wars* (New York: Columbia University Press, 1999); Mark I. Solomon, *The Cry Was Unity: Communists and African Americans, 1917–36* (Oxford: University of Mississippi Press, 1998); Gary Edward Holcomb, *Claude McKay, Code Name Sasha* (Gainesville: University Press of Florida, 2007); and Winston James, *A Fierce Hatred of Injustice: Claude McKay's Jamaica and His Poetry of Rebellion* (New York: Verso, 2000).

40  Kathryne V. Lindberg, "Rebels to the Right/Revolution to the Left: Ezra Pound and Claude McKay in 'The Syndicalist Year' of 1912," in *Ezra Pound and African American Modernism*, ed. Michael Coyle (Orono: The National Poetry Foundation, 2001), 12.

41  Holcomb, *Claude McKay*, 147.

42  Claude McKay, *Banjo* (San Diego: Harvest, 1957), 324. Hereafter cited as *B*.

43  Bertrand Russell, *Proposed Roads to Freedom: Socialism, Anarchism and Syndicalism* (New York: Henry Holt, 1919), 35, 54.

44  *Ibid.*, 132–3.

45  *Ibid.*, 133.

46  *Ibid.* Russell, however, does not favor a purely anarchist or syndicalist social structure, and he ultimately argues for a form of Guild Socialism, in which the state is retained "as consisting of the community in their capacity as consumers," while guilds, or workers' councils, would "represent them in their

capacity as producers" (*Proposed Roads*, 83). Presumably, this is why Ray does not wholeheartedly endorse Russell, in whose political vision the machine of state has not been completely dismantled; instead, it has "a few screws loose and some nuts fallen off" (*B* 325).

47 *Proposed Roads*, 83.

48 *A Long Way from Home*, 182.

49 Claude McKay, *The Negroes in America*, trans. Robert J. Winter (Port Washington: National University Publications, 1979), 5.

50 *The Passion of Claude McKay*, 236.

51 *Ibid*. Similarly, in his autobiography, McKay looks to the Finnish Federation and the Russian Federation of America as highly organized voting blocs within the American Communist Party – they are "the most highly organized units of the American party," and because "the representatives of these organizations voted *en bloc*," they outvoted the "Yankee" representatives every time on the question of party legality (*A Long Way from Home*, 177).

52 Sylvia Pankhurst, "Communism and Its Tactics," in Herman Gorter, Sylvia Pankhurst, Anton Pannekoek, and Otto Rühle, *Non-Leninist Marxism: Writings on the Workers Councils* (St. Petersburg: Red and Black Publishers, 2007), 137.

53 *Ibid*.

54 V. I. Lenin, *Nationalism* (Newtown: Resistance Books, 2008), 30.

55 Joseph Stalin, *Marxism and the National and Colonial Question* (London: Lawrence and Wishart, 1936), 50.

56 Leon Trotsky, *History of the Russian Revolution*, trans. Max Eastman (Chicago: Haymarket, 2008), 642.

57 *Ibid*. For an excellent account of the tensions between the Bund and the Bolshevik party, and of the attempt to create a "Sovietized Yiddish culture" (110) by way of party-aligned Jewish Commissariats and Sections external to the Bund, see Zvi Y. Gitelman, *Jewish Nationality and Soviet Politics: The Jewish Sections of the CPSU, 1917–1930* (Princeton: Princeton University Press, 1972), esp. 69–230.

58 Herman Gorter, "Open Letter to Comrade Lenin," in Gorter, Pankhurst, Pannekoek, and Rühle, *Non-Leninist Marxism: Writings on the Workers Councils*, 46.

59 See Winston James, *Holding Aloft the Banner of Ethiopia: Caribbean Radicalism in Early Twentieth-Century America* (London: Verso, 1999), which stresses McKay's organizing role in the African Blood Brotherhood and his service on its Supreme Council. Another point James makes, which is important to my own argument, is that the African Blood Brotherhood was a self-organized group, and not a top-down outgrowth of the American Communist Party.

60 Claude McKay, *Harlem: Negro Metropolis* (New York: E. P. Dutton, 1940), 39–40.

61 Karl Marx, *Grundrisse: Foundations of the Critique of Political Economy*, trans. Martin Nicolaus (London: Penguin, 1973), 453.

62 *Ibid.*, 488.

63  No doubt, McKay's is "an internationalism of the defective: the unregistered, the undocumented, the untracked". Edwards, *The Practice of Diaspora*, 224). (Brent Hayes Edwards, *The Practice of Diaspora: Literature, Translation, and the Rise of Black Internationalism* [Cambridge: Harvard University Press, 2003], 239). What I add to Edwards' excellent readings is the idea that it is also an internationalism of self-organizational processes and micropolitical forms of mutual aid. It is only this combination of international migrancy and local, embedded solidarities that allows McKay to imagine an internationalist alternative to the comprador state.

64  One might observe along with Michael Maiwald ("Race, Capitalism, and the Third-Sex Ideal: Claude McKay's *Home to Harlem* and the Legacy of Edward Carpenter," *MFS Modern Fiction Studies*, 48:4 [2002], 825–57) that Ray, like Jake in *Home to Harlem*, "finds his values outside of surplus value" (838). Does this mean that he also "rejects ... the economic as the central mode of human existence" (*Ibid.*)? Perhaps. But I explore the possibility here that Ray's reveries about trade and even Banjo's associational life point to alternative exchange processes, and alternative *economies*, not just a rejection of the economic writ large.

65  See Sheldon Pollock, Homi K. Bhabha, Carol A. Breckenridge, and Dipesh Chakrabarty, "Cosmopolitanisms," in Carol A. Breckenridge, Sheldon Pollock, Homi K. Bhabha, and Dipesh Chakrabarty, eds., *Cosmopolitanism* (Durham: Duke University Press, 2002), 6, 3.

66  Dipesh Chakrabarty, "Universalism and Belonging in the Logic of Capital," in Carol A. Breckenridge, Sheldon Pollock, Homi K. Bhabha, and Dipesh Chakrabarty, eds., *Cosmopolitanism* (Durham: Duke University Press, 2002), 100.

67  David Harvey, *The New Imperialism* (Oxford: Oxford University Press, 2003), 139.

68  Chakrabarty, "Universalism and Belonging in the Logic of Capital," 100.

69  *Ibid.*, 101–2.

70  *Ibid.*, 95, 106, 107.

71  Myriam J. A. Chancy is thus correct that in passages like these "McKay attempts to transcend his time and to view a future in which the 'Negro' might participate in the world economy" (Myriam J. A. Chancy, "Border Crossings: The Diasporic Travels of Claude McKay and Zora Neale Hurston," in *The Harlem Renaissance Revisited: Politics, Arts, and Letters*, ed. Jeffrey O. G. Ogbar [Baltimore: Johns Hopkins University Press, 2010], 131). My point is that the *agent* of this participation is not an emerging black bourgeoisie but rather the kinds of proletarian network McKay depicts in works like *Banjo*.

72  Chakrabarty, "Universalism and Belonging in the Logic of Capital," 83.

73  *The Practice of Diaspora*, 224. In the same context, Edwards calls attention to *Banjo*'s "fascination with the flotsam and jetsam of life, the goings-on at the margins, the pungent and busy 'wide-open dumps' of whatever any system must reject and extrude in order to function" (*Ibid.*). Since the black culture represented in the novel is a "resistive expression that evades the 'civilizing

machine,'" it "must be denigrated by the civilizing system with words such as 'primitive'" (*Ibid.*). In Edwards' incisive account, it is therefore no surprise that "those denigrated, those violently pushed out, such as the beach boys and Ditch-dwellers in *Banjo*, would claim such terms as their own, as the clearest proof of [their] resistance and resiliency" (*Ibid.*). Edwards therefore arrives at a model of reappropriation that is clearly in dialogue with the forms of political self-organization I analyze here.

74  *A Long Way from Home*, 68.

75  Hubert Harrison, *A Hubert Harrison Reader*, ed. Jeffrey B. Perry (Middletown: Wesleyan University Press, 2001), 210, 128.

76  *Ibid.*, 196.

77  *Harlem: Negro Metropolis*, 177.

78  As Michelle Ann Stephens notes, "McKay denounces the nationalist fiction completely, framing racial diaspora … as an alternative form of black masculinity antithetical to nationalism" (Michelle Ann Stephens, *Black Empire: The Masculine Global Imaginary of Caribbean Intellectuals in the United States, 1914–1962* [Durham: Duke University Press, 2005], 157). Though she does not engage with any of the theories of political decentralization I analyze, she does helpfully point out that McKay is searching for "other forms of black collective organization that could counter the powerful myth of nationhood" (*Ibid.*).

79  *A Hubert Harrison Reader*, 212.

80  Jeffrey B. Perry, "Introduction," in *Ibid.*, 119–20.

81  Peter Kropotkin, *Fields, Factories and Workshops* (New York: G. P. Putnam's Sons, 1913), 22.

82  *A Hubert Harrison Reader*, 122.

83  *Ibid.*, 122–3.

84  *Ibid.*, 125, 123, 123.

85  *Ibid.*, 228.

86  Peter Kropotkin, *The Conquest of Bread and Other Writings*, ed. Marshall S. Shatz (Cambridge: Cambridge University Press, 1995), 121.

87  *Ibid.*

88  *Ibid.*, 122.

89  *Ibid.*

90  *Ibid.*, 123–4

91  *The Passion of Claude McKay*, 228, 231, 228.

92  *Harlem: Negro Metropolis*, 198.

93  *Ibid.*

94  See Claude McKay, "How Black Sees Green and Red," in *The Passion of Claude McKay*, 58.

95  Arundhati Roy, *Capitalism: A Ghost Story* (Chicago: Haymarket Books, 2014), 10.

96  *The Passion of Claude McKay*, 58.

CHAPTER 3

# World Literature as Futurology: Melvin Tolson, T. S. Eliot, and the Poetics of Postcapitalist Governance

In the previous chapter, we examined two authors who, despite their geographical, temporal, and stylistic divergences, both participate in a shared world literature problematic: the attempt to imagine a nonstate internationalism, outside of the liberal internationalism that still fuels many of our debates about transnationality, and outside of the state-sponsored forms of communist internationalism that both Claude McKay and Arundhati Roy forcefully reject. This is a world literature problematic, I argue, neither because McKay and Roy are involved in global networks of literary prestige and canonicity, nor because their work embodies a project of universal humanistic understanding that, on some level, unites the literatures of the world. Both of these conceptions of world literature depend on what the Warwick Research Collective identifies as the "level playing field" thesis: the idea of an actually existing world-literary dialogue, in which writers of the Global South can participate in an atmosphere of friendship and equality.[1] Projecting "world literature" as the site of such a global process of sharing and reciprocity always risks ignoring the profoundly uneven distribution of social wealth and literary agency that currently exists worldwide, by imagining that an elite ethics of tolerance and understanding might compensate, on an ideal level, for the real forms of maldevelopment and neocolonial violence that persist on a global scale.

What if, instead of projecting world literature as the guilty "stand in" for incomplete projects of development and self-governance, we admitted that the concept of world literature belongs to the domain of the "not yet" – that the forms of self-determination and equality to which it is consigned have, as yet, only the most inchoate and precarious existence? World literature in this sense could be envisaged as a futurology, invoked too soon and far too incompletely by the apologetic ethics of global community. McKay and Roy encourage such a view of world literature precisely because of their suspicion about forms of internationalism that belong to the sphere of administratively implementable initiatives. They invite a conception of world literature based not in a canon or an ethos, but in multiple critical itineraries that aggregate works of literature on the basis of their ability to contribute to an archive of interpersonal strategies, techniques of association, and structures of feeling that exceeds a national scale. World literature, in this context, could be viewed as the cognate of a critical practice that views specific, seemingly "particularistic" struggles as part of a global interchange that currently may have few actual participants, but that could be seen, proleptically or counterfactually, as part of a transnational staging exercise.

The two authors I examine in this chapter, Melvin Tolson and T. S. Eliot, radicalize this future-oriented dimension of world literature by attempting to evoke the internal mechanisms of imagined, futural forms of nonstate self-government. Using highly fragmentary modernist techniques of parataxis and abstraction, they track the *longue durée* through which capitalist states develop irremediable crises and open up the possibility of post-state governance on a world scale. Unlike McKay's and Roy's narratives, however, which trace nonstate potentialities with reference to a mélange of contemporary extra-legal actors and proto-political associations, Tolson and Eliot engage in a far more speculative poetic itinerary, in which nonstate organization unfolds in a futural world, after state-sponsored development projects and modes of governance have reached their limits and imploded.

The fact that both Tolson and Eliot deploy extreme forms of modernist technique as part of this literary futurology thus broaches the question – which is surprisingly rarely asked – of what modernism's relationship to world literature is. Given the perplexing and abstract nature of poetry such as Tolson's and Eliot's, can it really be understood as part of a potential archive of socio-cultural practices and strategies?

Jed Esty and Colleen Lye suggest that such forms of modernism really do remain within an isolating technical bubble, "styliz[ing], even heroiz[ing] [their] baked-in failure to map the global system," whereas peripheral realist texts "invite their publics to grasp the world-system, via its local appearances or epiphenomenal effects."[2] No doubt, the magnificent array of scholarship Esty and Lye introduce with this argument proves how potent peripheral realism can be, especially in its capacity to "particularize and localize the laboring body" while at the same time framing it as part of the systemic forces which it mediates.[3] In this respect, peripheral realism should be seen as contributing powerfully to the world literature archive I describe – that palimpsest of knowledge-forms, tactics of self-development, and interhuman affective modes that allows us to measure human modalities of struggle against the effects of underdevelopment.

But, in this chapter, I hope to show that modernisms such as those of Tolson and Eliot do not simply project the capitalist world-system as "abysmal antimatter to literary description itself,"[4] but instead attempt to stage exactly the kind of literary futurology that can describe world-systemic tendencies and effects that may fully emerge only after many decades have passed. Modernist techniques of abstraction and parataxis could be viewed, in this context, as ways of evoking forms of relation and exchange that no ensemble of realistically imaginable characters could currently partake in. So, while I would not argue that all modalities of modernist technique possess this futurally-oriented dimension, in the case of Tolson and Eliot, modernist technique provides a way for counterfactual forms of governance and sociality to be presented simultaneously as a "not yet" and as a potential matrix of associational modes available to sensible intuition.

This is a way to imagine modernist texts as participating in a strong form in the conception of world literature that I outline – that is, as a situational staging exercise that frames even seemingly "local" or incipient social processes as part of an unrealized world-literary excursus. This does not imply, however, any need to broaden our conception of modernism to include all literature that focuses on "mobility, dynamism," and "rapid technological change."[5] The worst consequence of Susan Stanford Friedman's attempt to imagine everything from Tang Dynasty poetry to ceramics of the Abbasid Caliphate as embodying a "modernist" aesthetic is that it attempts to move beyond a Eurocentric conception of modernism by redeploying, on a global scale, a squarely Eurocentric definition of modernism – in other words, one focused on "movement, mobility … dynamism … mixing … innovation", etc.[6] What recent scholars' efforts to map the diversity of global modernisms in fact show us is that modernist technique is just as often mobilized to explore forms of enforced immobility, technological underdevelopment, and rural immiseration as it is to affirm forms of cosmopolitan exchange, industrialization, and urbanization.

Modernism, in this more precise sense, could be grasped as the attempt to register what Mary Louise Pratt calls the "*constitutive* relations between metropolitan modernity, on the one hand, and colonialism, neocolonialism, and slavery on the other hand."[7] I would add that the denaturing of traditional literary style that we associate with modernism must also be historicized along these lines, as a way of registering the uneven consequences of these encounters between colonial modernity and the vast regions of the world that suffer underdevelopment under its sway. Amos Tutuola's deforming of Yoruba folklore, for example, represents a different way of denaturing traditional narrative than the Tammuzi poets' deforming of classical Arabic poetry – even if both of these literary modes register the subsumption of social life by the modern capitalist world-system. All of this is to suggest that attending to the wide variety of locally-inflected forms of modernist practice allows us to see them as participating in specific world-literary problematics, with their own compendia of associational modes and forms of savoir-faire – as opposed to detached forms of experimentation that engage in socially unmarked forms of abstraction.

Approaching the experimentation of Tolson and Eliot with the analytic tools that analyses of global modernisms require allows us to register their extreme ambivalence about the forms of technological development, industrial expansion, and cosmopolitan mobility so often associated with modernisms of the Global North. Neither Tolson nor Eliot is content simply to document the exhilarating mechanical innovations and cosmopolitan lifestyles promoted in the imperial centers of modernity. Instead, their works often unfold as agonized meditations on how combined development, urbanization, and increased social freedoms in some areas have as their corollary industrial stagnation, immobility, and misery in others. At the same time, though, their poetry functions as a speculative instrument, allowing them to imagine how underdeveloped societies, under the full weight of imperial dominance, could harness, in moments of capitalist crisis, the forms of development and renewal denied them by current regimes of imperialist oppression.

This image of an anti-imperialist Eliot, concerned with forms of self-government in the colonial world, is counterintuitive, I know. For this reason, I center my analysis in some surprising passages from *Notes towards the Definition of Culture*, where Eliot advances a form of nonstate thinking characterized by anti-colonial revolt and a process of political self-determination outside of both the Wilsonian and the Communist models of internationalism on offer in the early twentieth century.

This reading is grounded in just two micro-examples on which I focus from "The Waste Land": Countess Marie's puzzling statement that she comes from Lithuania and is therefore "echt deutsch" and the image of Isolde being transported from her native Ireland to a forced marriage with King Mark. Both of these moments from "The Waste Land" possess the selfsame affective tonality that has been revived in the "cosmopolitanism without options" proposed by so many contemporary global governance think tanks. In the former case, Countess Marie's strange posturing is meant to evoke the wheedling attitude the German Empire assumed in its attempt to forge an alliance with Lithuania, a "small nation" that Germany hoped to use to destabilize Russia during World War I. The absurdity of Countess Marie saying that she is, in effect, part of this subject nation simply because of her sympathy for its plight is meant to shock readers out of the kind of imperial cajolery she represents. As Eleanor Cook's incisive reading suggests, World War I was for Eliot a war of rival trading empires with rival economic interests, not a war to liberate subject nations, as it was often billed at the time.[8] An "Eliotic" approach to contemporary governance thinking would, presumably, entail similarly blunt exposés of the crude economic calculus that lies behind its official rhetoric of partnership and cross-cultural understanding.

The image of Isolde resolving, with murderous fierceness, to have her entire ship consumed by waves rather than marry her oppressor, is the counter-image to this affective manipulation that Eliot provides. It is a gesture that occurs in the nonstate space of the sea, and which mobilizes affective resources altogether external to the geopolitical affair of the heart that King Mark proposes. In focusing on an Irish character who chooses to destroy herself rather than bind herself affectively to the despoiler of her people, Eliot offers an affective template for anti-colonial revolt – a revolt which must, from his perspective, annihilate within itself all attachments to the oppressor and prefigure, in its rejection of political maneuvering, a new form of internationalism, outside the elite global reformatting accomplished at Versailles and the Berlin Conference. These micro-examples in "The Waste Land" function as "luminous details," in the Poundian sense – concrete poetic images whose internal logic points beyond official history, toward a transformative grasp of seemingly disconnected phenomena. My analysis of them is not meant somehow to capture the full meaning of "The Waste Land," but rather to gesture in the direction of a new conception of Eliot as a world-literary voice, engaged with the problematics of decolonization and nonstate self-government.

Melvin Tolson is, in many ways, the inheritor of both this aesthetic of decolonization and the highly fragmentary, non-narrative modernist method Eliot helped pioneer – Tolson once even said, vis-à-vis Allen Tate's preface to his own *Libretto for the Republic of Liberia*, "at long last, it seems, a black man has broken into the rank of T. S. Eliot and Tate!"[9] But, as Michael Bérubé, Aldon Nielsen, and Matthew Hart have argued in their excellent analyses, Tolson is much, much more than an "imitator" of Eliotic modernism. Indeed, as Tolson himself notes, "My work is certainly difficult in metaphors, symbols and juxtaposed ideas. There the similarity between me and Eliot separates."[10] Far from exhibiting a "will to assimilation,"[11] Tolson's Afro-Modernism projects those aspects of the New Black

Poetry that Stephen Henderson has described – virtuoso naming and enumerating, metaphysical imagery, compressed and cryptic imagery, and hyperbolic imagery – onto a geopolitical space where they are imagined as nonstate forces of self-development of global scope.[12]

In this sense, Tolson participates in the kind of black internationalism Brent Edwards has in mind when he describes diasporic practices with a "shared logic of collaboration and coordination at a level beyond particular nation-states."[13] But what Tolson adds to this narrative that is so singular is the image of local, racialized populations developing nonstate productive regimes and forms of mutual aid on a scale that would allow them to present a challenge both to the imperial cosmopolitanisms of the Global North and to the nominally communist statism of the Soviet Union. The movement from local, racialized forms of identification to large-scale economic and political power blocs that Tolson envisions is thus not mediated by the kinds of tactical alliances with state communism that Edwards analyzes in his accounts of George Padmore and Tiemoko Garan Kouyaté, nor is it presented as a potential outgrowth of organs of capitalist cosmopolitanism. Instead, Tolson imagines the almost unimaginable process whereby regional industrialization projects and nonstate forms of multilateral political alliance could expand on such a scale that they begin to lay a claim not only to their own material wealth, cultural resources, and exchange processes, but to those of current political hegemons as well – and all this from a position of strength, not as a byproduct of cosmopolitan openness on the part of the Global North.

This geopolitical vision opens up an entirely new kind of poetics, one whose global range of allusions and multi-linguistic complexity stem not from what Arnold Rampersand calls poetic "gentrification"[14] but rather from a futural vision of the material, political, and cultural resources that become available to racialized populations when European culture is provincialized and confronted with emerging power blocs that contest its hegemony. The nonstate dimension of Tolson's poetry is, therefore, not just a mimetic engagement with contemporary diasporic networks and interstate migratory flows, but rather a futural vision of the productive regimes and cultural resources that become available when they are no longer concentrated in states, but are able to circulate according to robust nonstate exchange processes.

What such a nonstate regime of global exchange might look like, concretely, was difficult for Tolson to picture. It would require the kind of military defensive capabilities and political cohesion that the protection of fledgling markets requires, and that have historically been the provenance of state governments, but would eschew the class-stratified forms of accumulation of contemporary states. If such a governance complex is difficult to imagine, it nevertheless belongs to a speculative imagination that, I'd argue, is no more utopian than the forms of cosmopolitan governance that it challenges. Indeed, "nonstate development" is a major watchword of cosmopolitan governance thinking, the fantasy being that direct, investment-bank funding of nonstate entities such as village cooperatives, NGOs, or civil society organizations could stimulate autocentered production and forms of agricultural modernization made impossible by "state failure" or endemic corruption. Truly, nothing could be more utopian than such promises, made by interstate institutions that have been deliberately sabotaging all such forms of autocentered production and agricultural modernization for more than six decades – "development of the periphery" being, in Samir Amin's words, simply "not in capital's interest."[15]

As I'll explain in this chapter, Tolson's images of nonstate political and economic development are directly opposed to the cosmopolitan dreams embodied in such neoliberal "nonstate" partnerships, and in fact take shape punctually as part of the global economic crisis that he saw as their motive force and internal limit. Tolson's poetics thus confronts the cosmopolitan fetish of nonstate actors with something unthinkable from its own perspective: that nonstate development actually could succeed on the scale promised by interstate lending institutions, but only through transnational political alliances outside of the aegis of these organs of capitalist cosmopolitanism.

For Tolson, the Non-Aligned Movement of African and Asian countries represented a preface to this kind of development – a first step in the process whereby postcolonial power blocs could develop themselves, first as autocentered states, then – at some future point – as nonstate mobilizations of workers and peasants, evolving capabilities counter to both the Global North and the comprador bourgeoisies that service them. Tolson's poetic method is to acknowledge the importance of state-based development projects like those of the Non-Aligned Movement, and to reimagine the transnational alliances that they encourage as a template for a futural nonstate project. Precisely because leaders of the Non-Aligned movement such as Nkrumah, Nasser, Nehru, and Sukarno were so invested in state sovereignty, as a counterforce to both US and Soviet forms of underdevelopment, Tolson's own nonstate poetics unfold as a world-literary futurology: an attempt to imagine the world-systemic implications of full economic development on a global scale, both as a limit to capitalist forms of accumulation and as a possible prelude to nonstate governance models.

The kinds of nonstate structures that could emerge from this complex transition were only beginning to come into view for Tolson as he wrote in the 1950s and 1960s. But in many ways his poetry brings such nonstate capabilities into focus even more clearly than our own theories of global governance and the cultural attachés connected to them, despite, or more likely because of, the cachet that ungoverned spaces and nonstate actors have taken on in the discourse of transnationality.[16]

To recapture the sense of nonstate potentiality that Tolson experienced as part of his own era of militant decolonization, let's examine the cosmopolitan impasses he came up against and the ways he wrote around and beyond them.

## Non-Alignment and the Cosmopolitan Problematic

In the first book of his epic poem *Harlem Gallery*, Tolson provides a vivid image of what could be described as the cosmopolitan problematic – that is, a cultural internationalism staged against the backdrop of a "missing" political and economic internationalism. In the absence of such real organs of international self-government, he suggests, the cultural productions of postcolonial nations risk becoming what their economies so often already are: a flow of specialized commodities allowed entrance to Western markets under strict terms, and in a way that does not allow for the full development of the potential they embody. The decolonization movements of Tolson's day promised to interrupt this cycle of dependency; he refers to them *in genere* in his poem as the "Day of Barricades," invoking not only the strikes and street fighting that accompanied the decolonization of many Asian and African countries, but also the protective barricading of postcolonial markets against predatory incursions of Western capital. In this context, Tolson imagines the poet as pursuing a transnational itinerary, gathering up the cultural products of the postcolonial world with a view to alternative forms of exchange – global in scope, but purged of the structural violence of colonial underdevelopment:

> In Africa, in Asia, on the Day
> of Barricades, alarm birds bedevil the Great White World,
> a Buridan's ass – not Balaam's – between no oats and hay.
>
> Sometimes a Roscius as tragedian,
> sometimes a Kean as clown,
> without Sir Henry's flap to shield my neck,
> I travel, from oasis to oasis, man's Saharic up-and-down.

> As a Hambletonian gathers his legs for a leap,
> dead wool and fleece wool
> I have mustered up from hands
> now warm or cold: a full
> rich Indies' cargo;
>
> but often I hear a dry husk-of-locust blues
> descend the tone ladder of a laughing goose,
> syncopating between
> the faggot and the noose:
> "Black Boy, O Black Boy,
> is the port worth the cruise?"[17]

In this passage, Tolson deploys the image of culture as akin to wool – a raw material that must be carefully gathered and worked up into finished, wearable garments. But this poetic value-adding process is somehow derailed in the above passage. The obvious reference to Richard Wright's *Black Boy* signals Tolson's hopes that his transnational journey could build on itself, perhaps taking on a style of militant self-development similar to that which propels Wright's black *Bildungsroman*. But the devastating final line of the passage – "is the port worth the cruise?" – suggests that this transnational process of self-assertion confronts obstacles similar to those that postcolonial economies confront when they become involved in global exchange processes whose basic terms and structures they have not had a part in shaping.[18]

This is where the specter of Eliot emerges in Tolson's poem. "But often I hear a dry husk-of-locust blues" contains a reference, by way of Marvell, to "The Waste Land": "But at my back in a cold blast I hear/The rattle of the bones, and chuckle spread from ear to ear."[19] The image of a locust husk also evokes Eliot's sense of post-World War I European subjectivity as a husk, as in "The Hollow Men," and the many images of locusts, dryness, and infertility in "The Waste Land." Finally, Tolson's image of wool recalls *Notes towards the Definition of Culture*, where Eliot compares culture to wool – something that cannot be "put on ... ready made," since "you must wait for the grass to grow to feed the sheep to give the wool out of which your new coat will be made."[20]

To what extent is Tolson enlisting Eliot as an ally, as a similar diagnostician of geopolitical barrenness and the need for economic and cultural renewal? And to what extent is he critiquing Eliot for complicity with European world dominance, both economically and culturally? The question is central to an understanding of Tolson's poetics, since it is essentially a question about whether the allusiveness, density, and cultural ecumenism of his poetry is part of an internationalist vision that belongs to Eliotic modernism, or whether Tolson evolves entirely new forms of nonstate thinking.

As Michael Levenson argues, "The Waste Land" is fundamentally an "anti-finance poem," preoccupied with the way in which "politics descends into the unsentimental truths of economics."[21] Expanding on this perspective, Paul Stasi has noted that Eliot's poem is shadowed by a global imperialist order that "in the early twentieth century was already transitioning into the financialized forms of today's neo-imperialist order."[22] It makes sense, therefore, to read the image that Tolson echoes – the wind and the rattle of bones that we hear in "The Waste Land" – as an image of suspended wealth, wealth extraneated from a national source and set adrift as finance capital. Eliot, famously, associates this process with a kind of perversion – the chuckle in this passage – but also with the quite practical machinations of financiers, the "loitering heirs of city directors" (*CPP* 42) who have had commerce with the Thames maidens and departed to pursue their own opportunistic course of capital accumulation. The barrenness of the Thames – the "cold blast" and deathly rattle that Tolson cites – is therefore meant to evoke forms of cultural and material generativity that cannot be accessed and potentiated by the people who are their source.

There is much in this image that would appeal to Tolson. He too sees the postcolonial world as being drained of its wealth and suffering a crisis of agency as a result. Crucially, for Tolson this represents a crisis of the postcolonial state – it leads not to a desire to return to a stable, primordial national identity, but rather to a desire to evolve forms of nonstate thinking that could assert themselves with the variability and global reach that the globalization of capital was beginning to take on in his day.

Does Eliot have a positive model of nonstate politics that similarly counters the global reach of international finance capital? If so, how does Tolson borrow, rework, or contest this modernist internationalism? The answer to this question is not as straightforward as it might seem.

In his 1948 *Notes towards the Definition of Culture*, Eliot engages with several different models of internationalism: the liberal internationalism of the League of Nations, the revolutionary internationalism of Trotsky's *Literature and Revolution*, and the state-socialist internationalism of the Marxist political theorist and historian of the Russian Revolution E. H. Carr. Writing in the aftermath of World War II, Eliot indicates that, in the interest of world peace, "we are … pressed to maintain the ideal of a world culture" (*CC* 136), encompassing not merely Europe, but all the cultures of the world. Eliot admits that such a world culture "is something we cannot *imagine*" (*CC* 136) – that "we can only conceive it, as the logical term of relations between cultures" (*CC* 136). Nevertheless, "we must aspire to a common world culture, which will yet not diminish the particularity of the constituent parts" (*CC* 136).

Eliot's is thus in a certain sense a negative internationalism, conceivable but not *imaginable*, and many of his meditations on internationalism consist not of positive prescriptions for an internationalist world order, but rather of warnings against the "zealots of world-government" and their idea that "unity of organization has an absolute value, and that if differences between cultures stand in the way, these must be abolished" (*CC* 135). Eliot's internationalism thus mostly takes shape as a critique of cultural imperialism. Reading this critique today, it is hard not to be struck by the contemporary implications of Eliot's observations. His point is essentially that architects of cosmopolitan world government too often, "without knowing it, take for granted that the final world-culture will be simply an extension of that to which they belong themselves" (*CC* 135). He broaches "the *colonial* problem" (*CC* 137) in this connection, and critiques the British, "with their assurance that their own culture was the best in the world," for imposing their culture on India, which possessed "an ancient tradition of high civilization" (*CC* 138) of its own. Confronted with a culture they could not understand, the British behaved like a person confronted with an unfamiliar human being, who "exert[s] an unconscious pressure on that person to turn him into something that we *can* understand," in the process effecting a "repression and distortion, rather than an improvement" (*CC* 138–9) of that person's personality. Eliot concludes that "no man is good enough to have the right to make another over in his own image" (*CC* 139).

In another passage devoted to "the cultural effects of empire" (*CC* 165), Eliot describes the "piece-meal imposition of a foreign culture," in which "there is at the same time an assertion of superiority and a desire to communicate the way of life upon which that assumed superiority is based; so that the native acquires a taste for western ways, a jealous admiration of material power, and a resentment against his tutors" (*CC* 166). This gives rise to a complex, hybrid state, in which the native "is more conscious of differences" while at the same time "the partial success of westernisation" has "obliterated some of these differences" (*CC* 166).

At this point, however, instead of turning to the numerous anti-colonial revolts that had already arisen from this condition of discontent, Eliot cites the case of pre-World War I Germany as the first in which "culture-consciousness as a means of uniting a nation against other nations was …

exploited" (*CC* 165). For Eliot, Germany's national-cultural revolt becomes a cypher for the anomie and possible national-cultural revolt of a large array of *colonized* nations. Though this is a counterintuitive conceptual maneuver, it makes sense in that Eliot regarded pre-World War I German culture as one that "had developed in the course of a history of extreme, and extremely sub-divided regionalism" (*CC* 133). The scattered statelets of pre-imperial Germany emblematize an international array of regional cultures, whose autonomy Eliot strongly advocates in *Notes towards the Definition of Culture*. For Eliot, the violent self-assertion of German national culture in World War I is the consequence of the failure of the forms of internationalism Eliot is attempting to imagine in *Notes towards the Definition of Culture*. An international order that does not provide for the self-development and autonomy of all national and regional cultures, however small, is an order that promotes violent forms of national self-assertion both in Europe and in the colonial world.

What would it mean to read "The Waste Land" as an attempt to render a viable internationalist project imaginable? That is, to read its images of World War I, international finance, and colonization as the effects of a failed internationalism? Answering this question will help bring into focus the forms of black internationalism in Tolson's own poetry, and the ways in which it both rescripts and distances itself from Eliotic internationalism. The first thing to clear up, then, is an issue that has received less critical attention than one might expect, namely, what is the status of the colonial world in "The Waste Land"?[23]

## Unimaginable Internationalism

In the first two verse paragraphs of "The Waste Land" Eliot evokes four colonial locales in swift succession: Lithuania, Bosnia, Ireland, and India. Lithuania comes first, in Countess Marie Larisch's enigmatic statement that she is from Lithuania and is for that reason authentically German. Bosnia is next, its anti-colonial revolutionaries hanging like a shadow over the Countess' innocent recollections of Archduke Ferdinand – her innocent statement "and down we went" evoking both the assassination of the Imperial archduke by an anti-colonial revolutionary organization and the decline of empires brought about by World War I. Ireland is evoked next, in the strain from Wagner's *Tristan und Isolde* that focuses on the Irish Isolde being forcibly extracted from her homeland. Finally, pervading the scene is the image of impending rainfall, which is strongly tied to the replenishment of the river Ganges in the final section of "The Waste Land."

In the interest of economy, I will mostly focus on the role that Lithuania and Ireland play in the opening lines of "The Waste Land," since these examples will bring into sharp contrast the models of anti-colonial agency we find in Tolson's work. Critics have been baffled by Countess Marie's statement "Bin gar keine Russin, stamm' aus Litauen, echt deutsch" for some time (*CPP* 37).[24] Germans were a minority population in Lithuania and by no means serve as a synecdoche for the ethnic identities of Lithuanians, who are a predominantly Baltic people. The Countess' desire to distance herself from Russia is understandable, as the Austro-Hungarian Empire and Russia were imperial rivals. But why express this rivalry through an imagined identification with a small, colonized state like Lithuania (especially because the Countess was actually born in Germany, not Lithuania)?

Lithuania had been partitioned since the eighteenth century between Imperial Russia and Prussia. But Russia was clearly the imperial hegemon in the area, and, after the Russification policies carried out in the nineteenth century, became the principal target of Lithuanian nationalist agitation. Consequently, when territorial disputes between Germany and Russia began to become exacerbated in the lead-up to World War I, many Lithuanian nationalists sought to ally themselves strategically with Germany against Russia. Bismarck even promised Lithuania independence should Germany emerge victorious from World War I.

This is the background context for Countess Marie's puzzling statement that she is from Lithuania and is therefore "echt deutsch." Being "authentically German" in this context essentially means opposing the imperial designs of Russia – the affective charge placed on "Germanness" in the context belongs to a political project that aligns Germany with the burgeoning ethnic nationalism of Lithuania in the pre-war years. In this passage, "Germanness" means little more than non-Russianness; it is a floating signifier that emerges out of the *fin-de-siècle* wars of position prosecuted by colonial powers. It is less a positive cultural identity than a form of national chauvinism produced in opposition to another imperial power. The fact that Germany had its own imperial designs on Lithuania is concealed beneath an imaginary identification between Germanness and the anti-colonial imagination of Lithuanian nationalists.[25]

This strategic appropriation of anti-colonial ethnic insurgency on the part of imperial hegemons was not unique to Germany in the pre-war period. In fact, Eliot could not have avoided coming into contact with the British version of this peculiar colonial anti-colonialism, whose rhetoric is ubiquitous in publications such as *The New Age*, to which Ezra Pound, T. E. Hulme, and George Bernard Shaw were contributors.

For example, in a 1915 article in *The New Age*, A. S. Rappoport laments the poor treatment that subject nationalities received at the hands of Russia, stressing that "Russia's borderlands ... are inhabited by nationalities who are mostly non-Russians, and who have a distinct existence, a national consciousness, an historical past, a language and a literature of their own, and aspirations for a future."[26] He therefore observes "that the racial consciousness of nationalities reluctantly incorporated in the dominions of the Tsar is a problem of more than passing importance" ("RGF"). In this context, he mentions that Germany is "fomenting dissensions in Russia's borderlands" and asks whether through such alignments "the nationalities" (by which he means the insurgent nationalisms of small countries) might not "become pieces instead of mere pawns on the chessboard" ("RGF"). In this connection, he specifically mentions Lithuanians, who "have remained within their ethnographical limits" for centuries, "who have a language and a literature of their own" and whose "aspirations for an independent future have never disappeared" ("RGF" 372, 371). He even notes that Lithuanians differ racially from Russians, "being fair-haired and blue-eyed," and are, in fact, "practically related to the Prussians, who are to a great extent Slavo-Lithuanian renegades" ("RGF" 372).

This ethnicized alignment of "fair-haired" Lithuanians with German-speaking peoples helps explain Countess Marie's feeling of ethnic solidarity with the anti-colonial insurgents of Lithuania: she is projecting an imaginary ethnoscape in which Germans, physiologically akin to Lithuanians, serve as their protectors against the "semi-Asiatic" imperialists of Russia. This is by no means the only case that Eliot would have been likely to have come across in the pages of *The New Age* in which ethnicized anti-colonial revolt was made use of in imperialist wars of position.

In a 1913 article called "The Ukraine," George Raffalovich argues that Ukrainians are ethnically quite distinct from Russians, describing the "old village customs" they have preserved.[27] He describes their folk music, "filled with a boisterous kind of mirth very characteristic of the Ukrainian temperament," their religious celebration of the feast-days of both Christian saints and "many of the pagan gods of their ancestors," and their folk dances, which exhibit "the Dionysian poetry of a people as unfettered by convention as they are full of imagination."[28] This image of a semi-pagan ethnic Ukrainian is mobilized in order to invite English readers to position themselves as the protectors of Ukrainian national independence against Russia. Raffalovich's article even concludes with a bizarre fantasy about Winston Churchill being offered the crown of Ukraine and ruling it with sensitivity to its cultural uniqueness.

This image of England as another species of empire, sensitive to national differences, is evoked throughout the pages of *The New Age*. Rappoport, for example, contrasts England's "liberal policy" which gains the "loyalty and sympathy of their new subjects" to the ruthless imperialism of Russia.[29] Time and again in *The New Age*, readers are encouraged to imaginatively project themselves into the ethnic traits and folkways of small, insurgent peoples – in other words, to imagine the kinds of transnational affiliations that Countess Marie gives voice to in "The Waste Land." In many ways, Eliot's poem reflects the investment of such journalists in the regional cultures, pagan folkways, and even the carefully described soil types and agricultural habits of subject peoples. And yet, Eliot also sees the investment of imperial powers in the ethnic folkways of subject nationalities for what it is: a cynical attempt to mobilize these populations as pawns in the service of what are little more than inter-imperialist rivalries. Countess Marie's image of ethnic solidarity between Germany and Lithuania is *meant* to sound bizarre to the reader, because Eliot is attempting to expose the political cynicism that lies beneath such romantic imperialist evocations of subject peoples.[30]

The image of Isolde that follows in the next verse paragraph is Eliot's way of imagining a counterforce to such imperialist appropriations. As the Irish Isolde, her native land in ruins, is being forcibly conscripted to wed King Mark, she makes a fateful decision: to kill all aboard her ship. The passage that Eliot chooses to include from Wagner's *Tristan und Isolde* is precisely the one in which she is prompted into this violent opposition. Hearing a sailor's lament for his beloved in Ireland, "Frisch weht der wind/Der Heimat zu,/Mein Irisch Kind,/Wo weilest du?" (*CPP* 38) Isolde misrecognizes these words as a mocking reference to her own condition and forms her deadly intention. Isolde, in short, is the archetypal embodiment of the subject peoples of Eliot's own day – her land, her culture, her folkways have been destroyed through an act of conquest, and yet she is kept alive, appropriated by the conquering power as a signifier of the wealth and productive power of the subject population. Against the Countess Maries of the world, however, who would like to imagine a sentimental ethnic affiliation between colonizer and colonized, Isolde decides to destroy her oppressor, even if it means destroying herself in the process. Confronted with a voice that seems to mock her inaction, her tarrying, Isolde forcibly resists becoming anyone's "Irisch Kind," or perhaps, to pick up on the German word's etymological resonance, anyone's Irish kin.[31]

An image of anti-colonial revolt in "The Waste Land"? The suggestion should not surprise us, given Eliot's warnings about the consequences of colonialism in *Notes towards the Definition of Culture*. Eliot repeatedly reminds the reader of "the damage that has been done to native cultures in the process of imperial expansion" (*CC* 167) and insists that "any vigorous small people wants to preserve its individuality" and will voice "resentment against absorption" (*CC* 128). With respect to Ireland in particular, Eliot writes that "the 'flight of the wild geese,'" that is, the modern emigration of Irish to England, "is perhaps a symbol of the harm that England has done to Ireland – more serious, from this point of view, than the massacres of Cromwell" (*CC* 119). This is an overstatement of his case, but it reflects Eliot's hostility toward the process of cultural conscription and domination that the Isolde myth emblematizes.[32]

And resistance to this process of cultural imperialism, Eliot makes clear, should not be restricted to the realm of culture itself. Any preservation of "cultural autonomy" that neglected "political and economic autonomy" would "only be a shadow of the real thing," according to Eliot (*CC* 126). Therefore, "any local 'cultural revival' which left the political and economic framework unaffected, would hardly be more than an artificially sustained antiquarianism: what is wanted is not to restore a vanished, or to revive a vanishing culture under modern conditions which make it impossible, but to grow a contemporary culture from the old roots" (*CC* 127). For this to be possible, however, "it is necessary to investigate political and economic alternatives to centralisation in London or elsewhere" (*CC* 127). Regrettably, Eliot adds, "this is beyond my scope" (*CC* 127).

Once again, Eliot's argument opens upon a conceivable *but unimaginable* internationalism. Isolde's violent resistance to her cultural and economic appropriation could be said to constitute the horizon of this internationalism. It takes shape not as an entrenched revolt on the terrain of the *Heimat* itself, but as a setting herself and the other passengers on the ship adrift in the nonstate space of international waters. According to the logic of the myth, it is precisely this violent act of negation that *magically* transforms Isolde's destrudo into a force of love and positive creation – the poison she prepares to destroy herself and the passengers on board is transformed into a love potion, almost as if the willingness to destroy the oppressor's ship of state and one's coerced affective attunements to it is the necessary precondition for any larger, internationalist "growth" of culture.

Is this not precisely the double-movement of destruction and recombination that "The Waste Land" as a whole tries to make imaginable? In the poem, the sea is imagined as a space monopolized by imperialist trade – a space whose "internationalism" exists only as the violent expropriation of the material wealth and creative power of peoples. But for Eliot the imaginary solution to this imperialist deadlock is not a simple return of this wealth and creative power to the local, pre-capitalist rhythms of native locales, just as Isolde, as an emblem of this wealth and creative power, is never wafted back to the homeland evoked in the nostalgic reverie of the boatswain. Instead, Eliot stages a process of *self-annihilation* in which capitalist trade is imaginatively stripped of capital itself; "the profit and the loss" that govern its transnational rhythms are imaginatively swept clean from the earth. Nevertheless, just as the Phoenician trader *lives on* as a spectral intentionality that sustains and renews this process of self-annihilation, so too the internationalism of culture, which capital has largely made possible, *lives on* in this imaginary condition: its mythemes and native topoi become the currency, or the "current under sea," that will replace capital as the medium of international exchange.

An image of anti-capitalist internationalism in "The Waste Land"? Once again, the suggestion should not surprise us, given the phenomena Eliot enumerates in *The Idea of a Christian Society* as obstacles to a humane society: "the hypertrophy of the motive of Profit into a social ideal, the distinction between the *use* of natural resources and their exploitation, the use of labour and its exploitation, the advantages unfairly accruing to the trader in contrast to the primary producer, the misdirection of the financial machine, [and] the iniquity of usury" (*CC* 26). Eliot never makes it clear how these iniquities might be eliminated from the modern world, though he is certain that World War I, and "modern war" in general, "is chiefly caused by some immorality of competition which is always with us in times of 'peace'; and that until this evil is cured, no leagues or disarmaments or collective security or conferences or conventions or treaties will suffice to prevent it" (*CC* 77).[33] Despairing that the liberal internationalism of the League of Nations could ever prevent conflicts that stem from the very economic logic of competition-based societies, Eliot instead offers "The Waste Land" as sketches in the direction of an *imaginary international* – a formal structure in which national mythemes and topoi are abstracted from their regional sources so they might circulate as an international ensemble of appropriable powers, faculties, and organizational models.

It is not surprising, therefore, that a poet like Tolson, who is also committed to developing an anti-capitalist internationalist poetics, would borrow many aspects of Eliot's technique. His rapid modulation between different mythic traditions and national-linguistic topoi, his deployment of a high degree of conceptual abstraction and stylistic fragmentation, all place him in a dynamic relationship to Eliot's poetics and the concern with internationalism it embodies. And yet, at the heart of Tolson's poetics lies a critique of Eliot's modernism and the specific forms of internationalism it advances. What is the nature of this critique and what does it tell us about the forms of black internationalism Tolson was exploring in the 1950s and 1960s?

To answer these questions, we need to take a closer look at the forms of nonstate thinking Tolson employs in *Harlem Gallery* and its companion poem "E. & O. E."

## Racialized Space

In his 1951 poem "E. & O. E.," Tolson levels a fabulously complex indictment of the subjective model that subtends Eliotic internationalism. To do so, he first invokes the image of Hamlet, deciding whether or not he should choose death:

> If,
> eyeless in irony,
> to be
> is Scylla
> and not to be
> Charybdis,
> where is the dilemma?
>
> Is it not, oh,
> is it not because of my
> taste for *beccafico*
> my vassalage to an Act of *Poietes*,
> that I
> let this pleonastic red
> ink *bêche-de-mer* of the Dane –
> a Fysshstrete tinker's dam
> in zero's shadow –
> drain and drain and drain
> the spinal marrow
> of nth *comédie*
> from the *tragédie humaine*?
>                    (*HG* 134).

At first glance, the allusiveness, formal difficulty, abstraction, and mytho-literary ecumenism of this passage seem to place it firmly within the tradition of Eliotic modernism. Words culled from the Italian, Greek, French, and Middle English, and references to Homer's *Odyssey*, Shakespeare's *Hamlet*, Chaucer's *The Canterbury Tales*, and Balzac's *La Comédie humaine* are dazzlingly constellated in these brief twenty lines. Moreover, Tolson deliberately redeploys Eliot's "death by water" motif, whose importance to "The Waste Land" 's figuration of internationalism we have just examined. But what is the status of "death by water" in these lines? Does it point in the direction of the self-annihilation Eliot figures in terms of a negation of international finance capital and its magical replacement by a cross-fertilizing cultural internationalism?

The first thing to note is that Tolson aligns Eliotic death by water with the suicidal ruminations of Hamlet: the "pleonastic red/ink *bêche-de-mer* of the Dane." But why does Tolson describe Hamlet's monologue as pleonastic? And what does it have to do with "red ink" and sea cucumbers – literally, sea-spades: *bêches-de-mer*? Our first clue comes from Tolson's notes, where he refers us to an argument made by one Charles Gray Shaw in *Logic in Theory and Practice*, namely, that it is a mistake to stress the ontological problem in Hamlet's "to be or not to be," since Hamlet's concern is not really whether it is *practically* preferable to kill himself, but rather whether it is ethically or aesthetically preferable – whether it is *nobler* "in the mind to suffer the slings and arrows of outrageous fortune, or to take up arms against a sea of troubles and by opposing end them" (*HG* 205). From Tolson's perspective, this means that Hamlet regards death not as an ineluctable finality but rather as an occasion for an aesthetic performance of subjectivity: it is by playing at death that the subject tests and confirms itself, and the aesthetic is, in a sense, the byproduct of this play.

It is worth noting that Eliot observes something similar of tragic heroes such as Hamlet – what is most significant is "the self-dramatization assumed by some of Shakespeare's heroes at moments of tragic intensity."[34] In his death speech, Othello adopts a strangely "*aesthetic* … attitude, dramatising himself against his environment" (*SE* 111). Similarly, "Hamlet dies fairly well pleased with himself" (*SE* 113) – it is almost as if death is less a moment of absolute exigency than an occasion to exceed oneself phantasmatically, playing at the brink of nothingness, and in the process affirming the power of "Elizabethan individualism" (*SE* 112), to the extent of "identifying the Universe with oneself" (*SE* 120). This is ultimately why Eliot sees Hamlet's indecision, his playing at death, as a *social* symptom. It is the neurotic refuge of a social subject unable to "take part in the life of a thriving Greek city-state" or in the project of Christian ecclesiasticism – the inability to *objectify* oneself in "a set of objects, a situation, a chain of events" correlative to one's internal potentiality (*SE* 112, 124–5). As a character dominated by an emotion "in *excess* of the facts as they appear" (*SE*

125) Hamlet inaugurates a model of subjectivity *as excess*, as a pure capacity for investment *with no place to go*.

For Tolson, then, Hamlet's meditations are pleonastic because they do not really offer a choice between being and not-being. Instead, they testify to a modern Western model of subjectivity that evolves its potentialities in continual reference to a condition of not-being which it "takes up" as its motive force. On this score, Tolson's notes refer us to John Grier Hibben's introduction to Hegel's *Science of Logic*, which explicates a model of subjectivity in which death, not-being, negativity, is not a finality confronting being, but rather a power to alter the given world – a power that defines human being as such. This Hegelian subject is thus between being and nonbeing, at home in the vast sea of death, one might even say absorbing and "titrating" nonbeing, in the way the sea cucumber filters the sea through itself, before serving up the results of this process as an aesthetic delectation – significantly, *bêche-de-mer* refers only to the sea cucumber *as cuisine*; it is therefore an analogue of the aesthetic pleasure that Hamlet's playing-at-death affords.

The substance of Tolson's critique is that this entire model of subjectivity as self-annihilation and self-recuperation can sustain itself only by continually referring to and producing an alterior ontological space which the subject, perpetually in excess of itself, journeys into, probes for avenues of investment and returns from in a moment of self-realization.[35] This alterior space, this *tragédie humaine*, is a racialized space for Tolson – it is a space defined by the self-suspending, self-annihilating Western subject as "raw material" to be appropriated, "spinal marrow" to be drained, fuel for the ludic self-losses and self-realizations of the Western subject.[36]

In other words, Tolson suggests that this model of the subject as an excess with respect to its field of investment, a subject that must therefore suspend itself to realize itself, is in fact produced as the internal image of modern finance capital, at sea in the larger currents of transnational trade, and continually discovering and producing its field of investment in and as the colonial periphery. The "Fysshstrete tinker's dam/in zero's shadow" is thus the image of a metropolitan subject whose ability to imagine itself as a "nothing" (as a "tinker's dam," in the colloquial expression), can be won only by damming and draining the resources of the colonial periphery: the true socio-political "zero" that shadows the imperial subject as its racialized other.[37]

As in "The Waste Land," this is an image of the sea as a space of imperialist commerce. But Eliot's image of this imperialist space turning itself inside out, becoming a nonstate space of flexibilized investments, is not part of Tolson's vision. In fact, this image of voluntary self-annihilation is precisely what Tolson is critiquing in this passage. From Tolson's perspective, Eliot's image of anti-colonial agency is cast in the "native hue" of the colonizing agent – the agent who is in a position to choose death, to visit it, rather than the subject upon whom death is visited without choice or recourse. It is the image of an agent who takes up permanent residence on the shores of death, inhabiting a commercial "Fish Street," where the fruits of seaborne commerce can be enjoyed behind the safety of seawalls, protective tariffs, and colonial navies.[38]

Nevertheless, Tolson's project is to articulate a model of internationalist *agency*, and one, in fact, in which a certain model of Hegelian dialectics is retained. It is a model of agency that, like that of the "The Waste Land," retains an image of an aesthetic circulation of cultural signifiers – a model of *sui generis* creation which he wants to imagine as a contrast to his current, socio-political vassalage to the "Great White World." But Tolson wants to strip this circulation of signifiers of the character it has now – as something directed by the colonial center and the finance capital it controls, whose contradictions are magically "disappeared" by treating anti-colonial agency as structurally similar to the aestheticized self-negations of the capitalist subject.

But how can we imagine such an internationalism? To do so, we should attend carefully to the counter-myth that Tolson deploys as a response to "The Waste Land"'s death by water.

### "Unlaid Ghosts"

In sections V and VI of "E. & O. E.," Tolson rearticulates Eliot's image of the sea as a space of transnational capital. But instead of rescripting the Isolde myth as a willed "death by water" that brings about a magical transformation of capitalist commerce, he retells the story of Jonah and the whale.

How does this myth of anti-colonial agency differ from what we find in "The Waste Land"?

To begin with, the choice confronting Jonah in Tolson's mythic topology is not between violently resisting colonial power or complying with it. In fact, the choice Jonah confronts – to travel to Ninevah and make its population worthy of God's favor or to evade God's call and abscond to Tarshish instead – does not really "belong" to a constituted colonial subject at all. In reality, it is a false choice that belongs to capital itself, just as Hamlet's false choice belongs to a Western subjectivity that affirms and, in Hegelian language, *proves itself* through its capacity to tarry with the negative and produce itself as a self-suspending, self-positing agent. Along the same lines, capital must also *prove itself* by hazarding itself to the realm of colonial workers and industries, only to realize itself as the self-suspending power that animates and produces the colonial world itself. Marx's analysis of devaluation in the *Grundrisse* makes this crystal clear: capital cannot choose to abide within itself. Instead, its ideal status as the force that animates the economy is won only by devaluing itself – that is, by becoming wages and commodities. A moment of risk opens up here, which capital can overcome only by proving itself through consumption.[39]

Tolson's point in this connection is that in the neocolonial period, capital cannot choose whether or not to emigrate to the Global South. With consumption markets saturated in the colonial center, capital must "suspend itself" in the neocolonial periphery, reaping profits by dismantling native industry and driving wages down to an absolute minimum. The super-profits thus drained from the colonial periphery, however, come to constitute a growing mass of unrealizable capital: capital that cannot prove itself through expanded consumption or productive reinvestment, and which therefore (like Hamlet) *has no place to go.* Tolson evokes this floating capital as a transnational host of "unlaid ghosts": specters of capital that threaten it, from within, with a crisis it attempted to manage by producing the Global South as an immiserated exteriority: "I have seen/ the unlaid ghosts/of twenty sex-o'clock cities along/the White Whale's Acheron/freeze the dog/days, make/the crow's-nest hog/like the spine of a dated truth" (*HG* 139). The White Whale's Acheron here refers to capital's colonized periphery: a "river of pain" produced by the dynamics of imperial trade and serving to cut off the colonized world from international consumption markets. But the super-profits which temporarily made capital's realization crisis manageable have now started to accumulate unproductively – to "freeze the dog/days" – putting downward pressure on bullish markets. This, in turn, causes the all-seeing, all-encompassing "crow's nest" of the West's Ideal-I to "hog," to bow or hump, as if weighted down with "hogged" shares of global surplus product.

The result is economic crisis, which also precipitates a crisis of agency for both colonizer and colonized:

> 'Sdeath!
> The tail
> of doomsday struck
>
> I-*ness* in me
> between parentheses
> of my eternity:

ere one could do the five steps of a phrase,
my Tarshish odyssey
died in the scarlet viva of
a geyser: flung,
from perigee
to apogee,
to the crackling of thorns
under a pot, I,
a Momus scarecrow
with crossbones and horns,
dapped to Mt. Aetna's harpooned flesh below.
                                    (*HG* 139–40).

Notice how in this passage the crisis of floating capital is aligned with
a subjective crisis on the part of the aestheticizing, self-suspending poet.
As in the previous passage, where Tolson had difficulty resisting being a
"vassal" of the aesthetic, this passage discovers the speaker of the poem
cultivating an aestheticized, post-racial identity, whose ludic global itinerary is modeled on the free flow of transnational capital. Indeed, "trav-
elling to Tarshish" is Tolson's way of emblematizing the evasions of such
ludic cosmopolitanisms, their transnational journeys organized around the
refusal of economic and political necessity and the unfinished project of
politico-economic national liberation: the world-historical mandate that
the speaker, like Jonah, refuses to heed.

What interrupts this cosmopolitan trajectory is not a death that is chosen,
in the Eliotic mode, as part of a tactical self-negation and -recuperation: one
that structurally repeats the devaluation and self-realization of capital in
the age of imperialism. Instead, the speaker's subjective crisis is visited on
him from without, through a realization that he occupies the position of
what, from the perspective of global capital, can only be registered as a terrifying gap or absence: the moment of capital's migration into the Global
South, where its expanded return to the colonial center depends upon its
ability to maintain the political hypotrophy of the colonial periphery.

Tolson's image, therefore, is that of the postcolonial cosmopolitan who
realizes, in a moment of crisis, that the forms of ludic, transnational agency
he elaborates depend, for their impetus, on the draining of agency from
the colonial periphery: that the unseen support of the cosmopolitan project is the inability of colonial subjects to *float* their economically productive power on the international market, as a self-externalizing, self-realizing
force. Tolson's perfect pentameter line "ere one could do the five steps of a
phrase" speaks to the unrealized fantasy of his cosmopolitan speaker: that
a colonized people might pattern their collective subjectivity on the model

of colonial capital – that the colonized, too, might step out into the global space of international commerce and effect a return, a realization of their creative investment, that could then be reinvested on an expanded scale and give birth to a variable, self-suspending, *aestheticized* form of political subjectivity. Unfortunately, like the "crackling of thorns/under a pot" in Ecclesiastes, the playful self-suspension of the cosmopolitan subject is like "the laughter of a fool." In the final analysis, thorns, which burn quite poorly, are able to do little more than sputter unproductively, generating insufficient heat to cook food in a pot. This is Tolson's image of a form of ludic postcolonial aesthetic performance that has lost contact with the economies of human need that should be their generative source.

This is not to suggest, however, that Tolson foreshadows a return to national space as the proper terrain of anti-colonial agency. Instead, Tolson uses the myth of Jonah and the whale to articulate a vision of nonstate space in which postcolonial subjects could develop multivalent modes of transnational agency without the forms of social amnesia displayed by actually existing cosmopolitanism.

The key to this vision of nonstate space lies in Tolson's image of the postcolonial nation-state as a nexus of socio-economic and cultural forces that can achieve "realization" only through a supersession of the nation form itself.

But what does this mean?

## Financialization and the Post-state Horizon

In *Capitalism in the Age of Globalization*, Samir Amin defines floating capital as "profits derived from production [that] do not find sufficient outlets in the form of lucrative investments capable of further developing productive capacity" (*CAG* x). Amin's focus is on the last forty years or so – the period of neoliberal globalization, which began with the "erosion of the basis of postwar prosperity in the late 1960s," triggering a "collapse of opportunities for productive investment" (*CAG* 20) and the ultimate decision of the US Treasury to shift to floating exchange rates in 1971, which "allowed this gigantic mass of floating capital to find an outlet in financial speculation" (*CAG* 20). During this period, loans to underdeveloped nations were an essential part of this crisis-management strategy; they provided an outlet for "the overabundance of idle capital" (*CAG* 20) and were accompanied by structural adjustment programs that lowered wages in developing countries, opened their markets to US goods, and helped to cripple their national economic autonomy, temporarily bolstering the profitability of US corporations. The "financialization" of capital during this period is thus understood as a symptom of an underlying crisis of industrial overcapacity.

But as Giovanni Arrighi points out, massive expansions of floating capital, and the accelerated dynamics of speculation and lending they trigger, are not unique to the last few decades of capitalism. Periods of financial expansion structurally similar to that which began occurring in the early 1970s have occurred throughout the history of capitalism, from the switch of the Genoese capitalist oligarchy from commodities to banking in the fifteenth century to the free-trade imperialism of the British Empire after 1840 – indeed, at all times when "the investment of money in the expansion of trade and production no longer serves the purpose of increasing the cash flow to the capitalist stratum as effectively as pure financial deals can."[40]

The period of African decolonization which forms the backdrop of Tolson's writing marks the beginning of such a cycle of financial expansion. As Chris Hudson notes in his study of the mechanics of US imperialism, by 1952, the World Bank had already begun "to shift its focus from reconstruction loans to Europe to infrastructure loans to the less developed countries."[41] The earlier focus, from 1946 to 1952, on European reconstruction occurred at a time when material investment was still maximally profitable. But, already by the early 1950s, the United States' European allies "had been stripped of their marketable international assets," chief among them "the extractive industries of their former colonies, especially … Near Eastern oil" (*SI* 7, 10), which they had allowed to be sold to US investors. Commanding quantities of wealth that had yet to find a complement in the fragile national markets of Europe or the decolonizing world, the United States implemented a four-pronged strategy in the early 1950s: lending dollars to developing countries to allow them to buy up US manufacturing and agricultural surpluses; financing the development of electrical power and transport projects that employed US-owned contractors and primarily serviced US import markets; imposing austerity programs on developing countries; and contractually obliging developing nations "not to implement policies of domestic agricultural self-sufficiency," while "assuring the United States a guaranteed future share in their domestic markets" (*SI* 231).

As Hudson demonstrates, this regime of lending deliberately withheld funding for projects intended to modernize the agricultural sector of developing nations. In doing so, it bolstered the profitability of US corporations by siphoning off part of the massive agricultural surplus of the United States to the developing world, which resulted in the ruination of their now uncompetitive agricultural sectors, producing a flight to cities, resulting in lower labor costs and an inflation of food prices which benefited US importers. Rather than permitting developing nations to modernize their agricultural sectors in the way the United States had – through subsidies – countries which had been net food exporters immediately after World War II were transformed into food-debtor countries, subject to famine, and unable to repay their debts because their overproduction of non-food raw materials lowered the price of those commodities, leaving them with insufficient revenue to repay their loans.

This dynamic of underdevelopment, which we tend to associate with the capitalist globalization of the last forty years or so, was already firmly established in Tolson's day. By 1954 it had been enshrined in the Agricultural Trade Development Assistance Act, which allowed overproduced foodstuffs to be exported to developing nations on credit, rather than "burning them or dumping them into the ocean" (*SI* 229). In this way, the United States uses "aid" in the form of interest-bearing loans to liquidate part of its stagnant wealth (aid represented 36 percent of all agricultural exports from the United States in the 1950s), just as it uses aid to finance development projects geared toward exporting from other countries the raw materials it needs.

It is in this context of underdevelopment and floating capital that Tolson envisions the developing world as making "a mound of the Old World's decaying vegetables/to generate heat and hatch the eggs of the New" (*HG* 308). Tolson was aware of the immense difficulties such a project of development in the Global South confronted. "Capitalist nations have always exploited weaker nations," he wrote in a 1938 *Washington Tribune* column: "The sugar magnates needed Cuba; so we had the Spanish–American War. Uncle Sam, under the dictates of Big Business, barred up the Chamber of Deputies in black Haiti and ran the legislators out of the windows."[42] Writing in 1939, Tolson even describes World War II as "a war for the markets of the world": England and France, the "great imperialistic nations … cornered the best of the world markets"; naturally "they wanted peace after they had stolen most of the earth," but retaining their monopoly of imperial markets meant forcibly constraining the imperialistic expansion of the youngest power with pretensions of imperial power: Germany, "which came upon the scene rather late" (*CAC* 111).

Tolson thus had no illusions that capitalist powers had any investment in promoting democracy or development in the Global South. The interests of Britain, France, and Italy in the nations of "500,000,000 colored people" stem from only one source: the desire for "profits in gold and oil and rubber and agricultural products" (*CAC* 106). And yet, Tolson does not look to the Soviet Union as an alternative to capitalist exploitation. Indeed, Tolson's entire analysis of World War II signals his distance from Soviet orthodoxy, which called for cooperation with capitalist powers in the fight against fascism. Tolson's description of World War II as fueled by the competing imperialist interests of France, Britain, the United States, Italy, Germany, and the Soviet Union thus signals his non-alignment with either the capitalist or the state-communist powers of the world.

This raises the question of how the socio-economic rebirth Tolson anticipates could come to pass. From the beginning of the Cold War period, developing nations often looked to the Soviet Union as a trading partner and source of arms and economic aid in the course of their decolonization struggles. But in his 1954 *Libretto for the Republic of Liberia*, Tolson rejected the idea that Stalin's Soviet Union could be relied on as a friend of the decolonization struggle. Only an "ironcurtainless Kremlin" (*HG* 710) – something very difficult to visualize in the early 1950s – could be imagined as a partner in the struggles of decolonizing nations.

The vision of geopolitical self-development that Tolson evolves in *Harlem Gallery* is therefore one that is not aligned with either capitalist or state-capitalist powers. It is one that could only unfold through economic and political alliances between Non-Aligned nations of the developing world. In 1955, leaders of African and Asian countries who attended the Asian–African Conference for International Order in Bandung referred to this policy as "positive neutrality" and articulated its objectives: "provi[sion of] technical assistance to one another … in the form of: experts, trainees, pilot projects and equipment for demonstration purposes; exchange of know-how and establishment of national, and where possible, regional training and research institutes for imparting technical knowledge and skills"; "promotion of joint ventures among Asian–African countries"; and "Asian–African cultural cooperation."[43]

In the writings associated with the Non-Aligned Movement, we thus find a mixture of nationalism and internationalism that testifies to the transitional position Non-Aligned actors occupied – between the space of the nation-state and a future world governed by nonstate economic alliances. It is in this context that Tolson's internationalism comes to light – not just a cultural cosmopolitanism of sign systems, but an internationalism rooted in economic development and political solidarity.

It is no surprise, therefore, that one of the most eloquent contemporary theorists of Non-Alignment, Samir Amin, is also such a staunch critic of many of the cosmopolitanisms of contemporary theory. For Amin, both the "humanist universalism invented by Europe," which positions the West as the "world of tolerance, diversity of opinions, respect for human rights and democracy"[44] and the forms of culturism which are in many ways its corollary fail to articulate any new project for non-Western forms of autocentered development and self-sufficiency – a project which, while it must be "democratic and respectful of diversities" is not, fundamentally, a cultural one (*CAG* 104). The main thrust of this critique is that it is only when populations are in a position to shape and direct the processes of accumulation, resource allocation, and political decision-making that social life becomes based "on a diversity that is tirelessly produced and reproduced and not on a manipulated consensus that erases fundamental debates."[45] Depriving populations of access to these shaping politico-economic processes in the name of protecting "local cultures" is, for Amin, part of a neocolonial culturalism, which directly opposes the process whereby "the diversity of cultural and political differences among nations and peoples become[s] the means of providing individuals with strengthened capacities for creative development."[46]

Ultimately, for Amin, this kind of variability and self-positing is possible only when "democracy ... coming from those on the bottom, based on local government, rural communities, workers' fronts, citizens, etc." is articulated within "a framework of macro political and economic conditions that make their concrete projects viable."[47] At times, Amin suggests the state may be the only agent powerful enough to delink from neo-imperial processes and promote these forms of autocentered development. At other times, he warns that the state-centric "notion of power, conceived as being capable of 'achievements' for the people, but carried out without them, leads to the drift to authoritarianism and the crystallization of a new bourgeoisie."[48]

In the final analysis, Amin suggests that any balance between local forms of democracy and macro-political processes may only be capable of being consummated by nonstate forces. This is because, in the current phase of global capitalism, "the centers of gravity of the economic forces commanding accumulation have shifted outside the frontiers of individual states," and yet there have developed "no new forms of political and social organization going beyond the nation-state" (*CAG* xi, 2). The IMF and World Bank cannot serve this function, since they are interstate organizations "designed to provide the United States with complete control over its interventions" (*CAG* 18). Instead, what is necessary is a global "political and economic organization of controlled interdependencies" and the "negotiation of open, flexible economic relationships between the world's major regions which, currently, are unequally developed" (*CAG* 22, 6).

However, Amin repeatedly stresses that such a process is incommensurable with a world governed by capitalist nation-states. What he calls "Eurocentrism's impossible project" – that of a world-system in which all currently dependent countries would develop into autocentered capitalist powers, by way of "imitation and catching up" – is unviable in that capitalism functions as a system of wealth transfer from underdeveloped regions, countries, and populations to developed ones. Imagining an "equitable distribution" of underdevelopment-fueled wealth transfer is thus an untenable fantasy.[49]

If a world of generalized, autocentered capitalist production is a structural impossibility, since "further development of the productive forces in the periphery" would bring about "the destruction of the imperialist system of centralization of the surplus," such a global economic reorganization could be consummated only in a world-system no longer governed by capitalist states.[50] For Amin, the kinds of interstate alliance between developing countries that leaders like Sukarno, Nehru, Nasser, and Nkrumah first adumbrated in the 1950s are the first step in this direction, but the postcapitalist, post-state horizon of this process is extremely difficult for him to bring into view. He refers to the necessity of an "effective world political organization" making possible "the migration of people on par with the movements of products and capital" (*CAG* 49). But, in the absence of any current nonstate institutions that could foreseeably serve this role, Amin mostly focuses on transitional processes, such as the construction of "big regional entities in the various historic areas (Europe, ex-USSR, Latin America, the Arab World, sub-Saharan Africa, India, China, South-East Asia)" that could pave the way for genuinely nonstate forms of global political organization.[51]

This is where Tolson's nonstate poetics provides a speculative break with the forms of state sovereignty that are so crucial to the development projects of the Non-Aligned Movement. While leaders like Nasser, Sukarno, and Nkrumah focused mainly on shoring up state-sponsored development, and a theorist of Non-Alignment like Amin has difficulty imagining nonstate institutions of development, Tolson projects a future world governed by functioning nonstate forms of governance. He is thus confronting not only the limits of state-thinking in the Non-Aligned Movement of his day, but also our contemporary difficulties in imagining nonstate space outside of the rhetoric of "failed states" and the regime of NGO proxy governance, which so often, wittingly or unwittingly, promotes social service complexes answerable only to the private donors and Western development banks who provide their funding. According to the optics of these forms of proxy governance, what lies beyond the state is a political vacuum which must be filled through "humanitarian" interventions, loans, and aid programs, which substitute themselves for the forms of basic democratic representation and autocentered development which, under the right circumstances, states are in a position to promote.

Contemporary theories of globalization and transnationality therefore confront an impasse when it comes to imagining the political forms that nonstate self-government could take on – a failure, more than anything, of their capacity to imagine a large-scale organization of social life outside of state and interstate proxy institutions. One reason to approach Tolson's political imagination with the kind of rigor we bring to theories of globalization and transnationality is that, already in 1954, Tolson was thematizing the difficulty of conceiving of nonstate space as anything more than an apolitical void, and experimenting with different ways of overcoming this aesthetic and conceptual impasse.

In fact, in *Libretto for the Republic of Liberia*, he strongly satirizes those who can see beyond the state only a terrifying negative space:

> Between pavilions
> small and great
> sentineled from capital to stylobate
> by crossbow, harquebus, cannon, or Pegasus' bomb
> *... and none went in and none went out ...*
> hitherto the State,
> in spite of Sicilian Vespers, stout
> from slave, feudal, bourgeois, or soviet grout,
> has hung its curtain – scrim, foulard, pongee,
> silk, lace, or iron – helled in by Sancho's fears
> of the bitter hug of the Great Fear, Not-To-Be
> (*HG* 172).

The state, contends Tolson in this passage, has come to seem like the only guarantor of social coherence. Beyond its well-policed borders, it is difficult to detect anything but an onto-political void. But Tolson seeks to cast this clinging to state actors in a comic light. He compares it to Sancho Panza's fears that he will be killed as part of a fictional plot against the fictional isle of which he is the fictional governor. In a parallel fashion, modern subjects cling to the illusion that they govern themselves through the apparatuses of state command and that external threats are constantly endangering this condition of state-centric self-government.

It is in this context that Tolson resurrects the Eliotic image of Hamlet, as the embodiment of a modern Western subjectivity whose motive principle is a form of playing-at-death – a mode of self-positing in constant relation to an external finitude: the "Not-To-Be." Here, though, the exigency in relation to which the modern subject tests and confirms itself as an agent is explicitly identified as a nonstate space, a condition of extra-legal self-organization that constitutes the unimaginable horizon of modern individualism. "The Great Fear" is Tolson's way of designating this nonstate space. It is a term that invokes the fear of nonentity that subsumes state-centric thought when it confronts nonstate actors and institutions. But, more specifically, it refers to The Great Fear of 1789: the climate of upheaval in which self-organized groups of peasants and artisans armed themselves and took collective action against the nobility in the opening days of the French Revolution. The self-positing, self-claiming subjectivity of state actors is thus redefined as a neurotic attempt to denegate such nonstate organizational efforts, which, in Tolson's imagination, stand in for the nonstate organizational capacities of the decolonizing world as a whole.

But how are we to imagine these nonstate capacities? How might the efforts of national liberation undertaken by African, Asian, and Latin American countries be seen not as an historical end-point, but as the beginnings of a project of nonstate self-government? To answer this question, we should look more carefully at *Libretto for the Republic of Liberia* – a poem in which Tolson attempts to imagine the political agency of these anti-colonial nonstate actors.

## Nonstate Self-Government

On its surface, *Libretto for the Republic of Liberia* is a paean to a state – a state, moreover, whose poet laureate Tolson had the honor of becoming in 1947. Accordingly, Tolson celebrates the democratic promise of the Liberian state in the opening section of his poem and even addresses the state, with something approaching intimacy, in the second person: "No Cobra Pirate of the Question Mark,/No caricature with a mimic flag/ And golden joys to fat the shark:/You are/American genius uncrowned in Europe's charnel-house" (*HG* 160). The apparent aim of this passage is to reassure the Liberian state that it is not simply an extension of American imperialism, that its early trade with the United States did not simply enrich a country still growing fat on the slave trade, like the sharks that would follow slave ships in anticipation of the slaves who were to be thrown overboard.

And yet the long list of negations that opens his poem starts to over-whelm the positive characteristics Tolson attributes to Liberia and suggests his discomfort with his role as a spokesperson for the state. Though he claims Liberia is "No corpse of a soul's errand/To the Dark Continent" (*HG* 159), "No haply black man's X/Fixed to a Magna Charta without a magic-square" (*HG* 159) "No pimple on the chin of Africa,/No brass-lipped cicerone of Big Top democracy" (*HG* 160), "No waste land yet, nor yet a destooled elite" (*HG* 160), and so on, the impression Tolson creates is of a country tense with the contradictions that beset colonial powers that dis-rupt the languages, belief-systems, and governments of native populations. Tolson makes it clear that the Liberian state, though settled by Americans of African descent, is no exception to the barbarities of colonial rule, and that what is most hopeful about it is not so much its existence as a state as its nonstate potentialities: "You are/The iron nerve of lame and halt and blind,/Liberia and not Liberia,/A moment of the conscience of mankind!" (*HG* 160).

But how exactly does Tolson imagine this "not Liberia" that exists beneath or beyond the state form of Liberia?[52]

At first Tolson refers to this nonstate actor simply as "The *Höhere* of Gaea's children ... beyond/gold fished from cesspools, the *galerie des rois,/* the seeking of cows, *apartheid*, Sisyphus' despond,/the Ilande intire of itselfe with *die Schweine* in mud" (*HG* 174). This "higher power" is meant to evoke the suspended self-creative powers of the world's disenfranchised populations. If, as Tolson informs us, "the seeking of cows ... is the lit-eral meaning of the word 'battle' among the ancient Aryans who ravaged the Indo-Gangetic plains" (*HG* 198), the *Höhere* in this passage is meant to represent a political space beyond colonial and neocolonial dynamics: beyond the Sisyphean labor of the underdeveloped world to "catch up" to the Global North and beyond the solipsistic illusions of the industrialized world.

In the final lines of Tolson's *Libretto*, this nonstate space is imagined as a cosmic, futurist vehicle, part automobile, part train, part ship, and part airplane, known alternately as "the Futurafrique," "the United Nations Limited," "the Bula Matadi," "Le Premier des Noirs," and "The Parliament of African Peoples." While this vehicle is ultra-modern and cruises com-fortably through "the 70A subway" and the "blue harbor crossroads of Waldorf Astorias at anchor," she also mobilizes a transnational assembly of tribal peoples, allowing "television continents" to "hosanna the Black Jews from the cis-Danakil Desert, the Ashantis from the Great Sierra Nile, the Hottentots from Bushland, the Mpongwes from the Cameroon Peoples'

Republic, the Pygmies from the United States of Outer Ubangi" (*HG* 187). Tolson refers to this matrix of nonstate spaces as the "locomotive of history," the "flux of men and things," an image of the kinetic force that could metastasize nonstate forms of self-government on a vast scale (*HG* 206).

I would argue that, despite Tolson's grandiose language and occasionally comic tone in these passages, he is putting forward an image of nonstate economic cooperation and democratic self-government – an image that is meant to be taken seriously. For example, there is obviously no United States of Outer Ubangi, just as there is no Great Sierra Nile, no Cameroon Peoples' Republic, and no political entity known as "Bushland." When Tolson's *Libretto* was published in 1953, the Bayaka pygmies lived much as they do today, in nomadic, communalist groups in rainforests stretching across Cameroon, the Republic of Congo, Gabon, and the Central African Republic. They are a self-governing people, who pursue a hunter–gatherer style of life and resist assimilation to the states that claim their centuries-old hunting grounds for their own. Indeed, their resistance to state-sponsored resettlement programs is a good example of what James C. Scott calls "state-evasion."[53] Tolson's vision of a United States of Outer Ubangi thus seems like an absurd yoking together of modern forms of governance and local, customary forms of nonstate space.

But if we pause for a moment to consider the models of self-government that Pan-Africanist thinkers put forward, Tolson's integration of local, customary self-government and modern forms of governance seems less absurd. In his writings on the Ghanaian Revolution, C. L. R. James does not describe the customary organization of life in Ghana as a form of backwardness that must move aside for modern technology and social organization. Instead, he describes it as the basis for modern self-government in Ghana. James explains this as follows: "The sense of unity and common social purpose which for centuries has been imbued into the African by the family and the tribe is not lost in the city."[54] Instead, the "urban members of the family retain their intimate social and spiritual connection with the family left behind in the village" and "on a tribal basis ... formed unions and associations of all kinds, mutual benefit associations, religious groupings, literary associations, a vast number of sports clubs, semi-political associations or associations which provide in one way or another for one or some or all of these activities" (*N* 54) Nevertheless, James stresses, "these are not tribal organizations in the old sense"; rather "they are fundamentally a response to the challenge and the perils of town life in a modern community" (*N* 55). As such, "they make of the city a meeting place and solvent of the ancient tribal differences" (*N* 55).

James therefore views such nonstate customary forms of organization as "mutual aid societ[ies]" (*N* 220) whose local forms of production and democratic decision-making could serve as the basis for a modern system of national and international self-government. Indeed, in the final pages of his book on Nkrumah, James draws a parallel between the increasingly autocratic nature of Nkrumah's rule and the increasingly authoritarian character of the Soviet Union after 1922, and looks to local forms of self-government as the most potent counterpower to this centralization of power. To lend authority to this diagnosis, he examines Lenin's final writings on the Soviet Union, where Lenin condemns the Soviet "state apparatus [as] very largely a survival of the old one" (*N* 204) and recommends the organization of the population "into co-operative societies" (*N* 202) as the only solution to this residual statism. James carefully examines Lenin's recommendations that the centralized Workers' and Peasants' Inspection Committee be gradually taken over by workers and peasants from local districts – in other words, that the oversight of production be taken over by local producers themselves.

As James notes meticulously in his *State Capitalism and World Revolution*, this project of worker and peasant control ultimately fails in the Soviet Union, Stalinist statism standing as a "bureaucratic organization of accumulated labor, science and technology, acting against the working class in the immediate process of production and everywhere else."[55] But James is writing about Africa in his Nkrumah book, using Soviet models of self-organization merely as a general suggestion of the socio-political role he hopes nonstate customary organizations could play in postcolonial Ghana – that is, as self-governing units that could link the complex apparatuses of an industrialized economy with the local self-administration of actual producers.

This vision is a far cry from the condemnations of "tribalism" that appear in so many analyses of ethnic conflict and state failure in contemporary Africa. As Bill Berkeley points out, what we think of as "tribes" today do, in fact, operate as systems of clientelism and mutual aid, but these nonstate processes on the whole originated as self-protective responses to colonial rule, rather than developing organically from pre-colonial forms of self-government.[56] Indeed, the "tribalisms" of the colonial period are, at least in part, inventions on the part of the colonial power – part of a strategy of indirect rule intended to disrupt properly national forms of political organization. The recent "recovery of traditional authorities as a non-state legitimate alternative" to African states on the part of neoliberal policy-makers is thus, in many ways, a continuation of the "colonial idea of preserving . . . 'traditional'/'communal' land tenure."[57]

But, as scholars such as Kevin Ebele Adinnu, Dorothy L. Hodgson, and Renée Sylvain show, nonstate customary forms of affiliation have also taken center stage in many African struggles against neoliberal and neocolonial manifestations of state power. Organizations such as the Movement for the Survival of the Ogoni People, the Tanzania Pastoralist, Hunter–Gatherer Organisation, the World Council of Indigenous Peoples, the Working Group of Indigenous Minorities in Southern Africa, the Maasai Women Development Organization, The First People of the Kalahari, The Abuja Indigenes Youth Forum, and Abuja Indigenes Elders' Forum all represent nonstate mobilizations that have drawn on customary networks of the kind C. L. R. James describes to oppose state-sponsored forms of environmental degradation, forced resettlement, and social marginalization.[58] Such organizations constitute what scholars such as Gebru Mersha describe as African models of civil society confronting the postcolonial state's concentrations of power. If, as Mersha argues, "the post-colonial petty bourgeoisie elements in power demobilized and depoliticized Africans and used the rhetoric of anti-nationalism, shorn of its radical contents" to undermine "the growth of civil society," which "could be the breeding ground for opposition politics," such new forms of civil society organization represent the possibility of a revival and autonomous growth of nonstate networks that were so often the lifeblood of decolonization movements.[59]

The legacy of nonstate organization in Africa is thus highly contradictory, sometimes operating as an instrument of indirect colonial rule, sometimes allowing what Basil Davidson describes as "self-administration by local assemblies and their elected executives."[60] Tolson's vision of the Bayaka, the Ashanti, the Khoikhoi, or the Mpongwes integrating themselves into regional self-governing bodies as part of a modern apparatus of trans-continental self-government is thus not so outrageous – in fact, it corresponds to the views of Pan-Africanists who, far from viewing nonstate customary organization as a remnant of backwardness, saw it as one of the most important modern instruments of self-government. Tolson's incorporation of nonstate geographical features – the cis-Danakil Desert, the Nile Delta, the Bush, the Ubangi river – into the titles of these fictional governing bodies represents his attempt to imagine a form of democratic institutionality tied not to states but to the nonstate self-administrative practices of these African peoples.

Tolson's proposition is that such forms of global self-government could incorporate a wide variety of local forms of self-government: pastoralist communitarians, republics, and peoples' federations. The "television continents" he invokes are a way to imagine the forms of communication technology that would allow trans-continental economic cooperation between such different self-governing bodies. Images such as these encourage speculation about the forms of political affiliation that could sustain such an enlacing of local, nonstate networks with governance-complexes of continental and trans-continental scope.

But while Tolson's *Libretto* certainly invites such an epic perspective, the most intensive vision of nonstate organizational capacity comes not in the *Libretto*, but near the conclusion of "E. & O. E.," where Tolson imagines the long, complex process of political self-constitution that underdeveloped countries must initiate.

## Crisis and Self-Regulation

Like *Harlem Gallery*, "E. & O. E." presents the poet as conducting a transnational journey of the Global South, attempting to gather its cultural wealth into a nonstate process of socio-political *Bildung*. But this cultural itinerary lacks the state-centered power base, protected markets, and military striking power of the imperial core.

Its challenge to the imperial cosmopolitanism of the Global North is thus in danger of never evolving the real, socio-economic field of self-development that could anchor and expand a project of this kind. Tolson imagines this stranding of his internationalist project as its inability to test and externalize itself in a global power-system that excludes the underdeveloped populations represented by the poet. "I have not," Tolson writes,

> with a face
> card, introduced
> into the marketplace
> cos-lettuce from an aerie,
> and munched with rabbit glee
> beneath the *du-haut-en-bas* grimace
> of a dozen marble Caesars, as
> the sulky pike
> mocked the impertinent friskings of the dace
> against a Teverean dike
>
> (*HG* 143).

In this whimsical image, Tolson depicts an absurdly counterfactual situation, one in which underdeveloped countries could magically secure a place for their political voices, developmental agendas, and racialized subjectivities in the very heart of imperialist institutions of governance.

No doubt, something like this is at the heart of various cosmopolitan theories of cultural and political openness. Daniele Archibugi's ideal of an administratively created global assembly of representatives elected through international parties is one cosmopolitan ideal that comes to mind in this context. But Tolson insists on the structural inequalities that make such cosmopolitan fantasies hard to believe in. At a time when agricultural surplus from the Global North was overwhelming local producers in Africa and Asia, destroying the livelihoods of millions of peasant farmers and crushing autocentered modernization projects on a continental scale, Tolson imagines Arabic cos-lettuce magically floating into the markets of the imperial core, somehow bypassing the "Teverean dike" of unequal trade agreements that prevent anything but a select number of African commodities from flowing into European waters. Tolson suggests that the racialized "face card" that such a developmentalist agenda might present as part of this act of political and economic self-assertion might not enjoy the kind of welcome from imperial powerbrokers that cosmopolitan theories of cultural openness would recommend.

But, for Tolson, this very exclusion of postcolonial states from imperial networks of trade and decision-making prompts their populations to develop organizational capacities beyond the state, as a matter of political and economic survival. The Non-Aligned Movement envisioned such survival strategies, at least initially, as interstate alliances, and began putting them into practice. But if, as development economists remind us, capitalism is a system of wealth-transfer that could not be maintained in the context of full African, Asian, and Latin American development, then the kinds of development projects initiated at Bandung could become durable international institutions only outside the confines of the capitalist state.

In a column entitled "Masses of Negroes Are Ahead of the Whites!" Tolson makes an argument along these lines. "Since, in our great civilization, we can produce enough meat, bread, cars, houses for everybody," he reasons, "why should men fight over these things?" (*CAC* 79). In a global economy characterized by such massive industrial and agricultural surplus, the system of economic competition is obsolete. The true purpose of competition is to allow the ruling elites of industrialized nations to continue "pil[ing] up 'treasures on earth,' " which "means an everlasting series of wars between the Haves and the Have-Nots" (*CAC* 127). What is necessary, instead, is a form of global economic democracy, a "Parliament of Man, a Federation of the World" in which "the whites and yellows and blacks would be equal" (*CAC* 127). Only this kind of "interracialism and internationalism" (*CAC* 58) will make it possible to end the dynamics of class exploitation and racism that persist globally.

"E. & O. E." is an attempt to imagine how such a nonstate "Federation of the World" could come into being, and its extreme complexity mirrors the extreme complexity of this proposition. The most straightforward trope in the poem is Tolson's rewriting of the myth of Jonah and the whale, with the poet occupying the position of Jonah, traveling to Tarshish instead of to Ninevah, where his world-historical mandate should have carried him. Through elaborate analogic layering, Tolson associates Jonah's transnational journey with two things: first, his own poetic persona's premature attempts to articulate a "people's cosmopolitanism" while ignoring the urgent political and economic requirements of the Global South and, second, the cosmopolitan itinerary of global capital itself, which creates the illusion that these political and economic requirements have been, or could be, met without altering the fundamental imbalances of trade and political power that capital's global itinerary inaugurated. As I hope this formulation makes clear, Tolson sees these two analogic moments simply as aspects of a singular cosmopolitan problematic: an *aesthetic* regime, in the broadest sense of the term, in which a quantitative expansion and acceleration of the signifiers of globalized exchange is substituted for social capacities designed to mitigate the structural imbalances that this exchange process sustains and exacerbates.

For these reasons, Tolson's speaker is surprised in the middle of his cosmopolitan itinerary, devoured by a whale, which in turn becomes the gestational embodiment of a new, nonstate combinatoire:

As tonic spasms behind me locked
the Black Hole gate of teeth
to the *Weltschmerz* intervale
between sierras of quivering flesh ...

   .    .    .    .    .    .        .    .
                            ... I slid
like the wraith of scintilla,
between the jaws
of Calpe and Abila ...

   .    .    .    .    .    .    .    .
                    ... by Fear set free of fears,
though churned by entrail-dooms volcanic,
the *Weltschmerz* twisted me like the neck of a torticollis
in enzymatic juices oceanic ...

   .    .    .    .    .    .    .    .
                to die

> gyrating into the wide, wide privacy
> of the Valley of Hinnom's By-and-By …
>                    down
>                    down
>                    down
>         untouched by the witches' Sabbath of any wall
>         until the maelstrom womb of the underworld
>                    swallowed my Adamic fall!

*Ecce homo!*

         *Pero*

                 *yo ya no*

                        *soy yo:*

behold a micro-all-in-all
ashen as the ashes of saltwort
in Aguazall

                                   (*HG* 143–5).

Tolson's image here is of the speaker being swallowed by a whale – not a death that is chosen, as in Eliotic images of modernist self-annihilation, but a death that surprises him as he is attempting the kind of unattached, cosmopolitan wandering that belongs to capital in the age of global surplus. Because diasporic Africans and members of the neocolonial periphery cannot actually "float" their social surplus on global markets for a return, in the way that states of the Global North can, since they have been prevented from claiming a form of agency in which prospects for personal development are reflected in projects for economic self-development of transnational reach, the speaker's cosmopolitan itinerary collapses in on itself, just as projects for economic development in the Global South have collapsed time and again under the pressure of international trade deals and military interventions.

This is why, in Tolson's ingenious conceit, the digestive tract of the whale is imagined as a "*Weltschmerz* intervale," a river of pain created by the strictures of structural adjustment programs and extraction-oriented trade deals, and bordered on each side by mountains of "quivering flesh," the collective humanity of the Global South, imagined as a "surplus population" prevented from developing itself through autonomous economic activity. Fittingly, the juices in which the speaker stews are likened to the body of water that separates Europe from Africa: the Mediterranean Sea, which shuts off African commodities from European markets and whose "jaws" – the Calpe and Abila Mountains, flanking the Straits of Gibraltar – cordon them off from Atlantic trade.

In contrast to this image of political and economic containment, "E. & O. E." offers a vision of collective rebirth that stems from the regional control of social surplus produced by peoples of the neocolonial periphery. The whale's belly is thus both an image of the constraints placed on the neocolonial periphery by uneven trade deals and an image of a "maelstrom womb of the underworld" in which local populations of peripheral producers learn to coordinate their economic efforts in order to create new, autonomous trading zones, with a view to the "Adamic" autonomy that economic self-development affords.

Tolson imagines this regionally controlled surplus as "a micro-all-in-all/ashen as the ashes of saltwort/in Aguazall." Saltwort is an evergreen shrub whose roots have the unusual ability to filter out salt from coastal wetlands. For this reason, saltwort is burned to obtain the highly salinated soda ash it offers, which, because of its numerous industrial applications, is traded globally. But Tolson's image is of a saltwort that is still alive, in the aguazall, or swamp, with its valuable salt still suspended in its leaves and branches. This is a peculiar image of transnational economic self-regulation, but, compared with the many images of vegetal death and rebirth in the tradition of Eliotic modernism, it begins to make a great deal of sense. The hyacinths and narcissi that appear in Eliot's poetry evoke the flowerings of peoples that World War I was supposed to stimulate. The dying god who lives on after death in vegetal form is meant to evoke a power of life-giving, nonstate mediation that could become actual only after a period of crisis and death. But the life-giving power of organic self-regulation that his vegetation images evoke finds no real-world complement in Eliot's political thought. The place of such a nonstate actor is either left poignantly open or evoked through a magical non-personal actor.

Tolson's image of organic self-regulation points in a different direction. His image of the grains of salt that are titrated by the saltwort – the "micro-all-in-all" that it absorbs – is an image of the profit margins that neocolonial trade practices extract from peripheral producers and float, as surplus capital, on international markets. The humble saltwort, a plant that has inspired no myths of immortal agency, but which is perfectly adapted to its local conditions of existence, is an image of peripheral producers who have begun to resorb and contain their own social surplus, rather than having it extracted from them in an economic slash-and-burn procedure. Tolson's image of valuable salt ash that has not yet become salt ash, because it is still "suspended" in the body of the saltwort, nourishing the plant itself, is thus an image of local self-development, but not one that is isolated from transnational economic currents. The saltwort flourishes on seawater, drinks it in, diverts surplus from international waters, for its own development.

This is why Tolson uses the whale's belly as another way to imagine this site of protected development – a gestational space in which the forms of interiority and agency that local producers develop exist as a function of global, nonstate capacities for self-development. The "wide privacy" of the whale's belly is thus an image of transnational economic and political *Bildung*, but it is also an image of a nonstate "personality" that Tolson wants to imagine outside of the forms of racial inscription that belong to the Great White World. For Tolson, the process of "becoming global," whether it be in the cultural arena or in economic practices of global scope, is something that is difficult to imagine outside of the models of whiteness, or "ashenness," that have for so long masqueraded as models of universality. In other words, his approach to internationalism doesn't involve local cultures negating or destroying themselves, and then transforming themselves into featureless white ashes that circulate globally. It is defined, instead, by forms of political and cultural autonomy that would allow postcolonial nations to participate in a multipolar world culture whose terms of trade and forms of discourse would not just be impositions of neocolonial nations.

What Tolson's poetry insists upon is that this world culture has not come into being yet, nor can it be substructed through a cultural cosmopolitanism that leaves questions of underdevelopment, global inequality, and the structural violence of the state-form unasked. What it offers in place of this "status quo" world culture is a glimpse of the almost unimaginable process of transformation that would allow regional and trans-regional political alliances to play the economically protective and self-developmental role that it is difficult to picture outside of a statist optic. The Non-Aligned Movement was, for Tolson, one way to begin imagining how this alternative internationalism might come into being. But Tolson's abstractions are an attempt to imagine how Non-Alignment, as the constitution of an interstate power bloc, could be transformed into a global process of economic mediation steered by and composed of nonstate local communities of producers and decision-makers.

In our time, when not just the Non-Aligned idea, but Pan-Africanism and other models of regional and trans-regional alliance are being taken up with new energy, Tolson's poetry encourages forms of political speculation that are of profound contemporary relevance.[61] If we are still attempting to evolve a theoretical vocabulary able to grasp the nonstate potentialities which such large-scale alliances of the "rising South" offer, we can neverthe-less acquire a *sense* of the new solidarities, democratic methods, and forms of exchange they may yet bring into being. Poetry like Tolson's invites us to transform this sense – our sense of how such large-scale figurations might take shape, our sense of the forms of globality to which they may give rise – into a speculative organ as complex and multi-sided as theories of globality and transnationalism aim to be. In this context, the forms of aesthesis Tolson mobilizes may very well constitute not just the "insensible" of many of our theoretical problematics, but their future horizon as well.

## Notes

1 The Warwick Research Council, *Combined and Unven Development: Towards a New Theory of World-Literature* (Liverpool: Liverpool University Press, 2015), 22.

2 Jed Esty and Colleen Lye, "Peripheral Realisms Now," *Modern Language Quarterly,* 73:3 (2012), 285.

3 *Ibid.*, 281.

4 *Ibid.*, 285.

5 Susan Stanford Friedman, *Planetary Modernisms: Provocations on Modernity Across Time* (New York: Columbia University Press 2015), 58, 61.

6 *Ibid.*, 58.

7 Mary Louise Pratt, "Modernity and Periphery: Towards a Global and Relational Analysis," in *Beyond Dichotomies: Histories, Identities, Cultures and the Challenge of Globalization*, ed. Elisabeth Mudimbe-Boyi (Albany: State University of New York Press, 2002), 21–48, 29.

8 See Eleanor Cook, "T. S. Eliot and the Carthaginian Peace," *ELH,* 46:2 (1979), 349–50.

9 Quoted in Robert M. Farnsworth, *Melvin B. Tolson, 1898–1966: Plain Talk and Poetic Prophecy* (University of Missouri Press, 1984), 146.

10 Quoted in Farnsworth, 224.

11 Michael Bérubé, "Masks, Margins, and African American Modernism: Melvin Tolson's *Harlem Gallery*," *PMLA,* 105:1 (1990), 65.

12 Stephen Henderson, *Understanding the New Black Poetry* (New York: Morrow, 1973), 33, cited in Nielsen, who makes a strong argument that such forms of "Black linguistic elegance" are part of Tolson's cultural inheritance, against those who "would reduce 'Black' linguistic style to a very narrow register" (Aldon Nielsen, "Melvin B. Tolson and the Deterritorialization of Modernism," *African American Review,* 26:2 [1992], 248). Matthew Hart makes a similar point, mobilizing the concept of Afro-Modernism to argue that Tolson embraces modernist style "as a technology of cultural *moderni-zation* through which black poetry might address the historically determined problem of its own underdevelopment" (Matthew Hart, *Nations of Nothing But Poetry: Modernism, Transnationalism, and Synthetic Vernacular Writing* [Oxford: Oxford University Press, 2010], 147). In this connection, see Michael Hanchard, "Afro-Modernity: Temporality, Politics, and the African Diaspora,"

in *Alternative Modernities*, ed. Dilip Parameshwar Gaonkar (Durham: Duke University Press, 2001); and Kathy Lou Shultz, *The Afro-Modernist Epic and Literary History: Tolson, Hughes, Baraka* (New York: Palgrave Macmillan, 2013).

13 Brent Hayes Edwards, *The Practice of Diaspora: Literature, Translation, and the Rise of Black Internationalism* (Cambridge: Harvard University Press, 2003), 23.

14 Arnold Rampersand, *The Life of Langston Hughes, Volume II: I Dream a World* (New York: Oxford University Press, 1988), 193; cited in Nielsen.

15 Samir Amin, *Capitalism in the Age of Globalization: The Management of Contemporary Society* (London: Zed Books, 1997), 34. Hereafter cited as *CAG*.

16 Literally hundreds of volumes could be cited whose approach to transnationality derives from academic interest in neoliberal projects of governance; most relevant to my argument are titles such as Anne L. Cluham and Harold A. Trinkunas, eds., *Ungoverned Spaces: Alternatives to State Authority in an Era of Softened Sovereignty* (Stanford: Stanford University Press, 2010); Thomas Hale and David Held, eds., *Handbook of Transnational Governance: Institutions and Innovations* (Cambridge: Polity, 2011); Amitai Etzioni, *From Empire to Community: A New Approach to International Relations* (New York: Palgrave Macmillan, 2004); and Marie-Laure Djelic and Kerstin Sahlin-Andersson, eds., *Transnational Governance: Institutional Dynamics of Regulation* (Cambridge: Cambridge University Press, 2006).

17 Melvin Tolson, *"Harlem Gallery" and Other Poems*, ed. Raymond Nelson (Charlottesville: University Press of Virginia, 1999), 209–10. Hereafter cited as *HG*.

18 Jed Esty's analysis of the "antidevelopmental bildungsroman" is quite germane here, insofar as this genre "literalizes the problem of colonialism as failed or postponed modernization" (Jed Esty, *Unseasonable Youth: Modernism, Colonialism, and the Fiction of Development* [Oxford: Oxford University Press, 2011], 14). Like the novels Esty analyzes, Tolson's images of failed socio-economic *Bildung* "allegorize uneven development in a world-system rather than in a national context" (*Ibid.*, 15). But Tolson's staging of the explosion of individual biography as a suitable "container" for nation-centered models of development is performed in such a highly fragmentary poetic dimension that it departs even further from what Esty describes as "organicist claims [that] underlie a reciprocal allegory of development with the representative soul" (*Ibid.*, 26).

19 T. S. Eliot, *The Complete Poems and Plays 1909–1950* (New York: Harcourt, Brace & World), 43. Hereafter cited as *CPP*.

20 T. S. Eliot, *Christianity and Culture* (New York: Harcourt, Brace and Company, 1940), 200. Hereafter cited as *CC*.

21 Michael Levenson, "Does *The Waste Land* Have a Politics?," *Modernism/Modernity* 6:3 (1999), 9, 6.

22 Paul Stasi, *Modernism, Imperialism and the Historical Sense* (Cambridge: Cambridge University Press, 2012), 39.

23 One of the most powerful strains of argument concerning the status of colonialism in "The Waste Land" sees in the poem what Purnima Bose calls "end-anxiety": an anxiety of Britain's imperial decline (Purnima Bose,

"'End-Anxiety' in T. S. Eliot's 'The Waste Land,'" *Yeats–Eliot Review,* 9 [1988], 157–60). Similarly, Srila Nayak refers to "The Waste Land"'s "nostalgia for empire" (Srila Nayak, "Citizenship in Heaven and Earth: Contesting Nationalism in *The Waste Land,*" *Modern Philology,* 109:2 [2011], 230), and Paul Douglass sees the poem as expressing "anxiety of imperial decline" through its images of "moral decay, invasion by barbaric 'tribes,' [and] the corruption of the (imperial) center" (Paul Douglass, "Reading the Wreckage: De-encrypting Eliot's Aesthetics of Empire," *Twentieth Century Literature,* 43:1 [1997], 9, 10). Paul Stasi departs from this consensus, viewing "England's imperial status as the structural condition for the alienated crowd of the poem" – suggesting that the "death by water" staged in the poem is not necessarily a lament for British imperial decline but rather a warning that the mechanisms of overseas domination inevitably refract back upon the metropole itself (*Modernism, Imperialism, and the Historical Sense,* 51). In my own reading, I suggest, further, that Eliot stages an anti-imperialist critique in "The Waste Land," which derives both from the "anti-capitalis[m]" that Michael Levenson detects in the poem ("Does *The Waste Land* Have a Politics?," 9) and, paradoxically, from what I will describe momentarily: Eliot's conservative investment in unified, self-determining codes of behavior and feeling that are instinct in the various peoples of the world.

24 H. A. Mason notes that anti-Russian nationalism can be heard in the quote (H. A. Mason, "The Lithuanian Whore in *The Waste Land,*" *The Cambridge Quarterly,* 18:1 [1989], 68), whereas Pouneh Saeedi views it as reflecting an obsession with "'pure' German identity" at a time when "the concept of purity of race was about to fuel fanatic sentiments" (Pouneh Saeedi, "T. S. Eliot's *The Waste Land* and Surging Nationalisms," *CLCWeb: Comparative Literature and Culture,* 13:4 [2011], 5. http://docs.lib.purdue.edu/clcweb/vol13/iss4/14/). Calvin Bedient simply refers to the quote as "the wild-card line in German," hypothesizing that it "betrays a petty, in fact false concern with worldly purity, purity of race, national clean and proper boundaries" (Calvin Bedient, *He Do the Police in Different Voices:* The Waste Land *and its Protagonist* [Chicago: The University of Chicago Press, 1986], 19, 20). Marjorie Perloff takes a different tack, seeing the statement as testimony to Marie's status as a "deracinated cosmopolite" (Marjorie Perloff, *Poetry On and Off the Page: Essays for Emergent Occasions* [Evanston: Northwestern University Press, 1998], 194). But I can find no critical account that fully explains the geopolitics involved in Eliot's linking of Germany, Lithuania, and Russia in this passage.

25 According to my reading, however, this does not mean that Eliot is evincing the "distrust of nationalism" that David Roessel describes in his analysis of "The Waste Land" (David Roessel, "'Mr. Eugenides, the Smyrna Merchant,' and Post-War Politics in 'The Waste Land,'" *Journal of Modern Literature,* 16:1 [1989], 173). Roessel describes with admirable clarity Eliot's hostility to the post-World War I international power brokering which saw Smyrna taken from Turkey and given to Greece. But I see this hostility as rooted in Eliot's exasperation with the ineffective and imperialistic practices of the Wilsonian

interstate system rather than in any disagreement on Eliot's part with the specific claims of Greek nationalists.

26  A. S. Rappoport, "The Russo-German Frontier," *The New Age,* February 4, 1915, 371. Hereafter cited as "RGF".

27  George Raffalovich, "The Ukraine," *The New Age,* April 10, 1913, 549.

28  *Ibid.*

29  "The Russo-German Frontier," 372.

30  Jahan Ramazani also stresses the *usability* of Eliot's modernist technique in the context of postcolonial struggle in his attention to the ways poets like Kamau Brathwaite and Derek Walcott value Eliot as part of their own "quest to break through monologic lyricism, to express their cross-cultural experience" (Jahan Ramazani, "Modernist Bricolage, Postcolonial Hybridity," *Modernism/Modernity,* 13:3 [2006], 448).

31  Of course, framing this geopolitical narrative is the more local narrative of the hyacinth girl's failed romance, which Calvin Bedient argues has to do with a psychic process whereby "the 'subject'" is returned to "a fund of anguish" (*He Do the Police in Different Voices,* 31). Similarly, Jewel Spears Brooker and Joseph Bentley see this romantic failure as testifying to a Bradleyan form of "immediate experience" whose unattainability the Tristan and Isolde narrative only palely evokes (Jewel Spears Brooker and Joseph Bentley, *Reading* The Waste Land: *Modernism and the Limits of Interpretation* [Amherst: The University of Massachusetts Press, 1990], 76). My sense is that these Lacanian and phenomenological readings take on their fullest hermeneutic power when they are placed within the larger frame of the pre-World War I imperial "innocence" that Eliot is evoking in the beginning of his poem – an innocence, like that of the hyacinth girl's relationship, that is interrupted by harsh realities of inter-imperial war and colonial subjection. If, as Jewel Spears Brooker and Joseph Bentley suggest, the Germanness of the *Tristan und Isolde* passage may represent the presence of Britain's imperial rival in World War I, then it's easy to see the *Gemütlichkeit* of the hyacinth girl's romance as evoking a larger geopolitical innocence and desire for imperial perpetuity that the reality of national-cultural revolt and anti-imperialist struggle shatters.

32  What are the politics of Eliot's hostility to cultural imperialism? As Kenneth Asher notes, Eliot's politics were influenced by the Catholic fascism of Action Française – hardly a paragon of anti-imperialist thought. In this context, Asher describes Eliot's investment in "the subtle internal self-adjustments of the organic life of a people" (Kenneth Asher, *T. S. Eliot and Ideology* [Cambridge: Cambridge University Press, 1995], 93). But, according to my analysis, it was precisely this "conservative organicism" (*Ibid.,* 94) of Eliot's, the intellectual history of which runs from Edmund Burke to Joseph de Maistre, that became a factor in his hostility to cultural imperialism. If each people possesses a self-generated "*felt* life of the whole" (*Ibid.,* 96), then impositions onto this popular spirit are contrary to its spiritual oneness – a belief that leads Eliot, counterintuitively, to affirm the organicity of peoples, even "small," subject peoples, over and against the modern machinery of empire. It is to preserve

the integrity of these cultures that Eliot attempts to imagine an alternative model of internationalism – not a Wilsonian internationalism of states, but a nonstate internationalism of peoples. This gesture is commensurate with what Jed Esty describes as a "secondary universalism" based on "the representative status of a bounded culture," over and against the "myth-making imperial humanism" of an earlier era (Jed Esty, *A Shrinking Island: Modernism and National Culture in England* [Princeton: Princeton University Press, 2004], 14). That this kind of bounded universalism is visible in "The Waste Land," which in so many respects belongs to the kind of high modernist globalism that Esty sees as pre-dating the culturalism of imperial decline, suggests a real political continuity between this poem and the late works Esty analyzes in his study.

33 It is true that Eliot never goes so far as to claim that the profit motive is itself a social evil, only its "hypertrophy" into "a social ideal." This is not a surprise, since Eliot's anti-capitalism is a complex, hybrid phenomenon – a mixture of Social Credit theory, guild socialism, and social conservatism. From Social Credit he borrows the idea that "the fact that money is always forthcoming for the purpose of making more money, whilst it is so difficult to obtain for purposes of exchange, and for the needs of the most needy, is disturbing to those who are not economists" (*CC* 76). This leads him to a position that sounds even more radical: "I am by no means sure that it is right for me to improve my income by investing in the shares of a company, making I know not what, operating perhaps thousands of miles away, and in the control of which I have no effective voice" (*CC* 76). Beneath this political attitude lies an ethical uncertainty about economic speculation as a whole: "where the line is to be drawn between speculation and what is called legitimate investment is by no means clear" (*CC* 77). This uncertainty attracts Eliot to guild socialism, which is invoked in his idea that "the apprentice (ideally, at least) did not merely serve his master, and did not merely learn from him as one would learn at a technical school – he became assimilated into a way of life which went with that particular trade or craft; and perhaps the lost secret of the craft is this, that not merely a skill but an entire way of life was transmitted" (*CC* 116). Immediately, however, Eliot goes on to mention the family as another of these shaping institutions. In other words, he borrows from Social Credit, guild socialism, and social conservatism the elements of an anti-capitalist political model, while at the same time remaining agnostic about whether capitalism could be reformed to eliminate its social pathologies. His anti-capitalism does not, therefore, lead in a revolutionary direction, but rather into speculative territory that would see capitalism somehow voided of all the exchange relations that define its operations, but without the forms of class struggle and reappropriation specific to classical Marxism.

34 T. S. Eliot, *Selected Essays* (New York: Harcourt, Brace and Company, 1950), 110. Hereafter cited as *SE*.

35 The brilliance of Tolson's critique of this aspect of Eliotic subject-formation is confirmed by Charles Altieri's rich account of affect in Eliot's poetry. Accurately expressing Eliot's hostility to the "fictions of self-mastery" that are bound up

with "romantic expressivist notions of identity" (Charles Altieri, "Theorizing Emotions in Eliot's Poetry and Poetics," in Cassandra Laity and Nancy K. Gish, eds., *Gender, Desire, and Sexuality in T. S. Eliot* [Cambridge: Cambridge University Press, 2004], 153, 161), Altieri locates an alternative mode of agency in the way Eliot's poetry "establishes and tests ways of making affective investments" (*Ibid.*, 151). But in exactly the way that Tolson regards the "placeless" Eliotic subject as requiring an alterior zone of investment in which to test and reclaim itself, Altieri claims that "we earn identities by being active in relation to forces that otherwise would determine us" (*Ibid.*, 154), ultimately claiming that for Eliot value inheres not in affective states alone, but rather "in how the person comes to make investments in [the] awareness of his or her own capacities for focused investment" (*Ibid.*, 167). Such an approach offers penetrating insight into how Eliotic subjectivity aims to "will its own range of affects without having to thematize them and seek criteria from the outside" (*Ibid.*, 169), but by the same stroke validates Tolson's critique of Eliotic subjectivity as requiring, for its coherence, an abjected social space fraught with the determinations which the self-suspending, featureless individual will must simultaneously disentangle itself from and prove itself in relation to. If Altieri's is one of the most profound accounts of how Eliot imagines we can construct "new sensibilities and new emphases within cultural life" (*Ibid.*, 170) – and I believe it is – this just serves to highlight the profound contemporaneity of Tolson's critique of the self-suspending Eliotic subject.

36 As Denise Ferreira da Silva points out, this process is part of a "strategy of engulfment" that transforms "that which is exterior, the effects of the universal *nomos*, into products, moments, 'other' manifestations of the fundamental interiority that distinguishes the *homo historicus*" (Denise Ferreira da Silva, *Toward a Global Idea of Race* [Minneapolis: University of Minnesota Press, 2007], 100). In other words, what she describes as the "transcendental poesis" of the Hegelian subject does involve a dialectic of self-exteriorization in which the subject "risks becoming an object of universal *nomos*" (*Ibid.*, 75). But in the process, this self-exteriorizing, self-claiming "I" in fact generates as its substrate "a productive symbolic regimen that institutes human difference as an effect of the play of universal reason," and this regimen is precisely the "analytics of raciality," according to which "whiteness come[s] to signify the transparent I and blackness to signify otherwise" (*Ibid.*, 3, 8). This is easier to see when we realize that, before the racial violence that inaugurates modern subjectivity, there is no "pristine black subject fully enjoying its 'humanity,' thriving in self-determined (interior or temporal) existence, that can refuse to 'interiorize' and actualize violence" (*Ibid.*, 8) – that, on the contrary, "the racial produces modern subjects" (*Ibid.*, 3) as such, along with the "ontological context – globality – that fuses particular bodily traits, social configurations, and global regions, in which human difference is reproduced as irreducible and unsublatable" (*Ibid.*, xix).

37 Lyndon Barrett makes a similar point when he stresses that "the modernizing racial trajectory of the West is implicated in the revolutionary certainty that

functional human being – individual and especially collective – is inseparable from the ideally infinite arena of ideally infinite exchange" – in other words, that this modern subjectivity is produced out of the violence of "mercantile capitalism and its modernizing transfers of economic values and peoples" (Lyndon Barrett, *Racial Blackness and the Discontinuity of Western Modernity*, ed. Justin A. Joyce, Dwight A. McBride, and John Carlos Rowe [Urbana: University of Illinois Press, 2014], 28). This means that "the extended quarantining of the Africa-derived population largely and effectively promotes key turns of the imagination that naturalize the gulf between the social conditions of the labor yielding the commodity for exchange and the failure of the commodity to resemble those conditions in the exchange" – that, in short, "racial blackness forms the historical and enabling point of 'dis/integration' for the paradigms of Western modernity" (*Ibid.*, 8, 2), both as "raw material" that subtends the entire regime of civic liberties that define modern subjectivity and as the unacknowledged inverse of the "transparent" market rationality that supposedly governs its objectivations. For further insight into this dynamic, see Lisa Lowe, who argues that "the modern distinction between definitions of the human and those to whom such definitions do not extend is the condition of possibility for Western liberalism, and not its particular exception" (Lisa Lowe, *The Intimacies of Four Continents* [Durham: Duke University Press, 2015], 3) and Alexander G. Weheliye, who describes "the essential role that racializing assemblages play in the construction of modern selfhood" (Alexander G. Weheliye, *Habeas Viscus: Racializing Assemblages, Biopolitics, and Black Feminist Theories of the Human* [Durham: Duke University Press, 2014], 4).

38  Anne C. Bolgan's classic reading of "The Waste Land," therefore, is not incorrect – no doubt "the sacrificial death of the Quester Hero through which his transubstantiation is to be effected … culminat[es] … in what is really life-in-death … [a] self-generative and self-transcendent life" (Anne C. Bolgan, *What the Thunder Really Said: A Retrospective Essay on the Making of* The Waste Land [Montreal: McGill–Queen's University Press, 1973], 78). My concern here is to elucidate the racial and colonial substructure of the heroic subject that Bolgan analyzes, with a view to expressing Tolson's critique of the forms of agency it embodies.

39  See Karl Marx, *Grundrisse: Foundations of the Critique of Political Economy*, trans. Martin Nicolaus (London: Penguin, 1973), esp. 402–13.

40  Giovanni Arrighi, *The Long Twentieth Century* (London: Verso, 1994), 8.

41  Chris Hudson, *Super Imperialism: The Origin and Fundamentals of U.S. World Dominance* (London: Pluto Press, 2003), 185. Hereafter cited as *SI*.

42  Melvin Tolson, *Caviar and Cabbage: Selected Columns by Melvin B. Tolson from the Washington Tribune, 1937–1944*, ed. Robert M. Farnsworth (Columbia: University of Missouri Press, 1982), 105. Hereafter cited as *CAC*.

43  Kweku Ampiah, *The Political and Moral Imperatives of the Bandung Conference of 1955: The Reactions of the U.S., U.K. and Japan* (Kent: Global Oriental Ltd., 2007), 226, 223, 225.

44 Samir Amin, *Eurocentrism: Modernity, Religion, and Democracy*, trans. Russell Moore and James Membrez (New York: Monthly Review Press, 2009), 180.

45 Samir Amin, *The World We Wish to See: Revolutionary Objectives in the Twenty-First Century*, trans. James Membrez (New York: Monthly Review Press, 2008), 109–10.

46 *Ibid.*, 109.

47 *Ibid.*, 125, 119.

48 Samir Amin, *The Implosion of Contemporary Capitalism* (New York: Monthly Review Press, 2013), 116.

49 *Eurocentrism*, 184, 183.

50 Samir Amin, *Class and Nation, Historically and in the Current Crisis,* trans. Susan Kaplow (London: Heinemann, 1980), 252.

51 *Eurocentrism*, 91.

52 In Matthew Hart's excellent analysis of Tolson, he observes that parts of Tolson's *Libretto* contain a "vision of a world beyond national sovereignty" and "the unsettling of nation-centered vernacular communities," but suggests that in Tolson's poetry "even when such communities exceed national boundaries, they still speak the language of the state," and in particular of the kind of modernization projects he associates with state-sponsored development (*Nations of Nothing But Poetry*, 176). My reading also stresses Tolson's precarious position between state and nonstate forces, but argues that Tolson's investment was primarily in the nonstate social strata that exist in a conflictual relationship with the Liberian state; accordingly, in what follows I draw out and contextualize the forms of nonstate modernization and nonstate political alliance that were part of Tolson's poetic imaginary.

53 James C. Scott, *The Art of Not Being Governed: An Anarchist History of Upland Southeast Asia* (New Haven: Yale University Press, 2009), 8.

54 C. L. R. James, *Nkrumah and the Ghana Revolution* (Westport: Lawrence Hill and Co., 1977), 54. Hereafter cited as *N*.

55 C. L. R. James, *State Capitalism and World Revolution* (Chicago: Charles H. Kerr Publishing Company, 1986), 37.

56 See Bill Berkeley, *The Graves Are Not Yet Full: Race, Tribe and Power in the Heart of Africa* (New York: Basic Books, 2001), 12–13.

57 Mario Zamponi, "Betwixt and Between Custom and Modernity: Traditional Rulers and Rural Development in Southern Africa," in István Tarrósy, Loránd Szabó, and Goran Hyden, eds., *The African State in a Changing Global Context: Breakdowns and Transformations* (Berlin: LIT Verlag, 2011), 163.

58 See Kevin Ebele Adinnu, "State–Civil Society Contestations: The Case of Abuja Indigenes," in Luc Sindjoun, ed., *The Coming African Hour: Dialectics of Opportunities and Constraints* (Pretoria: Africa Institute, 2010); Dorothy L. Hodgson, *Being Maasai, Becoming Indigenous: Postcolonial Politics in a Neoliberal World* (Bloomington: Indiana University Press, 2011); and Renée Sylvain, "Disorderly Development: Globalization and the Idea of Culture in the Kalahari," *American Ethnologist*, 32:3 (2005), 354–70.

59 Gebru Mersha, *The State and Civil Society with Special Reference to Ethiopia* (Dakar: Council for the Development of Economic and Social Research in Africa, 1990). See also Mahmood Mamdani, "State and Civil Society in Contemporary Africa: Reconceptualising the Birth of State Nationalism and the Defeat of Popular Movements," *Africa Development/Afrique et Développement*, 15:3/4 (1990), 47–70.

60 Basil Davidson, *The Black Man's Burden: Africa and the Curse of the Nation-State* (New York: Times Books, 1992), 299.

61 On contemporary forms of Pan-Africanism, see Horace Campbell and Rodney Worrell, *Pan-Africanism, Pan-Africanists, and African Liberation in the 21st Century* (Washington: New Academia Publishing, 2006); B. F. Bankie and K. Mchombu, eds., *Pan-Africanism/African Nationalism: Strengthening the Unity of Africa and Its Diaspora* (Trenton: The Red Sea Press, 2008); Mammo Muchi, ed., *The Making of the Africa-Nation: Pan-Africanism and the African Renaissance* (London: Adonis & Abbey, 2003); and Tajudeen Abdul-Raheen, *Speaking Truth to Power: Selected Pan-African Postcards* (Cape Town: Pambazuka Press, 2010).

# Epilogue: Transnational Studies and the "Nonstate Turn" of the World Bank

A few years ago, The Centre for International Governance Innovation (CIGI) published an essay called "The Future Is Nonstate." Its argument is that, given the high cost and uneven quality of state-centric policing conducted in post-conflict states, lending agencies and donor organizations should consider "partner[ing] with nonstate actors for the delivery of policing services."[1] These police entities could include, among others, "youth groups ... entrepreneurs ... vigilante groups ... religious (especially Islamic) police ... ethnic or clan militias [and] semi-commercial anti-crime groups."[2] Acknowledging that such groups are "deemed culpable of abuses and corruption" and "lack[ing in] accountability," the author of the essay reminds his readers that even "formal state systems" have limited accountability to international NGOs.[3] He then mobilizes a language of sensitivity and openness that will be eerily familiar to those acquainted with postcolonial and transnational theory:

> Post-conflict states need not be viewed from the Western-centric perspective of failure. Post-conflict states can be seen as another (if more acute) version of the "hybrid state" typical of African and many other developing countries ... The hybrid state has a form of governance in which state and nonstate actors share the distribution of public goods. In other words, the state does not have a privileged position as the political framework that provides policing. It has to share authority, legitimacy and capacity with other structures.[4]

This appeal to "sharing," "hybridity," and the questioning of "Western-centric" perspectives is an obvious attempt to justify the dismantling of basic social services in non-Western countries. But the line of argument advanced here, for all its opportunism and superficiality, is not at all uncommon. It has been articulated time and time again, with relatively few variations, in papers delivered at the Council on Foreign Relations, the OECD, and the International Network on Conflict and Fragility, as well as in publications funded by the World Bank and the United States Institute of Peace. The CIGI itself has an International Board of Governors that includes multiple ex-IMF and ex-World Bank executives, and its founding member was the CEO of Research in Motion, now known as BlackBerry Ltd. In short, the concept that "the future is nonstate" has the support and the financial backing of some of the most wealthy and powerful individuals in the world.

In concluding this book, I would like to present the kind of nonstate spaces, structures, and mobilizations that I have been exploring in this book as counterforces to the newly hegemonic forms of nonstate thinking that the CIGI and its elite allies have begun to put forward. In this book, I have explored alternatives to the top-down, UN-inflected forms of administrative universalism associated with the heyday of cosmopolitan thought. But this 1990s-era cosmopolitanism, with its language of universal human rights and international law, has recently been superseded by a new worldview among international power brokers – one in which even the façade of universal codes of conduct and ethical norms has been dismantled. In its place we find a language of cultural relativism, contextual sensitivity, and openness to difference that has been a part of humanistic discourse for decades, and that is now being deployed to rationalize forms of underdevelopment and social fracture reminiscent of early colonial indirect rule.

One way to summarize the shift that has occurred among the international governing elite is that a UN-centered cosmopolitanism of states has been superseded by a nonstate cosmopolitanism. But what remains of the cosmopolitan project once its language of universalism and moral accountancy is liquidated? What is most noticeable in publications like "The Future Is Nonstate" is the *affect* that is deployed to make certain lines of argument seem plausible. The military obliteration of state apparatuses and the channeling of funding to religious police and other armed groups is recast, feelingly, as "engaging with alternative governance structures." One essay, "Understanding Armed Groups," even uses the language of *verstehende Soziologie* to describe this process: "Understanding such a group means more than merely having information about them. It means developing a deeper knowing, an awareness of their experiences and perceptions, an understanding of their logic or way of reasoning."[5]

Other publications are even more direct. An essay with the forthright title "How to Capture Non-Western Forms of Governance" proposes that we regard "private actors as equal to state actors when fulfilling governance functions."[6] It then cites Foucault and Derrida to help explain that "human rights [and] ... parliamentary democracy are Western solutions" to the problem of "political authority" – that they are Eurocentric in nature, and therefore make it difficult "to get away from the ideal of the Western nation state when observing governance in areas of limited statehood."[7]

All told, what remains of the cosmopolitan project in this context is an affect of tolerance and openness, against the backdrop of a brutal combination of military suppression and economic underdevelopment. For the vast majority of the world, this means a cosmopolitanism without states, without democratic representation, and without options – in fact, a cosmopolitanism with no "cosmos" and no "polis" at all. This is the worst outcome that the writers I analyze could have possibly imagined, since it projects a world in which the nonstate networks and extra-legal forms of decision-making they describe would be not simply quashed by the forces of the state, but, in the language of Security Sector Reform, "captured" – infiltrated, turned against themselves.

Of course, the rhetoric mobilized by such elite, imperialist theories of nonstate governance is almost always that of empowering local communities and extending tolerance and understanding toward hitherto misunderstood nonstate actors. For example, in his essay "Towards a Non-State Security Sector Reform Strategy," Michael Lawrence contends that "a non-state SSR strategy aims to empower communities (particularly civil society) to negotiate with local elites (security and justice providers)" – it is a "decentralized strategy of bottom-up provision at the local level."[8] Similarly, in a World Bank publication funded by its "Justice for the Poor" (J4P) program, entitled "Justice Delivered Locally: Systems, Challenges, and Innovations in the Solomon Islands," reference is made to the preference locals have for the nonstate *kastom* system of dispute resolution, which is "seen as representing a more indigenous approach to dispute management" that is focused more on "'cool[ing]' hostilities and restor[ing] community harmony rather than … determin[ing] guilt or innocence."[9] Most extraordinary in this trend is an OECD publication that promotes the funding of *privatized* local justice systems in "fragile states," and suggests that "because of the political sensitivity of justice and security" "donors may need to modify their funding mechanisms in order to channel money through local non-governmental organizations to nonstate/local justice and security networks"[10]

As policy suggestions such as these show, nonstate actors, resources, and spaces are beginning to take center stage in debates surrounding transnational governance sponsored by the World Bank and the OECD, and the language used in these circles overlaps broadly and unsettlingly with the valuative language that is deployed in the humanities as part of the transnational turn. The emphasis placed on local control, self-government, and cultural specificity within the domains of transnational studies and post-colonial theory, in fact, finds its disquieting complement in World Bank publications from the 1970s to the present which, as Vijay Prashad has observed, are intended to provide "a populist antidote to [the World Bank's] critique of the inefficient Third World state: the sector of the people, which would be harnessed through non-governmental organizations."[11] In such documents, Prashad explains, "the language of empowerment, the grass-roots, and people-power disguised arguments about the dismemberment of national economies and state-run welfare schemes."[12] As part of this effort, NGOs came to "provide neoliberalism with its community face" even as they "often became conduits of official (government) and unofficial (private donor) foreign aid, which was often canalized through the donor's interests and not the actual needs of the area where the NGO worked."[13]

What should we make of the fact that the World Bank's and the OECD's shift from nation-centered forms of neoliberal planning to nonstate schemas is contemporaneous with the humanities' shift in focus from national projects and literatures to transnational complexes and nonstate social formations? Is this simply a coincidence? Bret Benjamin has argued that, on the contrary, it is part of a larger cultural shift in which the World Bank has attempted to play a shaping role, "consciously traffic[king] in culture, placing increasing emphasis on 'the local,' 'the micro,' and 'the participatory,'" to the point of sponsoring its own literary contest, "soliciting, judging, and publishing the most poignant success stories about local ICT (Information Communication Technologies) initiatives in the developing world."[14] In a similar vein, Amitava Kumar has even suggested that "World Bank Literature" might be "a new name for postcolonial studies."[15]

All of this suggests that now may be a good time to reassess our investment in nonstate social formations and the larger discourses of transnationality and cosmopolitanism that have served as their theoretical elaborations. To what extent do such investments proceed from an attune-ment to "organized citizen resistance to ... perceived harmful economic programs associated with globalization and transnational capital"?[16] And to what extent do they reflect the "power of global capital to constrain and even force national states to adopt particular policies," such as "the dereg-ulation of a broad range of markets ... and ... the privatization of public sector firms and operations"?[17]

Do we possess a theoretical language that allows us to discriminate between the utopian and the dystopian ambitions of nonstate thinking?[18] And, perhaps even more important, in light of the World Bank's recent literary avocation and the Defense Advance Research Projects Agency's roughly contemporaneous mandate to "weaponize narrative," is the question of what kinds of narrative and image we mobilize when we imagine nonstate potentialities.[19] Do we draw on an archive of stories and images that amplifies nonstate populations' resources for self-development and self-government? Or do we, perhaps unwittingly, script nonstate spaces into imaginative wholes in which agency can only be imagined as proceeding from administrative networks and governance complexes remote from the shaping influence of these spaces themselves?

In this book, I have argued that imaginative literature can operate on a geopolitical scale wide enough to contest these new forms of governance thinking. World literature, I contend, can be imagined as more than a corollary of 1990s-era cosmopolitan universalism. And it is certainly irreducible to the celebrations of cultural incommensurability and neoliberal affect that we see in recent publications by the World Bank and the OECD. Instead, world literature can be viewed as an archive of democratic mechanisms, interpersonal modes, and affective complexes outside of the hierarchical mechanisms of the state – including organs of combined state power such as the World Bank and the OECD.

World literature, in this sense, can help us visualize modes of life and forms of relation that pose alternatives to the regime of legalized dispossession that goes under the name of globalization. The "world" in world literature could then be reimagined – not as a cognate of elite, globalized networks of literary prestige, but as a capacity to project alternatives to neoliberalism's itineraries of social fracture. World literature, in this sense, serves to remind all of us who have been told we possess an "organic incapacity for self-government" that we can order our affairs, our neighborhoods, our workplaces, and our larger societies in the absence of permanent political elites and the states they make use of.

Where is the evidence for our capacity to act on such a scale?

It resides in the world of struggles, capacities, strategies, and modes of comportment that constitute what we call "world literature."

### Notes

1 Bruce Baker, "The Future is Non-State," in Mark Sedra, ed., *The Future of Security Sector Reform* (Ontario: Center for International Governance Innovation, 2010), 208.

2 *Ibid.*, 208–9.

3 *Ibid.*, 214, 215.

4 *Ibid.*, 211–12.

5  Sue Williams and Robert Ricigliano, "Understanding Armed Groups," *Accord,* 16 (2005), 14.

6  Anke Draude, "How to Capture Non-Western Forms of Governance: In Favour of an Equivalence Functionalist Observation of Governance in Areas of Limited Statehood," *SFB-Governance Working Papers Series,* 2 (January 2007), 12.

7  *Ibid.,* 11, 18.

8  Michael Lawrence, "Towards a Non-State Security Sector Reform Strategy," *SSR Issue Papers,* 8 (May 2012), 29, 7.

9  Matthew Allen, Sinclair Dinnen, Daniel Evans, and Rebecca Monson, "Justice Delivered Locally: Systems, Challenges, and Innovations in the Solomon Islands," *World Bank Research Report* (August 2013), 66, 40. Available at http://documents.worldbank.org/curated/en/353081468308114790/Justice-delivered-locally-systems-challenges-and-innovations-in-Solomon-Islands.

10  Eric Scheye, "State Provided Service, Contracting Out, and Non-State Networks: Justice and Security as Public and Private Goods and Services," The International Network of Conflict and Fragility, Development Assistant Committee, OECD (June 2009), Paris.

11  Vijay Prashad, *The Poorer Nations: A Possible History of the Global South* (London: Verso, 2012), 128.

12  *Ibid.*

13  *Ibid.*

14  Bret Benjamin, *Invested Interests: Capital, Culture, and The World Bank* (Minneapolis: University of Minnesota Press, 2007), 138, 145.

15  Amitava Kumar, "Introduction," in Amitava Kumar, ed., *World Bank Literature* (Minneapolis: University of Minnesota Press, 2003), xx.

16  Paul Almeida, *Mobilizing Democracy: Globalization and Citizen Protest* (Baltimore: Johns Hopkins University Press, 2014), 7.

17  Saskia Sassen, *Territory/Authority/Rights: From Medieval to Global Assemblages* (Princeton: Princeton University Press, 2006), 224, 222.

18  I use the term "utopian" in the sense that Douglas Mao articulates so clearly: as a way to name "an unrealized there, a state imagined for the future or at least deemed still under construction" (Douglas Mao, "The Unseen Side of Things: Eliot and Steven," in Rosalyn Gregory and Benjamin Kohlmann, eds., *Utopian Spaces of Modernism: Literature and Culture, 1885–1945* [Basingstoke: Palgrave MacMillan, 2011], 196).

19  See Dawn Lim, "DARPA Wants to Master the Science of Propaganda," *Wired,* October 18, 2011. www.wired.com/2011/10/darpa-science-propaganda/.

# Index